T0012797

Praise for Leo Houlding

'Leo is an amazing climber and adventurer who's been pushing the limits for as long as I can remember. He's done some of the wildest climbs on earth'
– Alex Honnold

'One of the greatest climbers Britain has ever produced'
– Steve Backshall

'He is a brilliant climber and makes everything seem so incredibly easy. Leo is equivalent of an Olympic athlete only in a spore where losing can mean death'
– Sir Chris Bonnington

ABOUT THE AUTHOR

Leo Houlding is a world-class climber adventurer, filmmaker and popular public speaker. He lives in the Lake District with his wife and two children.

FILM AND TV CONTRIBUTIONS BY LEO HOULDING:

Wild Climbs

My Right Foot

Top Gear (Season 7, Ep. 2)

Take Me to the Edge

The Asgard Project

The Wildest Dream

The Prophet

Autana

Last Great Climb

Lost Worlds With Monty Halls and Leo Houlding

Mirror Wall

Spectre Expedition

Great Sheiks

House of the Gods

Two Point Four

CLOSER TO THE EDGE

LEO HOULDING

Headline

First published in 2022 by
HEADLINE PUBLISHING GROUP

First published in paperback in 2023 by
HEADLINE PUBLISHING GROUP

1

Jacket design by Patrick Insole
Front cover image © Matthew Pycroft/Coldhouse Collective
Back cover image © Mark Sedon/Leo Houlding collection
Author photo © Mark Sedon
Please refer to page 339 for internal image credits

Cataloguing in Publication Data is available from the British Library

ISBN: 978 1 4722 8871 4

Offset in 11.25/13.73 pt Janson MT Std by Jouve (UK), Milton Keynes

Printed and bound in Great Britain by Clays Ltd, Elcograf S.p.A.

HEADLINE PUBLISHING GROUP
An Hachette UK Company
Carmelite House
50 Victoria Embankment
London
EC4Y 0DZ

www.headline.co.uk
www.hachette.co.uk

To Jessica, Freya and Jackson.
To many more family adventures.

Contents

PART THREE: BIG TIMES

CLOSER
TO THE
EDGE

Foreword

Teetering on ancient sandstone above Arabian dust, a wiry figure in bright blue tiptoes along on invisible footholds. Fingertips clasp the scoops that were carved from the soft rock by ancient peoples many thousands of years ago. The craftsmen could never have imagined their scoops would one day function as handholds for a modern Spider-Man. Leo is leading up a blank vertical slab that has never been climbed before. Without cracks for protection, it's a serious proposition. We're a fair way from help if he takes a whipper, and it's a long drop down to the hard desert below. I can barely watch. There are very few people in the world who'd attempt a climb like this. Leo is doing it in Acid House dayglo yellow socks and trainers. He pulls through the crux, and we sprint up an ancient carved staircase to the highest and most sacred point of a forgotten civilisation, the rock emblazoned with indecipherable inscriptions. Standing in the sun, we take an epic selfie, and feel like gods. It was one of the sweetest moments of my life. It will not however be in this book. This magnificent climb would not rank in Leo's top one hundred. This book is made up of far better stories.

There have been certain athletes in the modern era who have redefined the way we perceive our world and our place in it: Reinhold Messner at high altitude, Tanya Streeter in freediving, Rush Sturges in a kayak . . . These pioneers have changed their sport by finding harmony with the environment. It's not about difficulty, it's about aesthetics. For the first time, we mortals have seen a human at ease in a place we once thought of as extreme, existing there as a wild animal might. Leo to me is the ultimate example of this. Leo is at home on big walls. He looks more at ease there than he does in our 'real' world. Yes, he can push grades, and pump and grunt his way up near-impossible cracks, but it is the effortless ease with which he flows across hard rock that makes him special. Watching Leo climb is like watching Nureyev dance.

In his early climbing days, Leo had a reputation. The old guard talked of him as a bold boy who was a bit big for his boots, with raw talent and apparent fearlessness being the only thing between him and disaster. Kind of like Jim Morrison with a chalk bag. In all the stories, a bottle of cheap Scotch, a punch-up and a foreign prison cell were never far away. In his teens, he forged his craft in the Lakes, North Wales and on the giant faces of Yosemite, with accomplishments that have stood the test of time. Leo first entered the public imagination when (with that pure gem of a human being Tim Emmett) he speed climbed the Verdon Gorge, racing against Jeremy Clarkson in a sporty Audi – the best sequence in *Top Gear* history. People still talk about it now, not least because in it Leo introduced the world to a new sport – para-alpinism – by BASE jumping off the top. The sequence portrayed him as cocky and brash, an 'adrenaline junkie who . . . calls everyone "dude"'.

When I first got the chance to climb with him, I was sideswiped. Granted, he was supremely confident, but he had very good reason to be. He had also put more thought into the philosophy of adventure and risk than anyone I'd met. Leo had rationalised every single element of his craft, of risk versus reward, and of where his talents and passions lay. Clearly he wasn't someone with a death wish; he was a natural, operating at a totally different level to everyone else. That was before Asgard, Autana, Ulvetanna and the Spectre, before he became one of the greatest expedition climbers of all time.

Leo was at the vanguard of the pro climbers, one of the first people to properly make a living as a dirtbag climber without having to resort to being a grumpy guide or doing other jobs in his downtime. He led the way for people like Alex Honnold and Nims Purja, mastering both the mountains and the media. A supreme storyteller and communicator, he has brought tens of thousands of young people to the sport, revamping the once unfashionable image of the hills, making it all unspeakably cool.

Climbing now is a young person's sport, with grades soaring to difficulty that would once have seemed pure fantasy. Leo, though, has kept himself at the cutting edge, continuing to innovate, to challenge the perception of what is possible. Many of his expeditions and expedition films broke new ground, and have led the way for all who follow. In recent years, Leo attracted controversy by taking his very young family up precipitous Alpine rock faces that to us normal folk seemed beyond foolhardy. The truth is that Leo knows ways of making those climbs safer than a playground climbing frame, and is operating so far within himself that there is always an escape route. With that skill set, it is surely folly *not* to give the kids those experiences.

The last and most important thing to say is that he is also damn good company. People at the cutting edge of endeavour can occasionally be . . . a bit dull. (It's not surprising, if you spend a year working one single pitch of rock, it may be hard to talk about anything else.) Nobody would ever call Leo dull. In fact, he is the perfect campfire companion, with a thousand different stories to make you gasp, giggle, then gasp again. How he decided which ones to include and which to leave out of this book . . . well, I'm glad I'm not the editor! We're all so glad though that he's finally done it. I've been on at Leo for years to write this book, to share these tall tales with the world. And now it's done, I urge you all – whether fellow climber or armchair adventurer – to spark up a campfire, pour yourself a glass of cheap Scotch and prepare for a roller-coaster ride with the ultimate rock star.

Steve Backshall

Preface

Some people are born lucky. Not because of wealth or status but because they find something that they are both passionate about and good at early in life. They know what they were put here on Earth to do. Life has clear purpose.

I am one of those lucky people. My passion: climbing. In particular reaching the most remote, wildest, steepest and inaccessible summits on Earth. To enjoy wild times with wild people doing wild things.

From humble beginnings in the Lake District my passion became my profession and has taken me to places I never imagined could exist, on adventures beyond my wildest dreams: skydiving into an expedition in the high Arctic; mind-blowing shamanic ceremonies deep in the Amazon; Mount Everest in 1920s tweeds; snow-kiting thousands of miles across Antarctica to climb a mile-high cliff.

It's been a dangerous path with many close calls and good friends lost along the way. But that risk is what has made the journey so exciting and has taught me much about facing fear, dreaming big and making the most of our precious time on Earth.

My friend Sir Chris Bonington has been encouraging me to write this book for twenty years and it is something I have always felt compelled to do, but as a lazy perfectionist who prefers to create stories than write them, actually putting pen to paper has been a major challenge. How do you begin to illustrate with words Mother Nature's finest creations – the Yosemite Valley, the Torres of Patagonia, nunataks of Antarctica or *tepuis* of the Amazon rainforest? Where do I start to try to explain the nuances of climbing style and ethics, the technicalities of BASE jumping or snow-kiting? Which of the many wild stories and characters do I include or, more difficult, choose to omit? I know the stories are good; I only hope I have been able to do them justice here. I'm pleased to finally share some of these wonderful places and wild experiences in the hope they will inspire readers to embrace adventure, push their own limits and live with less fear.

I have never considered myself to be an athlete. Athletes are disciplined people who train religiously in pursuit of optimum performance and tend to take things rather seriously. I have never trained properly or really pushed to climb at my physical limit. It was a conscious decision I made early on as I get bored quickly and was not willing to make the sacrifices necessary to perform at the very highest level.

I am an adventurer, an explorer, an undisciplined person blessed with more than my fair share of natural talent, burdened with insatiable ambition and driven to make the most of life. And above all to enjoy it, to eke as much fun as is possible from this one-take scene.

This book is about twenty-first-century exploration. About taking modern action sports to the ends of the Earth in search of ever greater adventure. Most of my explorations have taken place in the vertical realm, and the most striking have been to what we climbers call 'big walls' – the tallest cliffs on Earth that are measured in kilometres, can take weeks to climb and are often located in extremely remote, inhospitable environments like the polar regions, tropical rainforests or high altitude. It is full of stories of the kind of adventures I dreamed of as a boy, wanting to be Prince Theseus and fight the Minotaur, or Indiana Jones on some daring escapade in an exotic land. I must've hit every branch when I fell out of the lucky tree as compiling this book I repeatedly have to remind myself this is all fact and not fiction.

This is an autobiography, my life story in my own words. As such I've tried to identify the key memories, people and events that set me off on this life of extreme adventure and those that stand out most prominently when I reflect back over my first forty years on this planet.

As I reflect I can see a constant theme emerging, a philosophy that has both led to and been formed by all the climbs, characters and journeys into the unknown. Simply put, it is about daring to attempt your wildest dreams, aiming as high as you can without being afraid of failure or fatality, about having the self-belief and drive to make great things happen against the odds. It is about dealing with fear and coping with risk in all its guises, be that mortal danger where a small mistake will kill you or your friends, forsaking financial security to have a shot at the life of which you dream, or taking on massive projects that cost hundreds of thousands of pounds that even your closest confidants say are impossible and doomed to fail.

As well as to entertain with tall tales of high adventure, I hope this book inspires you to pursue your own dreams and adventures, to get out into nature and wild places, to leave home comforts and comfort zones behind and to push hard even when times are tough. But most of all, to not be afraid, to live life without unnecessary fear. It is also a coming-of-age story about finding balance – between risk and responsibility; extreme adventure and universally desired stability; dangerous dreams and a wife, family and comfortable home; a life less ordinary and the norm.

Something I've realised is that climbing for me is almost an excuse to spend extended periods of time in nature's wild places sharing intense, purposeful and powerful experiences with partners, small teams of friends and more recently with my young family. The people with whom I've shared the adventures have been equally if not more significant than the places or performances. Some of our most meaningful and memorable family times have been on outdoor adventures.

Stand-out memories from many expeditions are as often from the relaxed downtime as from the intense summit highs. Sipping morning coffee watching a sublime sunrise, or witnessing the Northern Lights while perched together on a desk-sized ledge thousands of feet above the ground, share equal space with the desperate lead climbs, adrenaline-charged BASE jumps or victorious summits.

As my great friend and climbing partner Jason Pickles, with whom I've shared many wild times and close calls, once said, 'Climbing is like going to church' – in reference to the reverence with which we approach mountains and nature and the deep spiritual reward we gain from spending time immersed in them. Jason also said in a photobook put together for my fortieth birthday by another friend, Alastair Lee, a gifted photographer and filmmaker, 'When I look back at all the wild things we've done and places we've been there is one stand-out thought – FUN – what a laugh we've had!'

There is no pot of gold on the top of a mountain, nobody there to cheer your successful summit – it is a purely emotional journey. The only reward is the memory of the experience and the feelings that remain, often of friendship and fulfilment. Mountains and outdoor adventures amplify emotions at both ends of the spectrum. Cold feels so much more gripping, fear so overwhelming; excitement so much more raw, joy so empowering. When things go wrong they go really wrong. But the successes are life-defining, the sense of satisfaction so much deeper than in everyday life.

There is a simplicity to life in the outdoors that appeals to fundamental instincts: shelter, warmth, companionship, camaraderie. For me, a big part of the adventure experience is about overcoming fear, leaving those home comforts and comfort zones behind, putting yourself into positions of commitment and exposure that force connection with deep, powerful emotions and give a different, higher perspective. These are things that cannot be bought, they must be earned through endeavour.

Prologue

Top Gear

One day in 2005, when I was twenty-four years old, my phone rang.

'Hi, my name's Alex,' the caller said. 'I'm a researcher for BBC's *Top Gear*. We'd like to race a car against a climber. We want it to be a genuine one-on-one race and we'll need to be able to drive from the bottom to the top of the cliff. Do you think that might be possible?'

This was an interesting opportunity, but I had to admit it might be quite difficult. I explained that rock climbing is not a very fast activity. Even speed climbing is slower than walking and there aren't many cliffs with roads at the bottom and the top.

Then a thought struck me.

'But BASE jumping is really fast,' I told the researcher. 'How about a race up and back down, that could balance it out?'

'LOVE IT!' Alex shouted. 'Where could we do that?'

'Leave it with me,' I said.

I phoned my friend Tim Emmett straight away. We had learned to skydive and got into BASE jumping together the year before and were both captivated by this new, dangerous and extremely exciting game.

Tim had recently jumped in the Verdon Gorge in the south-east of France.

'Mate, it's awesome! There's a car park at the bottom and the road skirts right along the edge at the top. Landings are a bit spicy. Only problem is the drive's not that far and the cliff's over a thousand feet. I don't think we'd stand much of a chance.'

'What if we get the car to drive a circuit the long way around the canyon? It's about fifty miles on windy roads. Should give us a chance?'

We showed photos of the Verdon Gorge and some clips of me speed climbing and BASE jumping to the *Top Gear* producers and got the green light.

Jeremy Clarkson and the director, Nigel, arrived two days before the rest of the crew. We took them to see the climb, the exit and a few other locations. It was September. The summer crowds had dispersed, the scent of herbs filled the air and the sun hung low in the sky, bathing the serene scene in delicious, golden light. A cloud inversion flooded the gorge below and vultures spiralled above.

'I've got a good feeling about this. It's going to be spectacular. Let's pull out all the stops. Get the best crew and give ourselves plenty of time,' Clarkson said back in our plush hotel. 'I will not be beaten by a man with a fourteen-inch waist and a hairband.'

In 2005 *Top Gear* was the BBC's most profitable show and one of the most widely watched TV shows on Earth, with devoted followings in the US, China and Japan and official global viewing figures of over 500 million.

'What are you going to be driving?' I asked Clarkson, half hoping it was going to be a beaten-up old shed to give us a better chance.

'Ah, yes, it gets better. We've just had confirmation that Audi will delivering a test model of their new RS4 fresh off the production line. Should be here tomorrow. Quite a beast, 420 brake horse, limited to 165 mph. They're very proud of it. They're only bringing one though, so we'd better not prang it until we've wrapped,' he said.

The next day Jeremy and Nigel drove the 53-mile circuit whilst Tim and I went to practise our route, aptly named *Les Marches du Temps* ('The March of Time'), a 300-metre mid-grade (7a/A0) route, and one of the few Verdon routes that ascends from the very bottom of the gorge to the rim. We'd already done it once and spent all day rehearsing the cruxes, running laps on some bits, chalking the holds and adding a few long quickdraws here and there to speed up our timed ascent.

It had already been decided that we would not film the race live. However, Jeremy stressed they wanted to keep it as real as possible.

'We'll race against the clock. You time your ascent and I'll time my lap. Then we'll spend the next week piecing together a mind-blowing sequence,' he explained.

The next day Tim and I did the route in one hour and fifty-eight minutes, just within our target time of two hours. Clarkson claimed to have driven his circuit, taking the long way round on the way up, in two hours and seven minutes, though there was no independent time-keeping of either.

People are often disappointed to learn that the final nine-minute segment of world-class TV was not 'real'. But just consider: how many camera teams would've been required to film a 50-mile course and 300-metre climb simultaneously? How would you cut from a tight shot of my fingers grabbing a hold to a wide shot of the cliff with no camera operator in shot? *Top Gear* is an entertainment show with no remit to be 'true' or 'real'. All television is a magic show, the art of using smoke and mirrors to create an impression of something, and these guys were master magicians.

It was an exceptionally well-resourced shoot. At one point there were twenty-two people on location and some of us were there for over a week. We had a helicopter on standby for three days and two Audi engineers whose job seemed to be to constantly polish the bright-red car. Most of the highly esteemed crew usually worked in the much more lucrative movie and commercial industries, only dipping into TV for the kudos associated with *Top Gear*.

My friends Keith Partridge and Brian Hall were the wall-filming team and we were left to our own devices for most of the week to film the climb. One day an unexpected and ferocious electrical storm rolled through whilst we were in the middle of the route. Every year people die from lightning strikes in the Verdon. In freezing wind and torrential rain Keith and Brian slowly climbed the fixed ropes with all the camera gear. Wearing shorts and T-shirts,

Tim and I were becoming hypothermic so I led the soaked route, pulling on bolts. Suddenly things had started to feel very real!

We saved the BASE jump until the very end. The landings in the Verdon are notoriously bad – tight, steep scree fields surrounded by trees, ankle-snapping boulders and a raging river that has claimed the life of more than one jumper. In case anything should go wrong, we wanted to make sure everything else had been filmed.

It was the first time I'd ever been filmed BASE jumping by a professional crew. There were cameras everywhere and loads of people running around getting ready. The helicopter got into position about fifty feet from the exit where I stood, geared up and poised to jump. I found it extremely stressful. Shaun Ellison, my friend and BASE-jump coordinator, came on the radio.

'You must be fucking joking! You can't fly a parachute next to a helicopter! How do you think the fucking thing flies! Down draft! You need to get way back and film zoomed in, you muppets.'

I was glad to have him on the crew.

'No pressure to do this, nobody wants you to get hurt,' said Nigel. 'But if you are going to jump, now's the time.'

'Three, two, one – see ya!' I dived off the cliff. Rapidly accelerating towards the ground, accompanied in the edit by a dramatic orchestral piece appropriately titled 'Speed me towards death', I hurtled down the wall before deploying my canopy, and more by luck than judgement landed effortlessly on the single-track trail right in front of the cameraman.

'One thousand two hundred feet in twenty seconds – beat that, Clarkson!' I said to camera, wide-eyed and giggling with adrenaline.

Before we left, I had to ask Udo, the German Audi engineer, if Tim, Shaun and I could go for spin in the RS4.

'In the last days, what I have seen you achieve is very impressive. I believe you are highly skilled, precise and calculated athletes. Here are the keys. It is very fast. Enjoy!' he said, to my utter surprise.

'Was that a good idea?' said Clarkson as we floored it down the hotel drive.

The show was broadcast in November. It was indeed an astonishing piece of TV that you could tell had been made by some of the best in the business. Clarkson loved the car, concluding the segment by saying he felt the RS4 was better than a BMW M3 – Audi's arch-rival and long the benchmark for supercars disguised as family saloons.

We had made a bet before the race up: double or quits on the way down. In the as-live studio link Clarkson paid up, catching me with his biting wit in his closing comment:

'Don't spend it all on crystal meth!'

Audi UK sold every single one of the right-hand-drive RS4s they imported on pre-orders in the next two weeks.

Just before Christmas I received an invitation to meet with the sponsorship manager for Audi UK at their swanky Mayfair showroom. I invited Tim to join me.

'I think we owe you boys a thank you,' said the friendly chap in the fine suit. 'It was mainly thanks to Clarkson's review, but what you boys did was jaw-dropping and certainly helped. I'm afraid we can't give you an RS4 but you can have anything in the range up to £40K. You have to give them back at 9,000 miles. How does a two-year contract sound?'

Up until that conversation, I had been driving a fifteen-year-old Ford Escort that you needed a screwdriver to start and had cost me £350 three years earlier. Life as a climbing dirtbag seemed to be working out.

PART ONE
First Times

I.

Valley of Eden

'The loveliest spot that man hath ever found . . .'
William Wordsworth on the Lake District

The next limb of the sycamore was just beyond reach. I was standing on a bough an adults' reach above the grass, some way from the main trunk, using tiny branches for balance. I'd contemplated this move many times and had fallen from higher before, so I composed myself and leapt. A resounding crack followed my gasp as the limb I'd jumped for snapped. I braced for my well-rehearsed crash landing. But I did not fall to the ground feet first as anticipated; instead, swinging head down in an arc, I came to rest suspended upside down, a shooting pain emanating from just above my right foot where a small spike had skewered my ankle. I screamed. My mum's face paled as she ran from the kitchen to witness what could have been a medieval torture scene. She unhooked me. The spike had left a small but vicious gash in my flesh. Without delay Mum took me to the home of the local doctor, conveniently located just across the road. Thankfully he was home, medical bag on hand and promptly administered my first five stitches. I was six.

I am from humble beginnings in rural northern England, in the aptly named Eden Valley, on the edge of the Lake District National Park, a green and pleasant land where I enjoyed a childhood full of love and outdoor adventure. I grew up in a dilapidated, rented farmhouse called Violet Bank in the small village of Bolton near Appleby, famous for its horse fair.

My dad, Mark, is a carpenter and my mum, Lindsey, worked in

social care. I have one sister, Carla, six years my elder. My parents came from the industrially declining Lancashire mill towns of Accrington and Blackburn. My mum was nineteen when Carla was born. In the late 1970s a friend of my dad's overdosed on heroin after my mum had kicked him out of their two-up two-down terrace in the depressed town of Oswaldtwistle when Carla was a baby, prompting Mum and Dad to leave Lancashire and family connections behind to start a new life in a rural farming community.

It was a bold move for a young couple not yet trained or skilled for the labour market, to cast off from the community and support network they knew to try to give their children a better place to start life. A move for which I am eternally grateful as the place they chose, that Valley of Eden, started me on a path to adventure that has led me on a journey to places beyond my wildest dreams.

I thought Violet Bank a great old house, my mum less so. It was a four-bedroom, detached Victorian affair with high ceilings and no heating, so was only partially habitable in the two rooms with fires. Plaster was peeling from the bedroom walls and dry rot ravaged the rest of the house. In winter I regularly woke with ice on the inside of the windows and a cloud of frozen breath. There was a big garden that backed onto an un-busy farmyard with huge barns full of hay for den building, roofs and rafters for exploring exposure and a stand of mature sycamore trees that provided my first canvas for climbing – and falling.

Surrounding the property were miles and miles of open countryside, little changed since the 1950s, pastoral stock-grazing fields enclosed by barbed-wire fences over which I loved to climb and hedgerows teeming with bird life that were hard to tunnel through. The ancient deciduous woodlands and dense conifer plantations were home to deer, foxes, badgers and countless rabbits, noisy rookeries, curlews, woodpeckers and all sorts of diverse ornithology.

Just a field away there was a small stream, Luzbeck, to dam, ford and bridge; a bit further was the mighty River Eden, where a kingfisher lived, in which to swim, raft and fish for salmon, trout and perch, though I mainly seemed to catch unpleasant, slimy eels.

The river is spanned by a beautiful, twin-arched sandstone bridge, that would later become my climbing training ground where I developed half a dozen boulder problems and short routes on the large sculpted stones.

I have always been an adventurous, curious and independent spirit, constantly out exploring these places that seemed to have been created for that purpose alone. Once, my mother tells me, I walked two miles out of the village to the house of a friend from playgroup *alone*, after my mum mistakenly granted permission thinking I was going to the friend's house next door. I was two. By the time I was four I had established an escape route from my bedroom on the upper floor of the house where I would sometimes be confined for my frequent minor misdemeanours: out of the sash window onto the rickety front porch and down the ladder-like lattice of its wooden structure to the ground.

I managed to keep my escape route secret for years until a neighbour saw me perched on the windowsill like a sparrow and called my parents.

Once, when I was four, my dad jumped out wrapped in a blanket sporting a Halloween mask to scare me. I knocked him out cold with the heavy wooden Saracen sword he'd made for my birthday. I was Prince Theseus, he was the Minotaur.

We spent most of our time in Violet Bank in the farmhouse kitchen, where a cast-iron stove burned coal almost constantly. On the wall there were large-scale, colourful political maps, one of the UK, one of Europe and one of the world. I spent countless hours staring at and studying those wonderful depictions of Earth, memorising the capital cities of countries, identifying the great deserts, rainforests and mountain ranges, and dreaming of exploring all of them. I have no doubt that those maps influenced my wanderlust and passion for travel.

A friend of my parents was a dustbin man and would occasionally donate interesting items somebody had thrown out. He once gave us a set of what must've been a telegraph-pole worker's rope rigging kit – some kernmantle ropes of varying lengths with fixed eyelets on the end, a baby-bouncer-type sit-harness and several very large clips, which I would later learn were oversized industrial carabiners. This was without doubt my all-time favourite toy and provided years of entertainment building rope swings and zip-wires, rigging rudimentary abseils and Tyrolean traverses high in the stand of sycamores behind the house. Soon I discovered an ability to climb higher than all my friends in those trees and was noticeably less scared than all of them whenever doing something dangerous, be it playing on the roofs of the hay barns, jumping from height into the river, taunting frisky bullocks in the fields or playing 'knock and dash' on the grumpy old man down the street who would occasionally be provoked into threatening us with his shotgun, though he never fired a cartridge. Once I made a para-chute out of bailer twine and polytunnel sheeting and leapt from the roof of the cow byre. It didn't work but the muddy landing zone broke my fall and I walked away unscathed.

Money was always tight and a cause of stress for my parents. The family car was always battered and at the end of its life; we never sold one to anyone other than the scrapyard. But what we lacked in finance was more than compensated for by love and affection. It was a happy childhood and though we lived simply we wanted for nothing. Our only extravagance was foreign holi-days. At least once, often twice per year, in the days before budget airlines, we would buy last-minute tickets to fly abroad, usually to somewhere hot and quite exotic, like Morocco or Turkey. We would always camp, sometimes in campsites, sometimes wild. Occasionally we would rent a basic apartment or hire a car for a few days.

My very first memory is of the souk in Agadir, Morocco. The dazzling array of colours and different peoples, the smells of Ara-bian spices and incense, all the interesting stalls of metalcraft and carpets and the hectic, in-your-face bustle. I was an incredibly cute, platinum-blond, blue-eyed, three-year-old boy, much like my own son, Jackson, is now. I was fascinated by snakes, having already posed with a python around my neck in the market square.

A smiley man on one of the stalls showed me a wooden dominoes box that was full of baby snakes. I was enthralled, wandering off into his Aladdin's cave to play with them. Unbeknown to me, to my parents this constituted a lost, probably kidnapped toddler. They went spare searching the notorious labyrinth of the great souk, eventually contacting the police and starting a full-scale child hunt, until I casually walked out of the back room of the stall into the alley, where I found my panic-stricken mum and asked her if we could buy one of the hawker's snakes to take home.

Those memories from so early in my life are hazy, confused with photographs of the souk and snake charmers, camels and desert. But I clearly remember the hawker's domino box full of those tiny snakes and the feeling of intense hustle, bustle, colour and fragrance. When I returned to that great souk, sometime in my mid-twenties, I had an overwhelming sense of déjà vu. It didn't seem to have changed much, other than the increase in easyJet tourists. The aromas especially took me back to infancy.

My dad has always been very skinny and bald as a golf ball for as long as I can remember. He sported a bushy moustache left over from the seventies until I was well into my teens. He never developed the typical British taste for alcohol and has been teetotal his whole life and not at all fond of pubs, leading him to be considerably less social than most. But he was an enthusiastic smoker, tearing the filters off Silk Cut Purples before moving on to Golden Virginia roll-ups until thankfully he quit in his mid-sixties.

After leaving Lancashire he had trained as a carpenter and throughout my childhood had a fantastic woodworking shop, a spacious, ramshackle old potting shed in a disused plant nursery in Appleby. I loved that workshop. The distinctive smell of wood-shavings and sawdust is one of my favourites to this day.

There was an ancient wood-burning stove in one corner, two long, sturdy wooden benches mounted with burly vices, always festooned with swirly woodshavings from his trusty plane, and a big, scary circular saw that is still his primary tool of trade. There were all kinds of interesting curiosities Dad had collected through life – stained-glass windows and rusting antique signs from old garages and shops from a bygone era; stuffed birds, a barn owl and a kingfisher, and animals, a badger and a fox; old glass bottles and ceramic jars and all manner of other worthless treasures.

He was a British-motorbike enthusiast and in one corner there were the leftover parts of his beloved Norton Commando, which he'd been forced to sell in need of the cash when I was little. Its black fuel tank with the ornate swirl of the Norton insignia painted in gold took pride of place mounted on a wall.

He had discovered outdoor sports later in life following their move to the Eden Valley. With my mum's elder brother, Graham, he had adopted mountain biking very early after its first appearance in the UK. Together they would build and modify bikes, making what I believe may have been the first ascent and descent by cycle of Ben Nevis in 1987.

Dad and Graham fabricated, before they were commercially available, a 'tag-along' system for me that mounted behind Dad's bike with its own pedals and crank so I could assist whilst riding. On this ingenious contraption, when I was six we undertook a strenuous cycle tour, along with my mum and sister, around the Amalfi peninsula in Southern Italy from Sorrento to Naples. Winding along the hilly seaside roads amongst stunning scenery, we wild camped on the rugged coast, once being moved on by the intimidating *carabinieri* police in their polished finery for pitching our tent in a town park.

Moved to a legitimate campsite on a breathtaking clifftop location overlooking the Bay of Naples, I requested permission to explore the fishermen's steps that led down to the coast. Half an hour later I returned, beaming, insistent that they all come and see the spectacular cave I had discovered. Once again my parents were aghast as I guided them down the decrepit, rusted remains of the metal steps that had all but disintegrated towards the bottom from the continued battering by corrosive salt water. Reaching the cave required precariously traversing above a raging sea, a level of scrambling skill that was beyond my mum. I was not allowed to explore unaccompanied again on that trip. We spent a couple of safer days in Pompeii, Carla and I playing gladiators in the amphitheatre and utterly spellbound by the ghostlike plaster casts of the Romans who perished during the eruption of Mount Vesuvius in AD 79.

When I was small we regularly went fell-walking as a family in the Pennines and eastern Lakes, occasionally venturing onto more serious scrambles such as Sharp Edge on Blencathra, Striding Edge on Helvellyn and my favourite, Pinnacle Ridge on St Sunday Crag above Ullswater. This highest-rated scramble, a Grade 3, was much steeper and harder than the others with one short section in particular that skirts the line where scrambling becomes climbing, for which many parties use a rope. That insurmountable, vertical step, the height of a bungalow, an open-book corner with a wide crack in the side, I remember as my first moves of rock climbing. My dad and I loved that route though Mum and Carla much less so. Carla would often complain, 'You smell of outdoors,' when Dad and I returned from the hills.

Though Carla and I have always been close and loving siblings, the six-year age gap meant we didn't really share childhood. Initially I was the cute, then annoying little brother to her and she was as much a parental character as playmate to me. She left Appleby Grammar School the year I started and had a job, a car and was out on the town whilst I was still playing with my He-Man figures and climbing trees. We are incredibly different. She likes to book her annual holiday a year in advance, has had a pension plan since leaving school, isn't fond of camping or heights and has never been into risking her life for fun. My wildest dreams are the stuff of her worst nightmares. I find it remarkable that two individuals who share the same genes and upbringing can develop such contrasting characters.

Though I was as active in organised sports as most nine-year-old boys, unlike most of my peers I never developed any fascination with football or other team sports or athletic disciplines. I suppose my fierce independence and anti-authoritarian character from a very early age pushed me away from the strict rules of these conventional activities.

The first really formative outdoor experience I remember was a two-week trip to Turkey aged seven with my dad and my eccentric uncle Graham, who, amongst many other things, did a bit of mountaineering. It was my first taste of serious adventure in a remote wilderness. We went to climb a 10,000-foot snow-capped peak called Akdağ ('white mountain' in Turkish) in the Taurus Mountains of southern Turkey, near Antalya.

We spent a week self-supported in that pristine region of Mediterranean forests of Turkish pine and Lebanese cedar, emerald alpine lakes and craggy limestone summits adorned with permanent snow cover. Back then in 1987 it was inhabited exclusively by welcoming, subsistence farmers whose lives herding goats, tilling dry earth lots with an oxen plough and tending to olive groves seemed more akin to biblical times than my life at home in England.

Early in the trek we forged a fast-flowing river. The cold, clear water came up to my waist. I was scared but exhilarated, braced against my dad and uncle for support. Once we were safely across the torrent a wizened old man, his face shrivelled up like a prune with a broad almost toothless grin, insisted we spend the night in his simple farmstead. He didn't speak a word of English but his welcoming intentions were clear and my hyper-intelligent uncle had already picked up enough Turkish for basic communication.

We drank deliciously sweet apple tea and shared a meal of goat and rice. The next day he sent us on our way with a load of enormous Turkish flatbreads, two feet across, some spring onions from his garden and seasoned dates from his orchard. I have a vivid memory of the walking stick he made for me, cut and sculpted with a curious horizontal-headed axe. We ate the potent spring onions wrapped in flatbreads spread with Nutella for days afterwards.

We arrived at our last campsite before the summit, just below the snow line. I was exhausted from walking uphill all day carrying what seemed like a monstrous load, though it was probably just my sleeping bag and some clothes. It was a magnificent spot, a flat grassy area with an expansive view down the mountainside to the valley and farmstead from where we'd started days earlier. A steep snow slope terminated right at our camp and after a short rest, whilst Dad and Graham set up camp, I set off post-holing up the snow that was softened by the day's heat from the sun. I found a new lease of energy, my first experience of the glorious feeling of almost floating that comes after unburdening a heavy rucksack, and before I knew it I was at the top of the snow slope, miles above camp where I could see my dad and Graham who looked like ants waving and hollering for me to come back. I turned around and began running in giant sliding steps down the snow, a technique I would much later learn is known as glissading. In no time I had bounded and bum-slid back down to camp. It was the most fun I'd ever had, my first taste of the magical sensation of gliding over snow that would develop into a passion for skiing in years to come.

We reached the summit the next day after a section of much more difficult terrain, scrambling over steep rocky ground using a rope. It was so much more engaging and enjoyable than the uphill slog of the previous days and it dawned on me that the more technical the terrain, the more fun it was. On the top I remember being a little disappointed to see that a much taller, more fearsome summit lay beyond, the highest peak in the massif and, as I saw it, clearly what we should be aiming for. I pestered Dad and Graham to push on but the continued ascent was a different level of severity, true alpine terrain and beyond the scope of their experience or skills, especially when accompanied by a child.

On the way down we crossed an enormous talus field and gained a tiny single-file goat track that traversed horizontally across the steep scree above a precipitous drop into a gorge. The trail led closer to the edge, where I watched a dislodged rock tumble from the path and gain speed down the slope before it plummeted into the void. Suddenly I realised that a misplaced step could send me the same way and became gripped by fear. Tension flooded through my body. A rising panic clouded my composure and, feeling exposed and vulnerable, I began to move awkwardly, unable to take my mind off the potential consequences of a mistake.

'Dad, I'm scared, can we put the rope on?'

My uncle, a widely travelled adventurer and the only university-educated member of my family, had studied archaeology and been on excavations in Egypt. He had worked as a policeman in Hong Kong and had cycled halfway around the world, amongst many other glorious escapades. He was somebody whom I looked up to greatly.

An unemotional man, he asked matter-of-factly, 'What's the matter?'

'If I trip, I might die!' I complained.

Bluntly he replied, 'Best not trip then. You've been walking sure-footedly for days, what makes you think you're going to trip now? We're walking, not climbing, you don't need a rope. Tread carefully and don't worry about the cliff. Now come on.'

And off he went, the rope in his bag. Looking back along the path, I realised we'd been traversing above the gorge for miles, skipping along merrily, and it hadn't been until I'd started to focus on the hazard and potential terrible outcome that I'd become scared.

I took his words to heart and continued down cautiously but with more confidence until beyond the terrifying drop we eventually reached the safety of the treeline. It was my first taste of the powerful, highly memorable sensation of great exposure and the debilitating, irrational fear it can bring. Of course it is not irrational to fear falling to your death, but the likelihood of that occurring while simply walking along a decent path is very low, so it is irrational to worry about it.

I was beginning to learn what I would later master: surrendering to fear greatly increases the likelihood of an incident. You become distracted from the task at hand for fear of the potential outcome should it go wrong, ironically raising the chance of that undesired result. Like acquiring the taste for beer, great exposure, danger and the fear it brings that at first seemed so repulsive, is something intoxicating that I would later come to savour and even crave.

Not everybody bonds with danger in this way. Most take active steps to avoid it at all costs. More often it is a male trait and most boys grow out of it as testosterone levels decrease with adulthood. But some thrive on it. We feel stronger, energised and more alive in the presence of danger. It is a warrior instinct that rarely in the modern world do we need to express in a fight to the death. Instead we seek less violent battles, leading us to surf big waves, jump off cliffs or to climb steep mountains.

The only other thing I remember clearly from our Turkey expedition is that I lost my treasured Swiss Army knife that Uncle Graham had given to me for my seventh birthday. I pinpointed the last time I'd had it, sitting on a rock by the river crossing, and was consoled by my dad's suggestion that it would be found by the kind farmer and he would probably treasure it more than me.

Following our big adventure we spent a week on the magnificent Mediterranean coast near Antalya. I found the Islamic culture enthralling. We explored Roman ruins and Turkish baths, my first hot springs and ate the strange gloopy ice cream so popular there. I remember feeling a sense of accomplishment and achievement from our time in the wilderness and on Akdağ that left a warming glow. My uncle wanted a Turkish carpet and we spent a whole afternoon in the pantomime that is carpet shopping in a traditional carpet shop. Endless rounds of apple tea, dates and banter whilst hundreds of skilfully woven, colourful rugs were unfurled and their respective qualities hard pitched before the drawn-out theatrical haggling to agree a price. I loved it.

Mass tourism was just encroaching this beautiful coastline. We camped on the shore of a splendid, wild lagoon of clear turquoise water called Ölüdeniz. At my uncle's encouragement we swam across it. It seemed very far although was probably only 500 metres. Halfway across I was exhausted and again had to learn to calm my fear and subdue my panic before holding on to my dad's back for the rest of the crossing.

Looking back, I have no doubt this trip, the influence of my fearless uncle, the bond I formed with my dad, those first flirtations with dangerous situations during our time together alone in the mountains, had a profound effect on me, seeding my deep desire for adventure, exploration and wild places, for travelling the world and experiencing alien cultures. But I was yet to discover my true passion, taking these things to altogether steeper, more extreme terrain, and greatly upping the stakes – rock climbing.

2.

Learning the Ropes

'Son, it's a truly lucky man who knows what he wants to do in this world. 'Cause that man will never work a day in his life. But there are a few, a precious few, and, hell, I don't know if they're lucky or not. But there are a few people who find something they have to do. Something obsesses 'em. Something that if they can't do it, it's gonna drive them clean out of their mind.'

Carrol Shelby – racing-car designer

Malcolm 'Pike' Cundy was a joiner, a builder, a husband and a father, but first and foremost he was a climber. The first I ever met. He was a vague friend of my dad's. Ten years older than him with unkempt grey hair, he too sported a moustache left over from the seventies. He had terrible eyesight, and squinting behind thick glasses gave him a mole-like appearance and a bumbling manner that concealed his wealth of climbing experience and time in the mountains. He was also one of the kindest, most selfless people I've ever met and I can safely say, were it not for coming to know Pike so early in life, I would not be writing this book now.

Pike was from Sheffield and had discovered his passion for climbing on the Gritstone Edges of the Peak District as a young man. A contemporary of Joe Brown and Don Whillans, he had never excelled at climbing but was nonetheless committed, viewing it as much as an identity as a sport. Most of his friends were climbers and most of his fondest memories were of climbing. He enjoyed all aspects of the mountains – rock, ice, winter and mountaineering. He had spent many season in the Alps, living in the notorious Snell's Field free campsite in Chamonix, and had travelled to climb all over North America, Norway, across Europe and in the Himalayas. Everything in Pike's life seemed to revolve around his passion: climbing.

My dad had a party for his thirty-fifth birthday and I knew Pike the climber and his charming wife, Di, were due to attend. I'm not sure why I was so obsessed with the idea of rock climbing. It must've been spurred by our scrambling and Turkey trip and I'd recently watched the televised, first ever International Federation of Sport Climbing (IFSC) Climbing World Cup, held in Leeds in 1989 – Brits Simon Nadin and Jerry Moffatt, both of whom I would later befriend, came in first and third respectively, and it was gripping. I was a precocious child, never shy to talk to adults, and at the party I made a beeline for Pike. I pestered him endlessly that night, all but forcing him to promise to take Dad and me climbing with ropes as soon as possible. In fairness, he didn't seem to mind and was very receptive to my energetic enthusiasm.

But I almost blew my opportunity on what was to be a pivotal day in my life. My keen adventurous streak and penchant for danger frequently manifested itself in what could simply be called bad behaviour. I discovered, when I was five, with an equally delinquent friend, a hidden room in the network of old farm barns by Violet Bank. There were all kinds of decrepit and fascinating things in those barns. Defunct farm machinery decades out of date, rotten trailers, piles of bald tractor tyres and rooms full of rusting tools and farm supplies inches thick with cobwebs and grime.

Unusually, the door to the hidden room was locked so we accessed it by breaking a window with a wrench liberated from the tool store and climbed through. Once inside we discovered a trove of enormous glass vats and vessels – dairy apparatus for milking cows. Although we genuinely thought they were as old and disused as everything else in the labyrinth of relics, that is in no way an excuse for what ensued. Having enjoyed the sensation of smashing the window, for the same reason a child draws on house walls or pours paint on the carpet, I took the wrench and struck one the vats that stood almost as tall as me. It exploded into a thousand shards like a glass firework. In a devastating frenzy lasting no more than a few minutes, we both destroyed thousands of pounds' worth of delicate glasswear until nothing remained intact and we were surrounded by piles of vicious shards. Of course our mindless vandalism did not go unnoticed as it transpired the equipment was still in use and belonged to the farmer who lived in a different village but passed through the yard most days. Having caught me dozens of times building dens in his hay barn or climbing around his roofs, I'm sure it didn't take him long to figure out the culprit. Though it made the local paper, somehow perhaps because we were so very young we seemed to get away relatively lightly, although I learned my lesson and have never since partaken in any form of vandalism or wanton destruction. Well, not on anything like the same scale at least.

The incident that almost got me grounded and to nearly miss my first day on rock wasn't quite as bad. I had been playing James Bond, my second favourite game after Indiana Jones, which involved being a secret agent on a mission to foil some evil plot. Having borrowed my mum's best gardening secateurs, I was climbing around the rafters of one of the old cow byres attached to our house that we used as a log store. I needed to cut the power to the villain's lair in order to undertake my daring plan to save the world, so I stood on top of a tall log pile and dutifully snipped through an electrical cable in the ceiling. It was a live wire, and a small explosion took a good chuck out of the secateurs' blade; I was electrocuted and tumbled down onto the hard concrete floor. Quite shocked but relatively unscathed, I was mainly concerned about the secateurs; I shouldn't have been using them for anything and there was no hiding the damaged blade and the singed, blackened metal, suggesting something more serious than catching some gardening wire. Plus the power to the log store was gone so when Dad went out that night to collect the evening fuel supply the light didn't turn on.

Thoroughly busted, I came clean. Mum was furious and threatened to forbid the day's climbing I'd been so looking forward to as punishment. I thought I was in trouble for ruining her secateurs and the lights in the log store, but I'm sure she was really far more concerned about my safety. I was a handful as a child and were it not for her love, support, guidance and self-sacrifice I could easily have stumbled down the wrong path.

Thankfully she calmed down and on my very best behaviour I went with Dad and Pike and my schoolfriend Alan Drummond to try rock climbing at a small but idyllic crag called Hoff Rock on the outskirts of Appleby.

Hoff Rock is about 30 feet high and set in a lush green meadow. It has a nice flat base and trees at the top that can be easily used as anchors for top-roping. A conglomerate outcrop, a kind of natural concrete with various sized pebbles and pockets set within, there are about a dozen good routes, several of them ideal for beginners.

I was a late developer and in the summer of 1990, aged ten, when I tied into a rope to rock climb for the very first time, I was barely 4 feet tall and skinny as a rake. The smallest child in my school year and, with a late-July birthday, the youngest. Perhaps this was the reason I never took to more conventional sports, with all the other boys much bigger and far more developed being difficult to compete with on the playing field?

But I took to climbing like a rat up a drainpipe. I breezed up my first route effortlessly and straight away wanted to push myself and try something harder, a common trait amongst climbers. I did another slightly harder one with a bit more effort before being stopped in my tracks by the hardest route at the crag, a climb called the Gromozal, E2 5c. There was one letterbox-sized slot in the middle of a 20-foot wall that was apparently smooth as a mirror to my novice eye and it seemed utterly impossible. Pike said he'd never seen anybody do it. Just a couple of years later, following frequent visits to the Hoff after school (and occasionally during), I had improved so much that I would frequently climb it solo, without a rope.

The psychical action of ascent came naturally to me. My prepubescent lack of upper-body strength combined with Pike's timeless advice to 'Think about your feet' encouraged me to use my lower body and balance to advance upwards. Immediately I grasped that, used correctly, climbing ropes, harnesses and all the other intriguing paraphernalia and meticulous systems could make this dangerous activity relatively safe. With a rope above you whilst seconding the lead climber or, as on this occasion, on top rope where the rope goes up to an anchor at the top of the cliff and down to a belayer at the bottom, there is virtually no risk of falling – in many ways it's safer than walking as you can't even trip over!

I was enthralled by the cerebral, problem-solving element of climbing, trying to figure out how to use your strength, suppleness and stamina to overcome a vertical obstacle with your limbs and a given set of available things to grasp and stand on. I believe we are born climbers – after all, we evolved from a common ancestor with apes, who are masters of ascent. Our bodies are very similar in design physiologically and it is utterly remarkable what we are able to climb with our four limbs, twenty digits and powerful brains with sufficient training and technique.

People often visualise rock climbing as like climbing the rungs of a ladder, but in fact it is rare to find such uniform steps in nature or to use such unsophisticated actions. There is a host of imaginative manoeuvres at our disposal. Our dexterous hands can pinch, jam in cracks, crimp with our fingers curled over tiny edges with thumb on top for extra strength, or hang open-handed on unimaginably sloping holds. We can use side pulls, under-clings and one-finger pockets. Forearms or shinbones can be barred across wide gaps, even whole-body bridges across wide chimneys can be used to ascend. We can heel- or toe-hook with our feet and with the sticky rubber of climbing shoes it's amazing how we can stand on even the poorest smears.

Low-angle slabs that look as smooth as glass to the unfamiliar eye can be climbed with the help of just a scattering of matchstick-size edges, pushing hands down and feet high to meet on the same hold, a move called a mantle shelf. Horizontal roofs hundreds of metres long that I'm sure would give any primate a run for their money can be free climbed, using ropes and gear for protection but not to aid ascent. With the right equipment we can climb fearsome fangs of rock a mile high in the most inhospitable corners of Earth that simply look impossible and where no other forms of life exist.

An infant instinctually uses climbing techniques before developing the advanced ability to balance and walk unaided. Just watch any one-year-old navigate a room holding on to furniture, side-pulling doorframes or pushing and pulling their way to a sofa. But from very early in life we are taught to fear falling and to be sacred of heights. The consequences of mistakes whilst operating at height are drastic. We quickly become aware of this, partly by intrinsic nature, partly by parental nurture, and without giving it chance to develop we soon lose our natural climbing ability.

Perhaps my independent spirit and mischievous adventures in the trees and barn roofs had allowed mine to continue to flourish? Or perhaps I am not normal, as I have so often been told throughout life when recounting my escapades? No doubt my mum and dad's liberal parenting helped. Another thing that grabbed me about this new and exciting game was the lightning-fast access travelling vertically gives you to real adventure. Often defined as a journey into the unknown, with an element of risk and an uncertain outcome, I had always fantasised about adventure.

I was obsessed with Norse and Greek myths and Hollywood movies centred around the classic narrative of the quest for adventure like Indiana Jones or James Bond. True stories of explorers like Meriwether Lewis and William Clark, Captain Scott and Ernest Shackleton, and Sir Edmund Hillary and Tenzing Norgay had gripped me since I could remember. I even did an award-winning primary-school project with detailed maps, scale diagrams and creatively written first-person reports of the infamous misadventure of George Mallory and Sandy Irvine's 1924 Everest expedition.

I was captivated by those brave men who disappeared into the cloud so close to the top of the highest mountain in the world, never to be seen again, almost three decades before it was finally conquered by Hillary and Tenzing. Little did I know that twenty years later I would climb Everest myself and take the role of Irvine, clad in identical gear for an IMAX movie, *The Wildest Dream*.

I dreamed of one day crossing oceans, of polar journeys, of climbing the highest mountains, of rescuing princesses, finding treasure and slaying dragons. All of which, as you will read in the coming chapters, were to come true either literally or metaphorically! But what that first climb and that friendly little cliff near my home taught me was that you don't have to undertake great journeys to the ends of the Earth, or even spend weeks and months in adversity to find those defining characteristics of adventure, you simply have to climb a few metres up a rock.

My friend Alan, who had a very loving but overprotective mother, reacted very differently to me on the same climb, more akin to the way most people do on their first route or when faced with danger. He was scared within moments of leaving the ground, didn't trust the rope, couldn't think straight or move freely, struggled in panic and was promptly lowered to the ground in a tearful mess.

We are a varied species who all enjoy or dislike different things. One boy's dream is another's nightmare. But in the sentiments of Carrol Shelby, the legendary American race-car designer, those of us lucky enough to find something that we are both passionate about and good at early in life are truly blessed, as for us the meaning of life is clear: pursue that passion for all you are worth. It is not even a choice but a necessity, for we will never be satiated without it. I had found mine: climbing.

Over the coming months and years, Pike, Dad and I would climb together whenever we could. Dad was captivated just as much as me and is still an active climber to this day, though starting so much later in life he never progressed into higher standards.

We mainly climbed around the Eden Valley, and in the eastern and northern Lake District, all within an hour's drive from home. I was probably the last generation to receive a very traditional introduction to climbing as indoor climbing walls were still very uninspiring, rudimentary affairs in the early 1990s. I learned to climb in a similar way, and often on the same routes as the pioneers of the sport in the late nineteenth century, but of course with the huge benefits of modern gear and knowledge. The first ascents of some of these climbs date back to the 1880s and are considered to be some of the earliest recorded rock climbs.

Pike lived in a hamlet called Brackenber on the lower flanks of Hilton Fell in the Pennines, just the other side of Appleby and about half an hour's drive from Bolton. We would visit him and Di quite frequently in their beautiful sandstone bungalow that Pike had built himself. Set on a hill in a big garden with extensive views in all directions, it was very much a climber's house, the walls decorated with paintings and framed prints of mountains and lots of photos of Pike and his climbing chums on adventures all over the place.

He had a magnificent mountaineering library. It is a curiosity of mountaineering that it is pretty much its own literary genre. Pike had all the classics: *The White Spider* by Heinrich Harrer, *The Mountains of My Life* by Walter Bonatti, *Conquistadors of the Useless* by Lionel Terray, *Touching the Void* by Joe Simpson, and hundreds more. Dad borrowed and read most of them over the next decade.

I wasn't a big reader as a child, preferring instead to be outside searching for any kind of adventure or mischief. There was however one book in Pike's library that I loved and pored over for hours every time we visited: Ansel Adams' *Yosemite and the Range of Light*, a huge coffee-table book of America's most famous landscape photographer's epic black-and-white, large-format photography. This was my first encounter with what those who spend extended periods there refer to simply as 'the Valley'.

The photographs showed a place beyond beauty. I never imagined somewhere so perfect could actually exist. And when Pike began to point out the walls, routes and features with a climber's eye I was transfixed.

'El Capitan is three thousand feet tall and takes most teams a week to climb,' he said.

A 3,000-foot vertical cliff! The Hoff is 30 feet tall and the big cliffs in the Lakes are 300 feet. The highest point of England, Scafell Pike is only 3,209 feet above sea level and that is a mountain! I couldn't conceive of the scale or imagine how you would climb such a monstrous wall.

'On the Nose there is a 100-foot pendulum, just here, called the King Swing. You have to run across the wall on the rope to swing between the Boot Flake and this crack that leads to the Great Roof.' He pointed to a clear boot shape halfway up the astounding promontory of El Capitan. 'And here, there's a ledge half the size of a tennis court that you can pitch a tent on and another here no bigger than a single bed that three of us had to sleep on.'

I knew that one day I was going to Yosemite and I too was going to climb El Capitan. That day would come and I was to spend many seasons in that mighty valley learning and refining skills that would lead me to greater adventures in even more grandiose landscapes.

We would sometimes attend slideshows about climbing at Ullswater Community College in Penrith. My first was by the most famous of all British mountaineers Sir Chris Bonington about an expedition he had just completed to unclimbed peaks in East Greenland. He had sailed there from the UK with the legendary Sir Robin Knox-Johnston, the first man to sail single-handedly non-stop around the world. These men seemed like a bridge to an earlier, more adventurous time when the blanks on the world map were only just beginning to be filled. Chris spoke of vast regions of still-unexplored summits in Greenland, Antarctica and the Himalayas.

Even back then in 1990 he spoke of his disdain for the commoditisation of mountaineering and of consumable adventure such as being guided up the Seven Summits, the highest point of each continent. He had had the chance to be one of, if not the very first to complete that challenge but had abandoned it to pursue his own, more pure dream of adventure on obscure, unknown summits about which nobody beyond a small community of dedicated climbers cared or even knew existed. I liked that idea of true adventure fuelled only by desire and not bragging rights.

After his lecture I spoke to him and he signed a postcard for me. Already a hero, later he would become a mentor and a great friend despite being my grandfather's age.

We went to another talk by Jerry Moffatt. Much younger and more of a rock climber than Sir Chris, he illustrated his travels to cliffs in astounding locations in Europe, America, India and beyond with stunning photography. He described his early years living in a cave at Stoney Middleton in the Peak District. He had climbed the hardest trad routes of the time, including an epic saga on a dangerous route called Master Walls in Wales that spurred him to move away from trad climbing into the new discipline of bolted sport climbing. He went on to establish some of the hardest climbs of that style, making him a strong contender for the title of best climber in the world for a time.

'Is Jerry the best climber in the world? What is the hardest route?' I fired questions at Pike.

'He's bloody strong, but all that poncing about on bolts isn't proper climbing,' said Pike dismissively. 'The hardest route is Indian Face [on Clogwyn Du'r Arddu in Wales]. It's E9 6c and there's no bolts. It was first climbed by Johnny Dawes and in my view he is the best,' Pike stated categorically.

Pike was close friends with Doug Scott, another legend of UK mountaineering who lived lower down the Eden Valley, where Pike would regularly do building work on Doug's big property. He enlisted Dad to help make some sash windows and I accompanied them to visit. Doug had a gear room full to bursting with fascinating equipment from his adventures: his oxygen apparatus from the first ascent of Everest's Southwest Face when he had become the first Brit to summit, and via what is still one of the hardest routes; heavy ironmongery, pitons and bongs that used to be the only gear climbers had to climb giant cliffs; loads of ice axes and boots, ropes and huge chains of carabiners. It was the most amazing Aladdin's cave, the toyshop of my dreams!

Doug was very distracted as he was organising a trip to Mount Vinson, the highest peak in Antarctica and one of the Seven Summits. There were mountains of equipment and supplies being sorted for his imminent departure to that faraway land of mystery. He looked stressed and explained to Dad that Antarctic expeditions were outrageously expensive and that most of the costs were priced in US dollars. He had raised funds in British pounds but the exchange rate was fluctuating wildly, putting the whole expedition in jeopardy. What a great problem to have, I thought!

My very first longer, multi-pitch route was 'Little Chamonix' at the charming Shepherd's Crag in Borrowdale, near Keswick. When climbing a cliff that is taller than a rope length it is broken up into logical sections that we call pitches. We usually try to stop on a ledge or the most comfortable 'stance' available. On steeper cliffs that sometimes entails simply hanging from the cliff, a hanging belay. At the top of a pitch the leader, exclusively Pike on those early climbs, would attach himself to an arrangement of safe gear or perhaps a tree as is often the case in the Lakes. Dad and I would then second with Pike belaying us up with a rope from above. This is the basic method that enables us to scale cliffs of any height using standard ropes, usually 60 metres long.

Little Chamonix is so named because although minuscule by comparison to its Alpine namesake, being set high on a hillside with majestic views over Derwent Water it does share the same sense of exposure that comes with taller climbs. I had another taste of that intoxicating sensation of high exposure, but this time it was exacerbated by being on a vertical cliff. At first it makes you feel small and insecure, but with time, for some at least, it becomes an emboldening, powerful and addictive experience.

The last belay on Little Cham is a small promontory that you straddle like riding a horse. The final pitch, graded Very Difficult on the confusing British rating system, is in fact a beginner's standard. It is only about 30 feet long but is very steep, almost overhanging, and the expansive exposure completely alters the feel of the climbing. Though I had enjoyed the more physical, sporting aspects of climbing on shorter 'single pitch' routes, this was something so much more, encompassing all the joy of those smaller climbs but with a whole added dimension of exposure, commitment and much more adventure.

My heart beat faster, I held on too tight. Even though I knew the rope was safe, being so high up made me irrationally question its security. But with some deep breaths and brave thoughts I composed myself and struggled up the steep face on big holds, surmounting the flat top that protrudes into the Lakes' most dramatic valley like the bow of a ship to reveal Pike's mentoring grin. He had done that climb countless times but he clearly savoured sharing the wonder of this great game with such an enthusiastic young apprentice.

'You're a natural talent, youth. You know, at this rate pretty soon you'll be ready for a much bigger adventure. Have you ever heard of the Old Man of Hoy?' asked Pike before we headed down to the delightful Shepherd's Café for brews and scones.

'No, who's he?' I naively replied, little knowing the idea that Pike was planning was to be a transformative and defining event in my life.

'It's not a person! It's a sea stack, Britain's finest adventure climb! A tower four hundred and fifty feet tall that sticks out of the sea in the Orkney Isles in the far north of Scotland. I think we should put a trip together after the summer when the midges bugger off if you're keen? I dare say you'd be the youngest to climb it. What do you think, Mark?' he asked my dad.

Old Man of Hoy
Orkney, Scotland
58.8833°N, 3.4167°W
Original Route
E1 5b 450ft.

⑤

Open Book
Corner
4b, 80ft.

④

Fulmar
Ledges
4b, 120ft.
(beware!)

③

4b, 80ft.

② Haven Belay

Coffin Crux
E1 5b, 80ft.

① Scary traverse
5a

4a, 80ft.

terrifying
free-hanging
rappel 200ft.

Shanlo Lampey

3.

Young Boy of Hoy

The following September of 1991, after a summer packed with weekends climbing together, Pike felt we were ready for the Old Man. I was eleven years old. He enlisted the help of his friend and greatly accomplished climber Guy Lee. Guy was the manager of an outdoor education centre near Keswick, where by chance I had met him on a school residential a couple of years earlier. He was a softly spoken fella who did not seem to be jaded by the many years of taking kids on adventures day in, day out.

Guy had been a climbing partner of the great British mountaineer Doug Scott during his heyday, and together they had been on exploratory climbing expeditions to Baffin Island in Canada, the Himalayas and beyond. Guy had also made several trips to Yosemite, a place that would become my second home for much of my twenties, where he had aid climbed El Capitan in the early seventies. It was he who introduced me to the term 'big-wall climbing' that was to become such an important part of my life.

With long, straggly hair and wire-framed glasses he looked a bit like John Lennon during his hippy phase, and I was Guy's new biggest fan. Throughout the week or so of the Hoy trip I talked his ear off constantly, grilling him about his escapades on these big walls. He told me a story about having to take a giant rope swing under an enormous overhang on the Leaning Tower in Yosemite to outrun a storm – a route that I would make the first free ascent of a decade later. He recounted sleeping on walls in hammocks or on natural ledges, something I couldn't imagine. I was utterly transfixed by his tales of Baffin Island in Arctic Canada, where he had made the first ascent of the South Tower of the iconic double-barrelled Mount Asgard, a name and landscape borrowed straight from my beloved Norse mythology.

'It's like El Cap, but instead of a hundred paces it's a hundred miles from the nearest road! And it's not in sunny California neither, it's in the Arctic! It can snow in August up there and there's more polar bears than people in that neck of the woods.'

I was in awe! What a life he had led compared to the farmers, dustbin men, accountants and other 'normals' I had thus far encountered.

Pike had suggested we could try to raise some money for charity off the back of my Old Man of Hoy climb, and Save the Children was our chosen beneficiary. We repeated Little Chamonix accompanied by a photographer from our local newspaper, the *Cumberland & Westmorland Herald*. He shot some beautiful images of me on that exposed last pitch and summit promontory and on another occasion on that very first climb at Hoff Rock. This was my first of many adventure photo shoots and I feel so fortunate to have such high-quality imagery from my early days, though I didn't realise then just how important this aspect is to the professional side of climbing.

Along with Pike, Guy and Dad our idea snowballed into a mini expedition. My mum came in a support role, as did Pike's wife, Di. Another solid lead climber called Ken Tilford came as we planned to climb in two roped pairs, Ken and Dad on one rope, Guy and I on the other, with Pike somehow joining us too (it is usual to climb in pairs). A photographer and film-maker called Tony Riley who had been on the first ascent of the mighty Trango Tower in the Karakorum Mountains in 1976 was enlisted to help document the action, but he was quite a miserable chap and didn't seem to like me pestering him so Guy remained the hero in my eyes. My dad's workmate and keen outdoorsman Trevor Lewis and his wife, Barbara, also came along for the adventure, but not to climb, as did a kindly old chap called Tom who worked in the little outdoor shop in Appleby where I was to spend many lunch breaks from secondary school thumbing through climbing guidebooks and playing with gear.

We had also managed to secure some support for our charity expedition in the form of sponsorship. This was my first encounter with getting stuff for free and sponsorship that would become the backbone of my finances as a professional climber. Steve Reid, local guidebook writer and owner of the excellent Needle Sports in Keswick, provided a top-quality, new Petzl kids' harness. Tony Bennet, a friend of Pike's who was the UK distributor of Edelrid gear, gave us a pair of fluorescent ropes, one pink, one yellow, that I only recently convinced my dad to stop using. In our household where every pound was accounted for and the weekly budget was always tight, freebies such as ropes and a harness were a big deal, like Christmas and birthday combined. We received support towards the cost of the rented mini-bus and fuel for the long drive to the Orkney Isles and still raised over £3,000 for Save the Children.

We made our way north and took the ferry across from Scrabster to Stromness on the main island of Orkney, and then another smaller vessel across to the wild isle of Hoy. We drove across the island and established a base camp by the characterful but dark and dingy bothy that overlooks the windswept beauty of Rackwick Bay's pebble beach. The notorious Scottish midges hadn't quite disappeared yet and I remember being shocked at how horrific they were when there was no wind. Thankfully an almost-constant breeze kept them at bay.

Our burgeoning entourage began the six-mile hike around Rora Head and across the moor early in the morning. It was overcast, windy and not the most inspiring weather. Guy was unfazed. 'This counts as a good climbing day up here, youth. You should see what it's like when it's bad!'

I shuddered to think.

The walk seemed to take for ever; I was impatient to get to the climb. I was never a fan of the boring walk-ins to crags as a youth. Hoy is derived from the old Norse word for 'high', the topography of the island being far more rugged and hilly than the gentle nature of the other Orkney Isles, though after an initial hill the approach to the Old Man is relatively flat.

We rounded a corner and caught our first glimpse of the tower's summit poking above the edge of the coastal cliff. I pretty much ran the final half-mile and arrived at the spectacular viewpoint on the promontory overlooking the Old Man with a stunned halt. It was terrifying. Unlike anything I had ever seen, let alone attempted to climb. It seemed to me to be overhanging on every side and overwhelmingly tall.

Though Pike assured me we had done longer climbs over the summer, they were easy, wandering affairs up low-angle mountain crags. This looked like a natural skyscraper protruding from the intimidating crashing waves of the North Sea, a 450-foot tower of crumbling Orcadian sandstone standing on top of a sea-level granite plinth. Giant seagulls encircled it, their nests perched on rubbly ledges all over the monolith. A huge crack split the top in two and it looked as though half of it might fall off, which one day it almost certainly will. The whole scene looked like something out of a mythological landscape. That thought excited me.

There are seven different routes to the top of the Old Man of Hoy, but the East Face, known as the Original Route, which goes up the landward side hosts almost all ascent parties. It was first climbed in 1966 by Sir Chris Bonington, Rustie Baillie and Tom Patey. It became famous in households throughout the UK in 1967 when Chris Bonington returned with an all-star cast including Joe Brown, Dougal Haston and Hamish MacInnes for a weekend-long, landmark BBC live outside broadcast called *The Great Climb*. This was in the days when there were only two TV channels in the UK and the show was watched by an estimated 23 million people, almost half the population, propelling Chris to climbing stardom and onto his path to a knighthood. The BBC went to extraordinary lengths to demonstrate the possibilities of outside live broadcast, including building signal repeater towers across the whole of northeast Scotland and drafting in the marines and their tactical landing craft to bring 16 tons of technical equipment to the remote island. In 1991 the Original Route was graded Hard Very Severe 5b (HVS 5b) but was later upgraded by consensus to Extremely Severe 1 (E1). This was about the limit of my dad's and my ability at the time.

'Don't worry, lads, there's only one short hard bit. The rest of it is much easier than it looks, you'll be 'reet,' reassured Guy.

Climbs are always graded for the very hardest section. The first part is reference to the overall difficulty and danger of the route, the second part, known as the technical grade, represents the single hardest move. It is all rather confusing in the lower standards but becomes a little clearer once reaching Extreme (E) grades. These span from E1 to E11. Normally an E1 would be 5b, an E11, 7a. A lower technical grade such as E1 5a suggests that the route may be quite bold; conversely a higher one, E1 5c, likely means there will be a single hard move that is well protected. Though far more complex than most other international grading systems, once you eventually grasp the concept the British two-part grade is a very useful way of representing the nature of a climb in numerical format.

Some climbs can be very sustained at a certain standard but on the classic route on the Old Man there is only one, 10-foot section of E1 climbing on the second pitch; the rest of the 450-foot climb, being much easier, was well within our capability. I couldn't even see a way to get down the coastal cliffs that led to the foot of the tower (technically not really a sea stack as it can be approached by land, the debris from the fallen arch that once attached it to the mainland forming a bridge).

The descent to the base is actually far easier than it looks. A climbers' trail winds its way through cliff bands without the need for a rope, though care must be taken on a few slippery sections above deadly drops. I think Dad was more nervous than me as we descended, concerned about his own safety and performance as well as mine.

We reached the base and I watched enthralled as our leaders Ken and Guy geared up and tied into the ropes. Looking up from the base it appeared even more overhanging and I couldn't fathom how on earth it could be climbed at such a relatively moderate standard? Something about the geometry and prominence of the Old Man of Hoy against the sky creates this optical illusion. I have been back several times since then and always marvel at this false impression of desperation. Ken set off first and climbed up to a good ledge about 100 feet higher. Dad followed, no longer worried about me as I was safe in Guy's hands and he had his own ascent to focus on.

My turn came to climb and with the rope running in a straight line directly up from me to Guy on the ledge above, I felt secure. Though I was unaccustomed to the sandy, damp rock and some of the holds felt loose, the climbing was indeed far easier than it looked. It was like there was a steep staircase, hidden amongst the rock features just waiting to be discovered by the cunning climber that I was, and I got up to the ledge without too much struggle. I was quite alarmed by what I saw. Above, the face really was very overhanging and impossible-looking, but already Ken had set off for the next pitch which actually went down a little and then horizontally right across a narrow ledge before he disappeared into a hidden chimney through a big roof.

Ken yelled down for Dad to start seconding. Guy left shortly afterwards on lead. Soon enough my turn came to follow. Climbing sideways is much less safe for the second than going straight up as if you fall you will swing. On this particular traverse the swing would've resulted in me hanging in space away from the wall, a long way above the crashing waves due to the overhangs above. To avoid this unappealing scenario Pike had climbed up to the ledge and belayed me from behind with another rope as I set off, which would prevent a swing if I fell. I was a very short eleven-year-old and I found the down climb hard. The traverse across the ledge no wider than a shoebox, though easy, was by far the most wildly exposed position in which I had yet found myself. I was scared but starting to acquire the taste for this strange brew and found my situation unbelievably exhilarating.

I found my way into the hidden chimney and squirmed upwards using various body-bridging techniques that were new to me, sometimes with one hand and one foot on each side, sometimes both hands on one side and both feet on the opposite, and at some points both feet on one side and my back wedged against the other. Eventually the chimney squeezed closed. The rope ran out of the chimney and around the corner and showed me the way to go. But for the life of me I couldn't figure out how to get out of the infamous coffin slot and around into the corner above. This was the hard bit.

It dawned on me that my fear had completely abated; I was so focused on the physical problem that I'd forgotten all about the wildness of my position. And eventually, after some effort, I figured out a way to pull around the corner and to my delight I managed to get my left foot onto a good hold and propel myself into the less strenuous corner above. I reached Guy and the others on the belay very chuffed with myself.

'Good effort, youth, it's pretty much plain sailing from here,' praised Guy. I beamed.

The next couple of pitches, though a bit green and slimy from all the bird droppings, were quite easy, rambling along good ledges that are not clearly apparent when looking across from the headland.

It was towards the end of the penultimate pitch that I wandered slightly off route, the easier terrain allowing one to climb anywhere. I pulled up onto a ledge and came face to face with one of the giant seagulls, a fulmar sitting obstinately on its nest. I had been warned about these fearsome birds and their uniquely vulgar defence mechanism whereby they projectile vomit a foul, fishy bile with surprising range and vicious accuracy. The big white bird gave me an evil look then thrust its neck forward whilst opening its beak wide to deliver its sickening blow. I closed my eyes, ducked away and braced myself for the appalling smell, notoriously difficult to get rid of.

But nothing happened other than an aggressive squawking, hissing sound. Feeling smug about dodging the vomit bullet, I backed away from the beast and found the correct path to the others. As I reached them on another small ledge I noticed a terrible odour of rotten fish and a nasty green stain on Ken's fleece. He was somewhat disgruntled but Guy and Dad were in stitches as they explained that a fulmar is a one-shot wonder, it takes time for her to produce the bile bullet, so it is generally the first disturber who falls victim to the impact – and that had been Ken.

The last pitch to the summit is a real gem and a fitting crown to what is undoubtedly one of the UK's greatest adventure climbs. A perfect 90-degree corner like an open book, vertical on both sides, with a crack in the back that widens as you ascend. Good hand- and footholds and safe protection for the leader create a fitting finale to one of the finest tower climbs anywhere.

I was the last to arrive on the summit as for some reason, perhaps to expedite the descent, Pike didn't do the last pitch – a sign of his selfless character as, even though he was the driving force behind the project, he forfeited his summit for the benefit of the team. He had climbed the Old Man a couple of times before, but it was nonetheless a truly altruistic gesture.

Ken, Dad, Guy and I all embraced on the top. I struck the iconic pose of the Save the Children logo – legs together, two arms raised in a Y shape – which is actually the international alpine distress signal. With the others out of frame Tony Riley took a photo from the headland with a telephoto lens.

Pike had told me that during the 1967 BBC broadcast the legendary Scottish mountaineer and explorer Hamish MacInnes, widely regarded as the father of modern mountain rescue, had rigged a Tyrolean traverse, a cable all the way from the headland opposite to the top of the tower where I now stood. I struggled to envision such a rigging marvel but wished it had been there then and that I could zip straight across.

Twenty-five years later, with the help of my great friend and rigging master Waldo Etherington, we would rig this very same Tyrolean traverse using much-improved modern ropes and set up an insane 150-foot rope jump. We leapt from the exact spot where I had struck my Save the Children pose and plummeted half the height of the tower on the giant swing before jumaring back up the rope and crossing to the headland.

Though we had succeeded on the route, unlike all the routes Dad and I had done thus far, there was no easy way to walk off the back of this climb. It is an oft-cited fact that the summit is only halfway, the most distant point of a climbing journey, and that more accidents occur whilst descending. I have never seen any hard data to support this, but anecdotally I believe it likely to be true. Often in the big mountains fatigue or exhaustion are a factor leading to accidents on the way down. On steeper climbs or descending cliffs, unlike during the ascent, where ropes and gear are safety back-ups in case of a fall, during the rappel descent you are entirely dependent on your equipment and, crucially, what the ropes are anchored to. I have known several people who are no longer with us due to rappel anchors failing or other mistakes on the way down. Though Dad and I had practised plenty of rappelling, or abseiling as it is also called, and had done a couple of multi-rappel descents, these had always been by choice as an easier alternative to the walk-off, never as a necessity like on the Old Man and never in such a dramatic, gripping environment.

The standard technique to descend a cliff face of any size is a retrievable rope rappel. Two ropes are tied together and attached to an anchor point that remains in place. The ropes can be pulled down from below, retrieving everything except the anchor. On popular climbs such as the Old Man the anchor points are already in place.

I rappelled the first few sections by myself, but secured by a back-up rope on belay in case I messed up and let go of my control rope. On the cramped ledge at the top of the crux, second pitch, Guy informed me that it would be best if he were to lower me to the ground from here with an extra-long rope he had brought for this purpose. We were about 200 feet above where the waves crashed into the rocky shore. It looked to me as if I would be lowered directly into the sea. The wall below was very overhanging so I would be hanging completely in space far from the wall, like a spider on a thread, all the way, something I had never experienced before.

Being lowered obviously means somebody else is in control of your descent. From Guy's experienced perspective this was the best option as he didn't have to worry about any mistakes I might make. However, from my perspective, relinquishing control of my destiny, even to my new hero Guy, in such an intimidating situation was very unappealing. I stepped awkwardly off the ledge into Guy's hands. Immediately I was free hanging and I began to spin as he lowered me.

The other end of the rope hung in space, thrashing around like a whip in the gusting wind, slowly creeping upwards as I descended. Halfway down I met the end of the rope. To my alarm there was no knot in it. By now I was just a child-sized dot in space, suspended by a rope no thicker than a finger, miles from anything and in the most abstract position I had ever found myself. I wasn't convinced the rope was going to be long enough to get me to the ground and I worried that the end might slip through Guy's belay and I would plummet to my doom. I suddenly felt very much the little boy that I was, in way over my depth and terrified.

Totally gripped, I grabbed the end of the rope in panic. My descent abruptly stopped. I was unable to hear the yells from the support team on the ground or from Guy above over the howl of the wind and crashing of the waves. So long as I held on to the end of the rope there was nothing he or anybody else could do to assist me. After a few long moments I realised this and managed to tie a knot in the loose end which gave me the confidence to let go. Soon after, I reached the large, slippery boulders of the ground, further inland than I had expected. Guy later assured me there was plenty of rope remaining but was impressed that I had the nous to knot the end of the rope, which is common practice. Everybody made it down safely and we headed back to base camp victorious.

My 'Young Boy of Hoy' ascent gained significant media interest with the iconic Save the Children pose photo featured in many national papers. The charity were thrilled with the exposure and the funds we'd raised, resulting in Dad and I being invited to their annual convention at the Barbican Centre in London, where we were formally introduced to their patron, HRH Princess Anne.

Far more exciting than a royal introduction to me was that I was invited to be a guest on the kids' TV show *Motormouth*, one of my favourite programmes. Back in 1991 most people in the UK had just four terrestrial TV channels. Very few had satellite or cable. Children's TV was confined to just a couple of hours after school on weekdays and mornings during the weekend. *Motormouth* was broadcast live on Saturday mornings and was one of the biggest shows of the era. Every kid watched it. And what was more – Johnny Dawes, the world's best climber (as Pike had informed me), was to be my co-guest! Johnny was already a hero of mine thanks to his classic film made by Alun Hughes – *Stone Monkey*, the greatest climbing movie of its era. He had also established, as Pike had also told me, the hardest trad route in the world, the Indian Face, E9 6c, on Cloggy in North Wales. A climb so hard and bold it was almost beyond comprehension.

The advent of bolt-protected sport climbing was still relatively recent at this time. All but removing the element of risk, bolts enable climbers to focus exclusively on difficulty and as a result standards were sky-rocketing. A different grading system is applied for sport climbing – the French system, as France is where the style originated. Currently the ratings go from 4a to 9c.

Ben Moon had recently climbed Hubble, the world's first 9a, ushering in a new level of difficulty that required long-term, specific training and is still today regarded as a world-class standard with Hubble a particularly stout example. But with the removal of risk comes the removal of adventure, and climbing becomes purely sport, hence the title 'sport climbing'. I have always enjoyed sport climbing, especially on the sun-kissed crags of southern Europe, and there is no doubt that if you want to climb hard routes of any style some sport pedigree is vital. But I realised quickly that what I loved about climbing was the whole package of adventure, the wild places, the uncertainty, the unusual scenes and without question the risk. I enjoyed the danger and that meant trad climbing.

The whole Hoy experience had a profound and defining influence on my life trajectory. Not only discovering my drive for adventurous climbs and inaccessible summits and learning of little-known natural wonders like Mount Asgard, Trango Towers and Mount Roraima, but meeting the inspirational Guy Lee and the idea of dedicating your life to a passion. Turning away from the expected norms of education, profession, wife, house, car. Working nine-to-five, forty-eight weeks a year, watching football and drinking in the pub at weekends with an annual beach holiday to Tenerife. Guy and Pike were men who worked to live, not lived to work, and created lives worth living.

It was my first taste of media exposure, something that would become so important and prevalent later in my career. More immediately, Johnny Dawes would soon open my eyes to an entire subculture and an alternative way of life centred around climbing.

4.

The Original Stone
Monkey – Johnny Dawes

We arrived at the studio in Maidstone, Kent, at the very opposite end of the country to where we lived. Seeing behind the scenes of a TV set for the first time was enlightening.

With so few channels and high advertising revenues for the host channel ITV, *Motormouth*'s budget must've been healthy. They had contracted the newly formed UK division of the world's biggest climbing-wall manufacturer, the French company Entreprise, to build a mightily impressive temporary structure that looked like a double-decker-bus-sized Arc de Triomphe.

The construction crew were still building it when we were taken on the studio tour the day before the broadcast. It seemed they had a lot to do and I suspect worked all night to finish it. Dad was even more fascinated by the structure and construction process than me. A scaffolding substructure supported a wooden frame onto which were fixed a modular cladding of preformed resin panels the size of beach towels that were textured with features like a rock face. Onto these panels were attached an array of colourful, removable bolt-on holds of different shapes and sizes that could be arranged and rearranged to create routes of different standards. It was by far the most impressive indoor climbing wall we had ever seen. The underside of the arch that was also covered in holds formed a particularly impressive feature.

Dad got chatting to the foreman of the crew, Steve Jones, mentioning his joinery skills and trading contacts. It transpired that amongst the construction crew were Lake District climbing legend

Paul Cornforth, who had established many of the hardest routes on our home crags, and another local young fella called John Wilson, a friendly climbing/ski bum character, aged right between Dad and me, whom we both immediately befriended. Dad would go on to work for Entreprise for years at the start of the indoor climbing boom and I even spent a fleeting spell in their employment after I finished school. Both Dad and I are still friends with Paul and John.

The morning of transmission came and we were ushered into the studio for a dress rehearsal. I was to climb one of the gable ends of the arch on top rope alongside presenter Gaby Roslin, who would be asking me questions on the way up. I was a dedicated disciple to climbing and had adopted the regrettable early-nineties fashion trend born from sport climbing of extremely garish lycra tights and tops. For insurance reasons, I was told I would have to wear a helmet. I protested as it was not the done thing whilst sport climbing and certainly not necessary for top-roping indoors, but to no avail. The fluorescent-yellow tortoise shell dwarfed my head, and accompanied with bright-pink high-top climbing boots my quite ridiculous appearance was complete. On the test climb I was at the top before Gaby had left the ground, so for the real thing the director kindly requested me to climb as slowly as I could to stay next to Gaby as she scrabbled gracelessly up the wall asking me questions.

Meanwhile Johnny Dawes was lurking humbly on the underside of the arch. Surprisingly short and stout, he was dressed in his characteristically eccentric manner in a tattered collared shirt with rolled-up chinos and sporting a tweed jacket along with slightly unusual-looking trainers in which he climbed, the original Five Tennie climbing approach shoes. Out the corner of my eye I saw him leap like a lemur between two holds a full body length apart on the underside of the arch.

'Dad, did you see that? He really is a Stone Monkey!' I said, jaw dropping having never witnessed anything so cool – a double dyno, Johnny would tell me later.

Dad hadn't seen and in fact had not noticed Johnny at all. This became apparent shortly afterwards in the green room where we sat with the other guests waiting nervously to be called into the studio for our live broadcast segment. I was playing with my chalk bag and Dad noticed the chap in the tweed jacket smiling towards me in an inquisitive, friendly manner, no doubt amused by my absurd appearance.

'It's chalk for climbing, same stuff gymnasts use to absorb the sweat from your hands,' Dad helpfully pointed out to 'the world's best climber'.

'Dad, I think that's Johnny Dawes!' I whispered to him as his face flushed crimson with embarrassment.

The transmission went ahead without incident. I was introduced to Johnny on camera and watched in awe as he showcased his unique, dynamic style, bouncing around the arch in a way I'd never seen before. The show cut to the next segment in a different area of the studio. Presenters, producers and directors all seemed happy with our bit and we were left to play on the wall.

Johnny was beamingly friendly, his playful, almost childlike attitude merging with my youthful enthusiasm and obvious climbing talent immediately forming a bond of friendship that lasts to this day. He taught me how to dyno, legs bent like a frog's on absurdly high footholds, a slight swing to build momentum and dive with absolute commitment, aiming to strike the target handhold with arms fully outstretched at the precise moment you reach the apex of the arch – the dead-point where you expel the least inertia and can catch a hold with minimum exertion. Before the end of the session I too was leaping full body lengths between holds, albeit that was little more than four feet.

Back in the posh hotel that night, our boisterous behaviour ultimately ended up with Johnny throwing me into the pool of the decorative fountain in the foyer and almost being ejected! We exchanged phone numbers and left for home. I was more psyched about climbing than ever. As soon as we got home I insisted my dad build me a climbing wall in my bedroom. He had already built me a captain's bed, like a bunk bed with a ladder but with a built-in wardrobe, desk and set of drawers instead of a lower bunk. We fixed two eight-by-four sheets of plywood on the wall opposite the bed and another to the ceiling. Dad made holds out of wood and fixed a huge 'jug' (climber speak for a good hold) in the middle of the roof. I eschewed the ladder for the rest of my childhood, instead going up the plywood and across the ceiling. Soon I developed a radical double dyno from low on the wall to the jug in the ceiling and in one continuous movement turned my body to swing into my bed using one more handhold. It was rad and I did it every night. Later when Dad started working for Entreprise he built an extravagant three-dimensional extension in another corner, effectively turning my entire bedroom into a climbing gym.

I'd just started my first year at Appleby Grammar School and my *Motormouth* appearance did my stature in big school a world of good. Being small, poor at football and reasonably intelligent I wasn't an especially popular kid, but I had fallen in with a good crowd of clever, fun, if slightly geeky and anti-authoritarian friends.

My best friend was Haydn Martin. A foot taller than me and almost a full year older, he started to grow a beard before my voice had dropped. He was extremely intelligent, programming his own computer game in our third year and eventually becoming a university professor. My academic success at school was in large part thanks to his friendship.

Pike, Dad and I continued to climb together throughout the winter in 1992. By then Dad and I were competent enough to climb without Pike's guidance. Dad would always lead, with me belaying tied to an anchor, even if I was on the ground. Due to our great weight differential, if he fell, which was very rare, I would be pulled up. However, safely anchored, I was quite capable of holding a fall.

On one occasion a guy Dad had befriended through Entreprise came to visit. Big Mark lived up to his name: a bear of a man, 6 foot 4 and 16 stone. He was a very strong climber with numerous E5s to his name. In our usual haunt of Borrowdale, Mark was keen to climb a three-pitch classic E2 5c called Vertigo at Black Crag. I was already seconding to a higher standard than Dad, and Mark had done the route, which was well within his abilities, years before, so we partnered up, even though he must've been almost three times my body mass. The crux second pitch of Vertigo has a stopper move pulling through a small horizontal roof 50 feet above the coffee-table-sized ledge on which I perched tied to a tree. Mark was not in his best shape and stalled below the crux. A move higher, his feet below the roof and hands above, he began frantically scrambling around for holds. His whole body began to shake, then in his distinctive Bristolian twang with an unmistakable hint of panic, he screamed, 'You got me? I'm off!' and plummeted downwards.

I held the control rope leading into my belay device with both hands for all I was worth and braced. I was catapulted up until my tether to the tree went tight, leaving me suspended in mid-air and Mark dangling against the wall below the roof.

'Well held, lad, I thought you were gonna get threaded through that first piece for a moment there,' Mark shouted, trying to play down his fear.

A deciding moment in my dad's and my partnership occurred on a climb at Tremadog in North Wales called the Plum. An E1 with two pitches of 5b. As usual Dad had geared up and gone up first. Halfway up the first pitch he was stopped by a hard move. He placed plenty of protection but, averse to falling with me belaying, he made a bit of a half-hearted effort before grabbing the gear and hanging on the rope. He tried the move several more times without success.

'Can I have a go, Dad?' I shouted up to him.

'Er, I suppose so,' he responded nervously.

I lowered him down, we switched ends of the rope and I racked the gear onto my harness. I quickly progressed with ropes above me to his high point and continued to breeze through the move that had stopped him, all the way up to the belay.

With no ledge to speak of the belay on the Plum is a hanging stance. I fastidiously arranged lots of gear as we would both be entirely dependent on my placements for our survival and I anticipated that Dad might fall. He battled through the section that had stopped him on lead; climbs always feel far easier with a rope from above. As soon as he arrived he lit a cigarette looking perplexed.

'I guess I'll lead the next pitch too, shall I?' I asked.

'I suppose you'll have to, I don't think I'll be able to do it if it's as hard as that one,' he replied sounding reluctant. 'Put plenty of gear in and keep a cool head in yer keks, son,' he encouraged as I set off, having retrieved from him the gear from the previous pitch and organised it onto my harness.

'Just a sec,' he said out of the side of his mouth whilst lighting another cigarette immediately following the last.

There was a 'runout' section at the start with no gear and some stern moves. I felt confident and progressed steadily through the hard section off the belay at risk of falling below Dad.

'Is there any gear? How about now? Get some gear in, son!' Dad yelled. His words were accompanied by a continuous cloud of smoke that drifted up to me. I was in the zone and climbing solidly. I took care to properly place all the gear I could and was soon at the top without any drama.

Dad had a real battle getting off the stance, and fell onto my belay several times before, eventually, with a tight rope, he made it to easier ground.

'Bloody hell, son! Good bloody lead! There's no bloody way I could've led that!' said Dad.

'Thanks, Dad, I really enjoyed it,' I replied, thrilled by his praise.

'And you climbed it really well, all the gear was bomber, some of it was really hard to get out. But it was bloody nerve-racking watching you there, mate! I smoked nearly a whole pack!' he continued.

From that day forth the tables had turned and I was now the leader in our father–son partnership. I was twelve.

I'd persuaded Haydn to get into climbing and taught him the ropes. Largely because climbing requires a partner and I needed somebody other than Dad or Pike to belay me, but also to share with my best friend the wonderful world of climbing. Haydn lived in a remote village called Sleagill. Handily there was a great little crag called Jackdaw Scar situated right between our two homes within cycling range of both. I would ride my mountain bike on a largely off-road route and he would ride his dropped-handlebar racer along the road. We spent many evenings at Jackdaw, a 30-foot tall, carboniferous limestone edge atop a band of soft sandstone in a pretty location above the River Lyvennet, and host to a massive jackdaw rookery in a giant beech tree and sixty routes of almost all grades from entry level moderate through to demanding E5s.

Throughout my school years I worked my way through all of them, though we often climbed the same, best lines. Eventually I would add my first new route, the hardest at the crag with the incredible title 'Leo's Line', a tough E5 6a. I'd often eyed the potential for a zip line off the top of the crag, all the way down the bank and across the river. Doug Scott had given Dad some old pulleys and jumars (clamps for climbing ropes), I suppose accepting that his bigwall climbing days were behind him. With these new tools I felt it would be possible to sufficiently tension two standard climbing ropes tied together to rig the zip line. Haydn and I were accompanied by our other climbing friend Paul Aitken and his burly farmer neighbour Rob Elwood. I tied an end of one dynamic, 9mm-thick rope high in a tree on the top of the scar. The steep bank below the crag was a thicket of nettles, brambles and saplings but we managed to get the rope over it and across the knee-deep river.

On the far bank we attached a running belay to another tree and Haydn put his intellect to work rigging a three-to-one mechanical advantage with the pulleys and jumars based on diagrams recalled from memory that we'd studied in Physics at school.

'Don't you think we should be using static rope for this? Climbing ropes are dynamic and are really bloody stretchy,' Haydn enquired.

'We haven't got any static rope. It'll be 'reet if we get it really tight and get all the stretch out,' I responded.

The four of us pulled with all our might and the line seemed to be guitar-string taught and at an appropriate angle. Our braking system was to be the knot holding the two ropes together that was above the river. I crossed the river and made my way up into the tree at the top of the cliff. Prudently I had decided to test our rig with a rucksack. I duly attached it with another pulley and let go. It whizzed down precisely as predicted and crashed into the knot above the river, springing violently around the rope on impact. I was happy with our test and once the others had retrieved the bag, I loaded myself onto the line.

'Three, two, one – here we go!' I shouted and launched.

Immediately I plummeted, striking the ground at the base of the cliff, some 40 feet below. Thankfully my impact wasn't that hard as I was just at the limit of the dynamism in the line before I was catapulted high into the air like the arrow from a bow. At the apex of the bounce, I once again plummeted, this time flying through the thicket, shredding myself on the brambles and snapping in half a sapling the width of my forearm. One final oscillation propelled me skyward again before I was dunked into the river, finally smashing into the brake knot and violently springing around the line, just as the bag had.

I had neglected to take into account the effect the mass of the load would have on the stretch in the system during my rucksack test. I was probably five times the mass of the bag and dynamic ropes stretch up to 40 per cent when shock loaded. I was quite stunned, covered in bleeding scratches and had the snapped sapling tangled in my harness. My three friends were literally rolling around on the floor in laughter. To this day they recount this tale with giggles.

The scenic Leeds–Settle–Carlisle railway that was fortunately saved from closure in the late 1980s has a station in Appleby. This was to provide a conduit for my unaccompanied travels to explore the world beyond Appleby and its grammar school, opening my mind and eyes to that much wider world, far earlier in life than most. Both Haydn's and my parents allowed us boys in our early teens an usual degree of autonomy and independence, though mine were the more liberal.

Haydn and I would travel north on the train to spend weekends camping at a sandstone crag called Armathwaite, which was set in an idyllic location right by the River Eden, within walking distance of the station and complete with a sandy beach and bivi cave that negated the need for a tent. We spent nights cooking on fires, sleeping in the sand and later experimenting with spirits liberated from parents' drinks cabinets and smoking joints. In the daytime we would swim in the river, jump from the top of the cliff into the water and, of course, climb.

Occasionally we would also travel south to the limestone country surrounding Settle and the world-class sport crags of Malham Cove and Gordale Scar, though this entailed taking bikes on the train as the cliffs were miles from the station. I soon learned that multi-sport expeditions add many layers of complexity to the organisation and execution of an adventure. Though I do find these trips can be the most rewarding and multi-faceted expeditions have become something of a trademark for me.

We made all the classic novice mistakes, like forgetting tent poles and having to whittle them from sticks, breaking glass jars of pasta sauce all over the contents of our rucksacks and pitching the tent in a seemingly sheltered spot only to discover that it turned into a stream during the night's rainstorm.

Though it was undoubtedly the climbing that compelled us to make these adventures, looking back it was the whole package that I enjoyed – the journey to get there, the independence and self-reliance, overcoming obstacles and solving problems large and small, a forgotten tin opener or missed train. They were micro-expeditions that taught us much and for me formed the foundation of the macro ones I would come to professionally organise and lead as an adult.

5.

Sheffield

After our *Motormouth* meeting I pestered Johnny with frequent phone calls over the next couple of years. Eventually, when I was just thirteen, I convinced my parents to let me go and visit him alone in Sheffield to climb on the fabled Gritstone Edges of the Peak District. Often overstated as 'God's own rock' it is a very coarse, exceptionally hard, dark-grey sandstone that was once used to make millstones to grind flour.

Exposed edges skirt the moors of Yorkshire and Staffordshire but those of Derbyshire are the most renowned. Many grit crags are sculpted like fantastical Gaudí creations, leading to a very unique style of climbing often involving holds so sloping you would not imagine it possible to grip them and footholds invisible to the untrained eye. It also hosts the UK's best crack climbing, a specific sub-genre of trad climbing that requires specialist and initially very painful 'jamming' techniques to climb.

I took the train from Appleby to Leeds and another on to Sheffield carrying little more than my climbing shoes, harness and chalk bag for a long weekend. Johnny picked me up at the station and we drove for half an hour directly to Froggatt Edge. I had been there once before with Pike and Dad but then we had been 'puntering' around on the low-angle, low-grade lines of weakness that were flanked by far more impressive, sparsely featured slabs of the high-friction rock. Rarely more than 50 feet tall, gritstone climbs are renowned for punching beyond their weight. Some of the classic hard routes are either completely devoid of protection, or only house a handful of gear placements.

This was in the days before the advent of the very useful

bouldering crash pad, meaning once you were more than 10 feet up, ground falls had consequences. The severity depended on whether the landing was flat or a pile of rocks. Often every move from the bottom to the top is difficult and requires advanced techniques, hooking heels, pushing with arms as much as pulling and jamming. Grit climbing is a contrasting mix of delicate, subtle balance and pure brute force.

Johnny had been dancing along these edges for two decades. He was a master of the art of grit and seemed to know every hold on every route like the back of his hand. We arrived at the famous Downhill Racer section of the crag. A crew of twenty- and thirty-somethings, climbing-bum friends of Johnny's, were already there. Nobody seemed to have a rope. Johnny strolled up to a difficult-looking *arête*, wiped his Tennies on his trouser cuffs and to my amazement began flamboyantly but graciously soloing it – one-handed! Using momentum, timing and balance, he moved dynamically but with precise control in a way I had never seen nor imagined. He skipped down a chimney like a monkey in a matter of seconds, one of the climbs that had taken Dad, Pike and me the best part of an hour to ascend with all the ropes and paraphernalia on my previous visit.

'It's just the first bit that's hard. It's piss from halfway,' he grinned.

I put my climbing shoes on and, using both hands, repeatedly fell from the first moves of what was indeed a hard bit. With some guidance from Johnny, eventually I managed to get my toe up onto the terribly sloping foothold by my hands and with a little hop from the other leg, use the momentum to smoothly transfer force through the sticky rubber of my shoe, finding the friction to make it stick. I reached a small positive edge, a hold I was far more accustomed to using and was suddenly was on a small ledge halfway up the wall.

'Nice one, Leo!' said Johnny, wandering off towards his next performance.

Meanwhile I was high up, without a rope or any gear, wondering what to do next. I wanted to place a piece of gear as I knew if

I fell to the ground from here my trip was over, and the upper section looked far from 'piss'.

One of Johnny's crew, a gangly fellow with long blond undercut hair, scruffy clothing and a huge joint in his lips, spotted my conundrum. He soloed up an easier crack beside the *arête* and casually wandered along the tiny ledge to assist me, toking his joint.

'Don't worry, lad, follow me,' he winked.

He moved back along the ledge and very slowly, taking care to show me precisely which hand- and footholds to use, though my reach was at least two feet shorter than his, he patiently guided me to the top. His relaxed presence removed my fear and the way he showed me was actually far easier than it appeared.

'You need to learn how to hand jam for that direct finish, mate! I'm Andy Pete, pleased to meet you. Now follow me, duck,' he said in a soft but heavy Sheffield accent.

He showed me an easy way down, passed the joint to somebody else on the ground and beckoned me to follow him around the corner to a bay of easier routes. For the rest of the afternoon I followed him up a dozen cracks that he methodically selected for their jam-tutoring properties, all with the major difficulties low down.

He demonstrated the nuances of hand, finger, fist and foot jams. What at first felt to me like a torturous joke soon started to be far less painful and very useful. I started to grasp what Pike had once told me – 'a solid hand jam is better than jug'. This had seemed preposterous, but now I began to see that the mechanical wedge of a hand jam required less strength and causes less fatigue than holding even the rung of a ladder. That means if your arms are exceptionally tired, or 'pumped' as we call it, causing your fingers to literally uncurl, you can still rely on the mechanics of the jam.

'Where've you two been?' asked Johnny when we returned.

'Jam school,' replied Andy.

'Oh, sorry, Leo, didn't think to ask if you could jam. Bet the top of that one-hander was exciting!' he giggled.

★

Johnny lived in the iconic S7 postcode of Nether Edge on the south side of Sheffield, which has long been regarded as Britain's climbing capital, largely due to its easy access to crags and the gritstone and limestone of the Peak District. Most of the best climbing areas in the UK are situated in national parks or rural areas far from large conurbations. Some of the best climbers of the day shared Johnny's postcode, including Jerry Moffatt and Ben Moon, who would name his climbing apparel brand S7, such was the stature of that neighbourhood in the climbing community.

Situated in one of the nicer parts of town on a quiet street lined with cherry blossom trees, from the outside Johnny's house appeared to be the typical red-brick, two-up two-down terrace with off-shot kitchen so common in Sheffield. On the inside it was far from typical. He had bought it in a dilapidated state with the intention of renovating it. But his years of living in North Wales climbers' squats, lack of finance, disparate focus and truly eccentric character meant that for best part of the decade I visited him, the house would've been considered virtually uninhabitable to most decent folk or even the DHS for that matter.

Bare brick walls and sanded but unsealed floorboards aimed for industrial chic but created more of an urban decay aesthetic. His kitchen was more like that of a base camp than a house and for many years his toilet and bath were on the landing. The furniture was an eclectic mix of heirlooms from his well-heeled roots – cracked-leather Chesterfield sofas and fine Persian rugs – juxtaposed against items rescued from skips and home-made eccentricities such as the massive 'moose head' mounted on the wall that was actually a tree stump and took some imagination to resemble a hunt trophy.

It was a fitting set for the cast of crusty characters who constantly came and went, some paying rent, some sofa-surfing and others just passing through. Most of them were climbers, though some were also artists, musicians, film-makers and others linked to climbing culture in some way. One of them, Martin Hoyland, was to play a significant role in the next chapter of my life. Johnny frequently hosted parties, where I met Ben and Jerry,

John Allen, Steve Bancroft and many other climbing legends. It was a window into a world I had never encountered before and I loved it.

Back in Appleby, the pretty little market town was beginning to feel incredibly small-minded. I started to feel different to my fellow pupils, like I knew a secret that they did not but didn't care to find out, too concerned with their football matches, who they fancied, whether to buy Nike or Adidas trainers or if they preferred *Neighbours* or *Home and Away*.

Most weekends I would get a lift from Mum or Dad to Penrith and then take the X5 bus to Keswick. From here I would meet my friend Adam Hocking, whom I had met at the Keswick climbing wall that Dad had helped to build. If the weather was bad, which it frequently was, we'd climb all day indoors at the wall. If it was good we'd hitch-hike down Borrowdale to climb on rock. Adam was also a really good climber, stronger than me but somehow I seemed better at piecing it all together on routes. We pushed each other with a healthy rivalry and both began ticking off some of the hardest routes in the valley. A highlight for me was a route called the Torture Board at a fiercely steep crag called Reecastle. There was a photo of Paul Cornforth, biceps bulging, in the Borrowdale climbing guidebook that I had spent countless hours poring over since starting out on Little Chamonix. In a few short years I had progressed from V Diff to E7 6c, one of the hardest routes in the book.

I also began to enter some competitions. Mum or Dad would diligently drive me to the six or eight nationals held at the best climbing walls in the country through the winter. Most were a long drive from Appleby. I won the junior event at the 1994 World Cup at the National Indoor Arena in Birmingham. This wasn't quite as cool as it sounds as the junior event was actually a national.

I had taken to wearing a baseball cap backwards for climbing, which I still do. During my climb in the final I knocked the cap, covering my eyes. I paused, adjusted it and, flicking my long blond hair flamboyantly to raucous applause from the large crowd, who were there to watch the senior world cup, climbed to the top of the route and to victory. Later I learned most of the other competitors had fallen from the move on which I adjusted my cap.

Competition success at a national level seemed to be easier for my non-climbing friends, school and wider family to understand than what I did on rock. I began to gain more respect and credibility for my talent at what was still a very niche, fringe activity at the time.

Over the final years of my schooling I visited Johnny frequently. Andy Pete and Martin were always around but other characters seemed to drift in or out of Johnny's magnetic field of influence. Johnny always made time for me and was unwaveringly kind and helpful. He would make the effort to introduce me to everybody at parties, give me climbing gear, pay for my meals in cafés and buy me drinks in the raucous climbers' pub The Broadfield, where nobody seemed to care I was clearly underage. He immediately adopted me like a nephew and I was wholeheartedly accepted into the Sheffield scene despite being but a precocious teenager, ten years junior to most of the others.

At first I was oblivious to it but gradually I began to notice that Johnny was either the life and soul of the party and superbly fun to be around or he would be very melancholic, introspective and at times bitter. Much later I learned of his battles with mental health during that period and the disheartening riches to rags story of his family fortunes that impacted his life so negatively. Though we are still friends, our relationship faded in later years in part because of my difficulty understanding his inner turmoil.

Hard gritstone climbing is best practised in the colder months and it was then that I would visit most often. Whilst still in my mid-teens, with the man himself I began climbing the famous, test-piece routes Johnny had established just a decade earlier that had created his legend. All the hardest ones I climbed in a style known as 'headpointing' – derived from the sport-climbing term 'redpointing', where a climb is practised and rehearsed extensively before being attempted in one continuous ascent from the ground to the top. The other, more traditional way to approach a climb is 'onsight', where you climb from the ground up, first go, without pre-practice. This is a far more demanding, applaudable approach that requires one to identify the line, find the holds, figure out the moves and protection as you climb. Crucially, you only ever get one attempt to do a route first go.

On sport climbs rehearsal can be practised in safety on lead by hanging on the bolts between attempts. On trad climbs a top rope is used until you feel ready to get your 'head' into gear for the actual ascent. Most hard grit routes involve sections where a fall would almost certainly have serious consequences.

My first hard grit route was one of Johnny's called 'Slab and Crack' at Curbar Edge that I dispatched in a weekend. It was graded E8 6c with potential for a ground fall from hard moves, high up and protected beyond only by RPs (tiny brass nuts the thickness of a pound coin, the very smallest climbers' hardware). I was fifteen and by far the youngest to have climbed at such a standard on such a serious route. The same year I also climbed onsight many less desperate test pieces from the generation that preceded Johnny's.

Millstone is an old gritstone quarry on the outskirts of the quaint village of Hathersage in the Peak District. The quarrymen of the previous century had inadvertently created a climbing wonderland: a perfect set of square-cut corners, towering *arêtes* and steep faces against which we climbers would later challenge ourselves.

It was a cold, damp, windy day. Conditions were far from optimal but I was psyched out of my tiny mind knowing I wouldn't be able to return for some time. I onsighted all five of the classic E5s of the crag in a single afternoon. London Wall, White Wall, Green Death, Great Arête and Edge Lane are all very different in character but each hold equally well-deserved reputations. An onsight of any one would constitute a good day, and all five a good season for any strong climber. Such a day for a fifteen-year-old was unheard of. Under Johnny's mentorship I headpointed many more hard grit routes, including the world-famous Gaia and End of the Affair, both E8 6c, and many more E7s, as well as onsighting loads of other E5s and a few E6s. I was beginning to make a name for myself.

Johnny had decided to become a film-maker and got hold of an early MiniDV video camera. It was the beginning of the digital video revolution in film-making. For the first time, broadcast-quality camera equipment and editing suites were readily available at affordable prices, democratising the art of film to all where formally it had been the preserve of professionals with access to expensive equipment and advanced skills.

Fortunately for me, Johnny or others had filmed many of my hard ascents. Eventually after years of delay Johnny completed his long-awaited film, a beautiful ode to gritstone crack climbing, *Best Forgotten Art*, that featured my big day at Millstone.

More significantly for my future career, film-makers Mark Turnbull and Richie Heap captured a section with my E8 ascents and an interview in their movie *Hard Grit*. Released in 1998, *Hard Grit* was instantly an astounding success, immediately attaining cult-classic status. It was hailed as the best climbing film ever made, in part thanks to the eccentric Seb Grieve's spectacular, hair-raising falls from infamous E9s, but also because of the insightful, anthropological approach the film took to the subculture, assisted by a banging electronic soundtrack. It won a dozen international mountain film festival awards, sold thousands of copies back in the days of VHS and spawned a massive boom in the popularity of hard grit ascents and similar styles of climbs around the world. It also launched my name firmly on the international climbing scene.

6.

North Wales Revelation

By the summer of 1995 I was outgrowing both Appleby and the centreless Lakes climbing scene. Unable to convince any of my friends to join me and once again benefiting from my parents' liberal support, I set out alone to spend the seemingly endless summer holidays in the hotspot of UK trad climbing, Llanberis in North Wales.

I took the west coast mainline train from Penrith to Crewe and another to Bangor in the northwest corner of mainland Wales. With a minute allowance, a giant old rucksack with all my climbing gear, camping gear and everything else I needed to spend six weeks in climbing paradise, I set off to battle. I caught the bus from Bangor to Llanberis and hitch-hiked up the pass to the picturesque wild camp sites where I had previously stayed with Dad and Pike.

I found a magnificent, secluded spot behind a boulder a five-minute walk from the road with commanding views down the valley and up to the mighty fortresses of Dinas Cromlech and Dinas Mot, home to some of the best trad routes in the UK. Travelling alone, I was banking on meeting climbing partners at the roadside Chromlech Boulders, a popular evening venue for local and visiting climbers, or in the definitive climbers' pub, The Heights in 'Beris.

In between the major half-dozen features of the Llanberis Pass lies a plethora of smaller crags and outcrops, many of which are far bigger and more impressive than they appear from afar. Armed with the new Pass guidebook, on my first day I decided to explore an area ominously called the Gravestones that I would be climbing solo and onsight.

Not much to look at from the road, the Gravestones is a collection of scattered buttresses over a wide area of hillside towards the lower end of the pass. On closer inspection the prominent steep outcrops of compact rhyolite range from 30- to 100-feet tall in what could be imagined as the giant headstones of a church graveyard. There is much good bouldering and many of the shorter routes have a distinctly gritstone character. I set off light on the hour's walk from my campsite, carrying just my climbing shoes and chalk bag on a belt around my waist, the guidebook and a flapjack in my jacket pocket and a bar towel to lay on the often boggy ground to dry my feet at the base of the climbs.

I did a few excellent boulder problems on an outcrop of gradually increasing height. The rock and style of climbing very much suited me and I progressed along the routes of the face with increasing height until I transitioned from bouldering to soloing short routes. I felt I was being careful, methodically climbing up, finding and chalking the holds, discovering the most efficient sequence of moves then climbing down to the ground to rest before attaining my previous high point with far greater ease and less fatigue.

Down climbing is often harder than going up and inevitably there comes a point of commitment. This is one of the games we climbers play, deciding whether or not we feel capable and confident enough to pass the point of no return, to commit to a move you cannot reverse, leaving the only remaining options to climb to the top, to be rescued or to fall. Climbing solo with nobody else around really only left me one desirable outcome.

It is an educated gamble with astonishingly high stakes for no tangible reward, but within lies the essence of why we climb: a deep, apparently meaningless internal journey of discovery, projected onto the face of a rock or mountain that provides those that are inclined with powerful, life-defining emotions when successful, or potentially life-shattering outcomes if we fail.

Climbing without a rope, drastically more so onsight, is the most distilled nuclei of this concept: at some point there is moment of commitment. I reached that moment on an innocuous little route called King of Rumpy, E6 6a, perfectly described in the guidebook as 'A solo proposition above a back-breaking drystone wall and brutal fin. From the wall, move up into the groove and teeter nervously to the top.'

I committed and indeed teetered nervously to the top. I felt empowered, emboldened and indestructible. I moved on to another, taller buttress called the Hidden Wall, set in a dip behind a hummock, obscured from view from most perspectives.

Soloing above 30 feet, if you fall you are unlikely to walk away; above 100 feet you are unlikely to survive. Hidden Wall ranges from 50 to just over 100 feet in height. I used my methodical approach to climb a HVS, an E2 then an E3, each progressing in difficulty and height, feeling in control and trusting my judgement. Next I did an E4 with a hard move that created the moment of commitment low down but was much easier above.

Next came the classic of the area: Rimsky-Korsakov, E5 6a, one of the high routes and what was to prove one of the low points and most harrowing near-misses of my barely begun climbing career. Over multiple attempts, I climbed up and down, gaining height each time until identifying the point of commitment, what I thought was the crux of the route. It was too high up to fall. Spurred on by my successes and the relinquished difficulties following the crux of the E4, and full of reckless teenage courage, I rested for a long while before attaining my high point and committing to the crux. I did the moves and continued on better holds up slightly overhanging rock to a body length below the top. To my horror there was a final hard move. I tried all I could to uncover a hidden hold or secret move that would ease me to sanctuary, but there was none.

I had covered a lot of rock that day with repeated attempts at each route and my arms were beginning to give out. Not only was I free solo, 100 feet above a rocky landing, I was alone on a hidden wall. Nobody even knew I was there, long before the days of mobile phones. Horrible thoughts ran through my mind. Even if I survived the impact, how the hell would I crawl down? It is not a popular venue, far from any hikers' radar, and even in the climbing honeypot of the Llanberis Pass it could be days or even weeks until somebody found me. The handwritten advice of Joe Brown, who lived just a few miles away, flashed before my eyes – 'Don't solo.' As the grains of energy ran through the hourglass of my forearms I was left with a simple choice: do or die. Summoning strength that seemed to come from beyond myself, I did.

Perched on top I felt sick, my arms burned with lactic acid and I sobbed, thinking of my mum, my dad, of Pike. Of all the adventures I had planned and all the places I wanted to see. I pictured myself crumpled and bleeding on the rocks below, what so nearly could have been. I sat there for an age, watching the sunset framed by the steep sides of the pass, contemplating my foolishness. There and then I decided never again to solo. A dictum that for the intervening twenty-five years I have largely adhered to on all but easy or unprotectable climbs, with just a couple of notable exceptions. The immediate implication of my conclusion not to solo meant I needed to find a partner. With the psychological recovery time of a fourteen-year-old, climbing-obsessed risk-seeker, that meant before tomorrow. I headed directly from my perch down to the road and hitch-hiked to The Heights.

The pub was a hive of energy. At that time The Heights was the quintessential climbers' pub, the best I've ever known. The walls were decorated with large, iconic framed photos of rock heroes on local climbing odysseys: John Redhead on Margins of the Mind, Johnny Dawes on Indian Face, Ben Moon on Statement of Youth. It even housed an aged first-generation Bendcrete climbing wall made of moulded concrete in a room right by the bar (although it seemed to be used more for sneaky romantic encounters than climbing by that time).

As soon as I walked in I caught the eye of a tall, muscular, pretty girl with big wavy hair in the unmistakable attire of a climber. She smiled at me. Perhaps she noticed my wild-eyed, near-death survivor's energy. Far too young-looking to be served at any bar, I only made it into the place because it was so rammed that people spilled onto the patio outside.

I walked straight over and introduced myself, more to ask her to get me drink and if she would like to climb tomorrow than to chat her up.

'Hi, I'm Leo. Are you a climber?'

'Yeah, I'm Jo, nice to meet you,' she said in her charming Geordie accent with a slight slur, swaying noticeably on her feet, which suggested she was already several pints in.

Before I could say another word a muscle-strewn hulk with bleached-blond hair, wearing a Stone Monkey tank top (the brand of choice in that era) that displayed bulging biceps and veins popping out of his forearms, bounded in between us like Tigger.

'Hi, I'm Tim, this is my girlfriend.' His beaming friendliness and positive energy quickly replaced his prickly chat-up-intervention tone. My childlike appearance obviously presented no real threat.

'What grade do you climb?' were pretty much the first words I spoke to Tim Emmett. Something he likes to recount often. He was six years older than me, very much the 'naughty public-school boy' and was studying for a degree in Marine Biology at Bangor University. He would quickly become one of my best friends and climbing partners. Over the next fifteen years we would share hundreds of climbs, BASE jumps, parties, escapades and misadventures in Wales, across the UK and beyond.

He bought me a pint and introduced me to as many of his crew as were in earshot. Amongst them were renowned expedition climbers Paul Pritchard, Noel Craine and Adam Wainwright, and up-and-coming talents Chris Wentworth, Chris Hope and many others. It was a wonderful, welcoming vibe and I quickly found an audience as I recounted my near-death experience from only hours earlier.

'You onsight soloed Rimsky-Korsakov, you nutter!' seemed to be the general response.

I was a total lightweight with alcohol and suffered from excruciating hangovers whenever I drank more than one beer until I managed to drink my way through them by my mid-twenties. However, that never dissuaded me from getting swiftly hammered if there was a party, though I didn't drink habitually. By last orders I was a wobbling mess as the entourage with whom I'd become ingratiated wandered back to a large, shared house called Woodleigh, just down the road, where I assumed some of them lived. More drinks were poured and joints rolled.

'Where are you staying?' asked a slightly older guy called Simon, who turned out to be one of the hosts.

'In a tent by the Cromlech Boulders,' I told him.

'Ha! Good luck getting there in your state, mate! You can stay here if you want,' said Simon.

I spent the rest of the summer there without a single night in my tent. I climbed loads of hard routes with Tim, Chris Wentworth and others in the Pass, at the atmospheric Gogarth sea cliffs and in the vast Dinorwic slate quarries that scar the landscape above Llanberis in a strangely beautiful way.

The following summer of 1996, after completing my GCSEs and compulsory education, I returned to Llanberis. This time I already had a network of friends with whom to climb, principal amongst them Tim. I'd finally gone through puberty, grown a lot taller and become much stronger in the year since my last visit.

That summer was an exceptionally warm, dry one and I had the most amazing time of my life so far climbing with Tim, Noel, Chris and a host of others. I climbed almost every day, if not dawn 'til dusk then certainly noon 'til dark, only stopping for rest days when my fingertips wore down to a bloodied mess. The biggest problem in my life at that time was that my climbing shoes had completely worn out to the point where my bare toe protruded from the front. Climbing shoes are expensive and a full-price pair would've annihilated my entire eight-week budget. I somehow procured another pair of the same model, Five-Ten Anasazi lace-ups, my all-time favourite shoes, but they were a full two sizes too big. This didn't matter too much on easier routes and I took to wearing two pairs of socks inside them. But on harder routes where the footholds are smaller it made a drastic, negative difference.

Occasionally I'd convince my partner to lend me theirs if I was leading and they were a better fit. But mostly I persevered, fighting my way up many hard routes with my floppy shoes that added at least a grade to most of the climbs.

Amongst the many great routes I did that summer, almost all onsight, one stands out in my memory head and shoulders above the others: Jerry Moffatt's Master's Wall, an E7 6b shrouded in history almost to the point of mythology, on Clogwyn Du'r Arddu (or 'Cloggy'), high on the flanks of Snowdon. Cloggy requires a long spell of dry weather to come into condition and the two-hour, uphill approach means it is never busy, despite the astounding quality and quantity of routes, including some of up to 1,000 feet, the longest in the UK.

Master's Wall is situated on the East Buttress of Cloggy on a gorgeous shield of stone known as Great Wall, the showpiece of the crag. All the routes are steeped in history but none more so than the controversial Master's Wall and its more direct, true finish Indian Face. The saga has become folklore in British climbing. The larger-than-life John Redhead, a climber and artist, was the first to attempt this visionary, faint scoop up the right side of the wall in 1983. He made several attempts from the ground up, taking one drastic fall, before eventually abandoning his attempts and rappelling down to commit sacrilege by placing a bolt at his high point.

'Like a dog pissing to mark his territory,' John later wrote.

The next year, new kid on the block and soon-to-be climbing megastar, one of the first truly professional climbers, Jerry Moffatt came down on a rope from the top for a brief inspection, breaking the unwritten rule of climbing new routes ground up. He concluded the face above where Redhead had placed his bolt, where the scoop turned a blank wall, was too difficult, but found an alternative, right-trending line from a little lower down the scoop. After onsight soloing the easiest line on the face Great Wall, E4 6a, to test his head, he promptly chopped Redhead's bolt and led his line. He was climbing as well as anybody in the world at that time but still endured a traumatic battle on the climb.

The next chapter was written by my friend Johnny when he came down from the top to inspect the direct finish, deciding that he possessed the skills and the head to lead it. He duly did, creating Indian Face, the world's first E9, and ushering in a new era of difficulty and boldness. I knew this history well and was captivated by these tales of wanton bravery, especially Redhead's audacious ground-up attempt. I wanted to add the final chapter to the saga by onsighting Indian Face but knew I was not yet ready.

I partnered with a guy from The Heights called Angus Faid who the very next year died in a climbing accident in the Alps. Arriving at the lake below Cloggy for the first time, witnessing the Great Wall, a natural monument to climbing history, the tales of the greats written in the stone, I was spellbound. I too wanted to solo Great Wall onsight like Jerry, even after my awful experience on Hidden Wall the previous summer. However, Angus wanted to climb it too and was keen to lead the harder first pitch, and understandably wanted a rope. I belayed as him as he worked his way up with great effort and much time until eventually he reached the belay. I seconded without tying into the rope, effectively soloing though the rope hung right next to me. That would offer no help in an unexpected fall but the get-out option radically alters the feeling of commitment. Angus was tired from the first pitch and didn't want to lead the top one so I did it without placing a single piece of gear. Again effectively soloing, but this time with the commitment-reducing get-out of placing a piece at any point should I have desired.

Though definitely not a true solo, my motivation was the same as Jerry's had been: to test my head and master my fear before trying Master's Wall. Ironically, following my absurdly dangerous non-solo of Great Wall, I felt confident I was in good enough psychological order for my next test on the face: A Midsummer Night's Dream, E6 6a. This time my baggy boots gave me much grief and I found it way harder than Great Wall. Really taking my time, I led both pitches, and though it was thought-provoking I never felt pushed anywhere close to my limit. That terror was reserved for my next ordeal, Master's Wall.

It was late in the day but I was psyched and Angus was willing to belay. I set off up the initial groove, the history that so enthralled me almost palpable in the scent of the lichen and texture of the rock. I entered the scoop reaching the fabled 'old style rock 6 in sideways' that had held Redhead's fall, an obscure piece of gear that I had procured especially. I placed it and carried on up the groove with increasing difficulty.

Completely in the zone, I felt I had attained what has more recently been termed the state of flow, completely absorbed in the moment, 100 per cent focused and without fear. After a while I noticed the scoop ran out not far above and that I had transitioned onto Indian Face. For a split second I considered continuing on that route, but knew the crux was near the top and extremely foot intensive, not one to be attempted in my hindering footwear.

I reversed some distance, scouring for an option leading up a rising line rightwards as Jerry had. I spotted some tiny holds though there was no real line of which to speak. I progressed painstakingly up those holds, hard move following hard move, up the slightly under vertical face on positive but minuscule footholds. I cursed my floppy, oversized shoes the whole time as I had to hold on way harder with my fingers and constantly adjust position as my feet rolled inside them.

Eventually I saw a feature to aim for, a thin diagonal line of edges, but just a single move below them I hit a dead end. By now dangerously far above the last gear, I dreaded to think what would happen should I fall. There was a hold that I had used for my hand that I could get my foot on in an awkward position just above hip height, but my hands were too low to rock onto it. Though the rock was heavily textured, I couldn't find any handholds high enough to make the move. I was getting tired and the footholds that I stood on seemed to be getting worse by the minute. I spent what seemed an age there and considered asking Angus to take me off belay, scramble around to the top and drop me a rope. But that would require untying and dropping one of the ropes, which I didn't think I could manage and besides, accessing the top of Master's Wall is an involved, time-consuming process that would take at least half an hour – I didn't think I had that much energy remaining.

I had hit my limit, that ephemeral, invisible line. Panic rising, I desperately tried to stay on top of my fear. Feeling close to critical, I closed my eyes and felt around the area of rock where I needed my hands to be, like a blind man reading Braille, until my fingers connected with a character that felt good enough at this desperate point on which to pull. Too scared to look at what I held, I went for it and made a massive rock over to the distant edge. My fingers stuck to the Braille and I grabbed the hold. To my dismay it was wet, as were the next couple of far better crimps. Now I knew I had thoroughly crossed the line and was beyond my limit. Without stopping I scrabbled my feet and pulled on the wet holds, praying my fingers wouldn't grease off. The next moves were like an out-of-body experience, again powered by a force beyond myself, until I came back to reality with my feet established on better holds and my hands on positive but filthy features.

To that point, my memory is vivid. Beyond, I don't remember anything of the last, easier section of the pitch, nor if Angus followed or if I rappelled to retrieve the gear. Perhaps it was temporary amnesia caused by shock? Or maybe just that twenty-five years of hard living has clouded all but the most entrenched synapses of long-term memory.

What I do know is that I have only reached and crossed that personal limit whilst leading a rock climb on very few occasions since and never with such grave potential consequences. Flirting with your limits is the most rewarding climbing experience, but to push those limits too far, too often, on serious climbs only leads to one place and that is one place I do not wish to explore!

What stands out in my memory as much as the climbs of that summer was the thriving Llanberis climbing community of the era. Not just the individual characters but the whole vibe of the time. It was the tail end of the Thatcher-sponsored, UB40-backed generation of British climbing, when dole payments could be drawn remotely by post and literally hundreds of climbing bums congregated in hotspots like Chamonix, the sport crags of Provence, in Sheffield and in Llanberis for years at a time.

Though not sufficient funds to live comfortably – discomfort is a common theme within climbing – the measly government payments provided plenty for the very basics of the climbing life: food, beer, fags and occasional bits of gear. The mass unemployment that led to these easy if meagre pay-outs spurred a boom in climbing standards. When Johnny climbed Indian Face in 1986 there were as many as thirty full-time climbers operating at E6 and above in the village of Llanberis alone. They lived in virtual squats and in real squalor, devoting themselves to climbing. Many eventually found employment and meaning elsewhere in life, some are still lurking in satellite villages, eking out a modest living however they can, and a few took the skills they mastered during that time to climb the hardest routes, greatest walls and most savage mountains around the world.

That life appealed to me. I wanted to be a climbing bum, to live off the dole and turn my back on the rat race. I didn't mind sleeping on a floor and eating tuna pasta every night if it meant I could pursue my passion and climb every day at the cost of all else. My bold, onsight ascent of Master's Wall made waves throughout the climbing media in the UK and was even featured in *Climbing* magazine USA, the most widely read and influential publication in the sport.

After that mind-blowing summer of social revelation, having reached a world-class standard of climbing, I returned to begin my A levels at Appleby Grammar School. I had performed well in my GCSEs with an almost clean streak of As and A*s and had every intention of going to university, in Bangor, in two years' time. All my close schoolfriends and most of my wider network had also stayed on for sixth-form education.

Within weeks I knew this was no longer my place. When I asked how people had spent the summer, nobody had done anything of any interest. Haydn had done a mildly interesting kayak trip down the Ardèche Gorge with his dad, a few had been on beach holidays to Majorca or Tenerife, but other than that all they seemed to have done was hang out, get drunk and swap girlfriends. It was a stifling feeling; like a caged bird, I was ready to fly but was trapped in an academic prison surrounded by small-minded people with narrow horizons. Like Frodo returning to the Shire after crossing Middle Earth, I had fire in my heart and was ready to express myself on the battlefields of climbing.

Martin Hoyland, one of Johnny's crew, had recently moved to the outskirts of Bangor and the last time I'd seen him had mentioned he had a spare room that I was welcome to rent for £25 a week.

'Mum, I want to move to Wales to do my A levels in Bangor,' I said one morning at the breakfast table. In my head it would be just like going to university two years early.

'Do you think you'll be self-motivated enough to finish your A levels?' Mum asked. 'The workload is far higher than for GSCEs and you struggled to focus on those.'

I assured her that I would, and before half-term I was living with Martin and had enrolled in Coleg Menai further education college in Bangor. Even more promptly and acutely than when I'd returned to Appleby Grammar School, I realised that it too was not the place for me.

Throughout my time in Wales I had almost exclusively hung around with expat English climbers. There were a few Welsh amongst them but in my eyes they were primarily climbers. I had noticed a slight nationalist undertone in Llanberis – the lady in the post office who always spoke Welsh and to whom English seemed very much a second language, the gnarly-looking truly local crew who hung out in the back corner of The Heights looking menacing and never smiling or saying hello to anyone. But I hadn't understood just how separate a country Wales is, nor how the English are sometimes resented there.

My college life was nothing like Tim and my other friends' university lives. They were in the melting pot of higher education where people from all corners of the country met for the first time.

There were freshers' weeks, all kinds of uni clubs, halls of residence, shared houses and legal drinking in bars and clubs. I was in what was basically an extension of school.

Throughout school I was fascinated by Chemistry and Physics, at which I had excelled. I had enrolled in these same classes in Appleby then Bangor. All the other students at college seemed already to know each other, no doubt having been at school together with established cliques and friendship circles well forged. They were all Welsh and though never outwardly hostile they were far from welcoming. I struggled to make any friends, something that usually comes very easily to me. On occasion during a class introducing a complex physics theory, a student would raise their hand and ask a question in Welsh. The teacher would respond in the same throaty, rapid tongue that was as alien to me as Mandarin. A minute later I would raise my hand and unbeknownst to me ask the exact same question to sighs and rolled eyes from the rest of the class and sometimes even the teacher.

I discussed things with my parents and explained that what I really wanted to do was try to make a go of it as a professional climber. After some consideration they responded, 'If you think you can make a go of it, we'll give you £200 a month for a year. If it works out and you start to earn a living from climbing by next September, brilliant. If not, then we want you to go back into education.'

I am blessed to have such supportive parents who could see my passion and drive so early on. As you may have guessed, things did work out. I dropped out of college before the end of winter term to pursue a path as a professional climber.

7

Passion Becomes Profession

Whilst still at school I had picked up contractual sponsorship from climbing brand DMM and the youthful, blossoming, UK surf brand Animal, known for their watchstraps and funky T-shirt designs. The founders of Animal, a pair of committed young surfers and talented graphic designers, had developed a Velcro watchstrap for surfing, a catchy logo and made some cool T-shirts. With clear entrepreneurial insight they marketed themselves as an extreme sports brand, sponsoring skateboarders, kite-surfers and snowboarders as well as surfers. This was during the mid-nineties, when the term 'extreme sports' first entered the mainstream lexicon. Redbull had just entered the UK market and snowboarding in particular was booming into the next big thing. Soon Animal were making watches, an entire clothing line – and millions of pounds.

I had introduced myself to Animal at the infamous Camping and Outdoor Leisure Activities (COLA) trade fair that used to be held bi-annually in Harrogate. I too had twigged on to the equity in 'extreme sports' and felt that climbing was every bit as cool as snowboarding, and was in fact the original extreme sport but had an image caught up with the leather boots, red socks and flasks of tea brigade from a bygone era.

I was here to change that. Bouldering as a sport in its own right was taking off, sport climbing was well established and regarded as cool. I introduced myself to the guys at Animal as an extreme sports athlete with attitude whose discipline was climbing. I showed them some photos, magazine clippings and competition results. Natasha, their attractive and kind marketing lady, took a shine to me. Animal were going through rapid growth and with booming budgets I joined their athlete team.

Early in the relationship I visited their offices in Weymouth, Dorset, for an athlete meet, which gave me invaluable insight into the world of professional extreme sport as well as to why Animal's founders soon had to sell a controlling share of their company. Natasha introduced me to the other athletes, or 'riders' as we were known. Most of them were up-and-comers like me, but apparently a couple of them were famous in their own scenes. They were a bit older and had a more self-assured swagger, but not being a snowboarder or surfer, I didn't know who they were. We were given the tour of the spangling new office. There were grown-ups' toys everywhere: longboards, surfboards, skateboards and awesome posters of the team doing their thing adorning the walls. Half the staff were beautiful girls and the other half were out the office surfing as the swell was up. Half-empty bottles of tequila and shotglasses festooned desks, with the odd rolled-up banknote lying around.

I'm not sure if there was any real purpose to the meet other than to introduce us all. Natasha took the time to explain to me how extreme sports marketing worked and was quite candid with the figures involved.

'Professional surfers like Kelly Slater earn millions of dollars a year. We are nowhere near as big as his sponsor Quiksilver, but we pay our top snowboarders professional salaries,' she told me.

'Like how much?' I asked.

'Some of them are on £30K per year,' said Natasha.

My jaw dropped. That was more than my than my mum and dad earned in a year combined.

'Now you're just starting out and climbing isn't a key market for us, but we like what you're doing and think you're going places, so we'll start you off on an incentive deal and down the line we'll look at a retainer,' she said.

I signed a deal that would pay me incentives for photos published in magazines where their logo was visible, for podium competition results and for requested appearances on their behalf. It was small amounts, about £500 for a front cover, but I didn't need much. I had a similar deal with DMM. At the end of the day we partied in the office, which sounded like a nightly occurrence. Tequila shots free-flowing and there was Redbull by the bucketload. I made friends with an Australian snowboarder called Drew. He wasn't an athlete but a photographer and editor of the influential *Onboard* magazine.

'It's all about the imagery, mate, photos and film. Doesn't matter if you're the best in the world in niche sports like snowboarding and climbing. Nobody cares. Brands sponsor people to make them look cool and help sell their shit. It's business not charity. You gotta give 'em something to work with and that's imagery of badass shit,' Drew enlightened me. 'If you're a footballer or an Olympic athlete, all you have to do is be good. Managers and agents will monetise it for you as there's enough money in it for them too. But in our games you gotta be smart. Keep doing what you're doing, but start working with photographers and get yourself out there, mate.'

That night we went clubbing. Unfortunately I got pulled up by the bouncers for being underage and had to go back to Natasha's place by myself. As l lay alone feeling disgruntled, my head spinning from the shots but unable to sleep from all the Redbull, Natasha and Drew's advice ran through my mind. I began to realise that climbing could be an actual career path and that I might be able to become a professional.

I wasn't interested in making my fortune from climbing, I was just looking for a means to an end, a way to enable myself to climb full-time and to travel to all those epic places I'd heard of to practise my passion. Once you have your gear, climbing is pretty cheap. I was perfectly happy to live in a tent as long as it was pitched near a cliff and I had enough money for food and the plane ticket to get me there. I wanted to climb, I wanted to explore, I wanted adventure!

The start of my life as a pro was nothing like I had imagined. Wales in the winter is a depressing place. To my astonishment it rained even more than the Lakes. That first winter it rained every day for three whole months and though it never put down more than a scattering of snow on the summits it was always cold. The nights were long and the days were short. In the off-season even the thriving scene of The Heights was reduced to just the menacing local crew at the back and a handful of the more hardened drinking climbers who actually lived in 'Beris. The endless sunny days of summer seemed a lifetime away.

My new home with Martin was a tiny, funny little house in a hamlet called Tal-y-Bont. It was only a couple of miles from Bangor but was serviced by infrequent buses. At sixteen I was too young to drive and besides, the costs of running a car were far beyond my means. A real blow struck when my bike was stolen from outside Tesco's within weeks of arriving, and even replacing that was beyond my budget or the already strained finances of my parents.

Martin did not drive and turned out to be far less of a climber than I had thought. He was a big man in his early thirties, starting to go bald, with a broad chest and ever-broadening waistline. He lived with his girlfriend, Emily, who had enrolled as a mature student at Bangor Uni, which is what had brought them from Sheffield to Wales. Though very intelligent, well read, a talented artist and seemingly worldly wise, often recounting tales of his days as a merchant mariner, Martin never seemed to do much of anything except smoke weed. Nevertheless he was good company and a great cook. Both of them were kind, and welcomed me under their wing, sharing their weekly groceries, teaching me to cook and the ways of independent living.

A saviour during that wet winter were the incredible club nights that Bangor Students' Union then hosted – wild, electronic dance parties, only one stop removed from the warehouse raves that gave birth to the dance music revolution. Back then, drinks were a pound for a pint or a shot, though the club nights were more fuelled by Ecstasy than alcohol.

Illegal outdoor raves were still happening at that time during the summer, in disused quarries around the 'Beris area. They would last all night and sometimes all weekend before they all started to get busted and shut down by the police. I discovered a love of dancing and partying that appealed to my wild heart and rivalled my thirst for adventure. Both are about enjoying life, living it to the full and going hard. Tim and I were a potent partnership on both fronts.

One regrettable night, walking back from a club night, Tim decided to demonstrate his climbing prowess by climbing a 50-foot-tall uni building that had decorative bricks protruding from a wall in a regular geometric pattern. It was extremely easy, perhaps E1, but Tim was barely able to walk and inevitably he fell from halfway up and landed on a flight of concrete steps, shattering his kneecap. Of all my years in Wales climbing hard trad and pushing the adventure envelope, that was the only time we ended up in A&E. After surgery he made a swift recovery and we both learned from his accident, if nothing else then never to climb whilst pissed!

My final farewell to my Appleby years was another ascent of the Old Man of Hoy, this time with Haydn. Before dropping out of school I had signed up to a sixth-form trekking and volunteering trip to Nepal. We had each to raise the £1,500 cost of the trip ourselves by a combination of sponsorship and parental support. Amongst the fundraising classics of car washes, sponsored walks and car boot sales, I suggested Haydn and I did a sponsored ascent of the Old Man. This time I would lead and we would likely be the youngest team to climb it.

The school were not at all supportive of the idea for obvious reasons of risk and culpability. But in 1996 health and safety liability was not as strict as today and our Geography teacher Miss Howard, who would be accompanying the Nepal trip, was a vocal advocate. She kindly offered to drive us all the way north and act as logistical support. As a non-climber, and with rescue services for Hoy located across the sea on the mainland, I don't think she could've helped much in an emergency. Nevertheless her selfless offer certainly helped to secure the school's blessing.

Standing at the foot of the Old Man, five years after my last ascent, though almost two feet taller and with a wealth of climbing experience under my belt, I was still impressed by the imposing silhouette the monolith cut. It was mid-October, late in the year for such a climb so far north. We had started the walk-in far too late after over-excitedly staying up late the night before and spending ages faffing in the morning. It was well past noon when we got to the base. But our real problem was that there was a full-scale gale hammering the tower. The sea was angry, the biggest waves spraying us with wash far above the shore where they crashed.

'Er, is this really a good idea, Leo? It's gonna be dark in few hours and it's forecast to piss down tonight,' Haydn, with harrowed brow, shouted at the top of lungs over the howling gale though I was standing right next to him.

'Don't worry, mate, it's miles easier than it looks, we'll fly up it. We'll have to give back all the money we've raised if we don't even try,' I convinced him.

Whilst he pondered, I set off and was at the top of the first pitch before he could see sense. We had a rucksack full of stuff that was way too big to climb with so ended up having to be hauled. This was a major hindrance and we did not fly up the route. Wind is a menace to climbers and at that strength a real danger. You can't communicate, it freezes you, makes you feel flustered, stressed and scared. Halfway up, one of the ropes got blown all the way around the side of the tower and snagged. Haydn had to untie from it so I could pull it all the way up. Then the bag got horribly stuck and I had to rappel down to get it. Meanwhile Haydn, whose warm and waterproof jackets were in the bag, started to become semi-hypothermic. It was dark before we reached the top but we had made it! That is, made it halfway.

The descent was my first real epic. The wind continued to rage and the forecast rain arrived. The ropes got stuck repeatedly on the retrievable rappels because of the wind and required some dangerous antics from to me to rescue them. Haydn's head torch stopped working. The camera tether snapped and it was lost for ever. With 60-metre ropes it is possible to descend directly from the top of pitch two to the ground, the same place where Guy had lowered me to my alarm years earlier. Haydn and I had 50-metre ropes which were the standard back then and that required a complex and involved sideways rappel to reverse the traverse of pitch two, to get onto the other side of the tower with the aid of a rotten old rope left in place for this purpose. It took me ages to get down first and Haydn even longer. Inevitably the ropes got horribly stuck again when we tried to pull them from around the corner. Only 100 feet from the ground, cold, wet and exhausted, we would have been in a very serious predicament were it not for the fact that before the ropes jammed we had pulled through just enough to fix a line that reached the ground.

'We'll have to come back and I'll go up to the top of the second pitch and get them tomorrow,' I said to Haydn, realising I was rather relishing the intensity of the epic experience – a trait that has proved useful throughout the many epics I have endured or enjoyed since.

We fought the long way back through the darkness of the storm to the bothy. Returning the next day in less horrific conditions, I left Hadyn, who was exhausted, on the ground. I managed to make my way up to the top of the ropes utilising some harrowing prussiking techniques I had not yet mastered, sort out the mess and get down, this time with our ropes.

Again the national media picked up on our success. Photos of us at Hoff Rock, with me wearing my Animal hat, were published widely, earning me a handsome return from my photo incentive with the brand. The school, who had so reluctantly allowed the ascent, hailed us as heroes and were thrilled with all the publicity. Haydn, appalled and mildly traumatised by the experience, did not climb again for almost a decade.

I continued to compete in national climbing competitions. I won most of them, and the 1996 national junior title, largely thanks to my long-time friend and rival Ben Bransby, who had always been, and continues to be, the better climber, being a year older and having progressed to the senior category. These wins and the Hoy media earned me enough from my Animal and DMM incentives to just about scrape through that winter of 1996.

I attended half a dozen European and world youth championships where I met and competed against future world champions and heroes of our sport like Chris Sharma and Patxi Usobiaga, who were about to usher in a new era of sport-climbing standards. I made it to a few finals but never the podium and realised that my newfound love of partying and distaste for serious training would have to be addressed were I to stand any chance of competing with this new breed on the international indoor stage. The boring format of competition climbing and the complete lack of adventure meant I was unwilling to make those sacrifices. I knew this was not the path for me and soon after stopped competing.

Around this time there was marked shift in the North Wales climbing scene. Tony Blair's New Labour had just won power for the first time in a generation, the economy was booming, unemployment was falling rapidly, the Spice Girls were a global phenomenon and Cool Britannia was on the rise. Perversely, the impact of this progress on 'Beris climbing culture was, at least from my perspective, a resoundingly negative one.

Moving to Wales, I had envisaged those heady mid-eighties days where dozens of hard-climbing, hard-living, squat-festering dolies climbed together, pushing each other and standards every day in some kind of hippy climbing-commune utopia. The economic growth of the mid-nineties had brought with it a burgeoning new industry – industrial rope access.

Construction companies specialising in large construction sites, tall buildings and oil rigs, had realised that there was a far more cost-efficient way to build and maintain the exterior of large structures or difficult to access areas at height than using traditional scaffolding. Many of the first generation of rope access companies were founded by climbers tired of living the dirtbag dream. They had realised that techniques climbers used regularly – rappelling, jumaring and aid climbing – could be modified and applied to any number of industrial tasks.

In a few short years, rope access became a multimillion-pound industry. Suddenly the climbing bums of 'Beris who already had the basic skills for rope access became a sought-after labour market and went from being unemployable to being in high demand and able to command £500 a day or more. Overnight it seemed every-one disappeared to work on the ropes.

With much of the work onsite or offshore, people would work for a few weeks, earn more money than they had earned in the previous year and then take a few weeks off to climb. This could be extended to work for a few months and then take off the rest of the year to travel and climb anywhere in the world. As my dreams of climbing professionally floundered financially I too considered doing my IRATA course and joining the tide.

However, money quickly brings with it increased expectations. People used to hitch-hiking could within a few weeks afford a Subaru Impreza. Those who had lived in squats could secure £100K+ mortgages and soon began to upgrade their standards of living at the expense of free time. Indoor climbing began to gain in popularity with climbing walls appearing in every major town and city, giving birth to another new industry and career path for climbers constructing these walls. As I saw it, these economic advances had a devastating effect on the 'Beris scene; I had nobody to climb with and didn't want to work.

8.

End of the Beginning

In early 1997 I was full of enthusiasm and dreams but lacked the finance and opportunity to chase them. Though he was supposed to be in full-time education, Tim too had aspirations to be a professional climber and was also sponsored by DMM. He had a car, a beaten-up old VW polo, and he was my lifeline. He would pick me up and we would go to the fast-drying slate quarries or microclimate of Holyhead, home to Gogarth, to climb whenever the weather allowed.

Following Drew the snowboarder's advice, Tim and I had begun working extensively throughout 1997 with a local professional adventure photographer called Ray Wood. He was well connected in the UK climbing scene, highly motivated and willing to shoot anything that looked good or was newsworthy. If published we gained exposure and returns from photo incentives and Ray owned the photos for which he would be paid.

The highlight of this collaboration for me was a new route on an impressive *arête* that I climbed headpoint in the Ogwen Valley, called Rare Lichen and graded E9 6c, the highest standard of the time. After my ascent Ray took some awesome photos that secured my first magazine front cover.

By now Tim was in his final year and had to actually do some work if he was going to scrape through uni with a degree, so he had far less time to climb. Everybody else was off seeking their fortunes on the ropes.

Noel Craine was one the eighties crew that had taken his skills to climb some of the greatest walls in the world. Along with Paul Pritchard, another of my childhood inspirations, Noel had done a host of serious trips to Asgard, Patagonia and Trango. He was eccentric, energetic, warm-hearted and an academic at Bangor Uni, meaning he had flexible working hours and hadn't partaken in the mass economic migration. He had a car, a clapped-out old Audi 80 that had once been a fine vehicle. He was very proud of its German engineering even though the boot didn't open. He became my regular climbing partner.

Never having put time into sport climbing, Noel was not very strong, though perhaps because of his experiences on those fearsome remote walls, he wasn't too fazed to attempt onsight almost any of the hard Welsh adventure climbs that, even though I was much stronger, I found daunting.

He would usually go up first and spend hours diligently working his way up some Gogarth horror show, placing copious amounts of gear, before running out of energy by the crux and lowering down. I would then go up on his gear in a fraction of the time with plenty of energy and more power to do the crux and finish the climb in a combined onsight ascent. We employed this tactic on dozens of hard routes and from Noel I learned much about how to climb extremely hazardous terrain far more safely than you might imagine possible. Though I learned equally as much from Noel about how *not* to do things, especially with regards to expeditions.

He continued to fire my imagination like Doug Scott and Guy Lee before him, recounting his tales of those remote, great big walls that I had dreamed of since I first started climbing.

The approach that Noel, Paul Pritchard, Adam Wainwright, Andy Cave, Johnny Dawes and others had taken to their big trips sounded pretty gung-ho. Shoe-string budgets and loose planning often resulted in avoidable, godawful epics but a surprisingly impressive success rate – a testament to their tenacity and grit.

In my soon-to-commence Yosemite years I noticed the far more thorough and rigorous approach to expedition planning that my future American friends like Conrad Anker and Jimmy Chin employed. When El Cap is your local crag and you spend winters living in the big mountains of the Rockies you tend to be pretty tuned in to the demands of remote wall climbing. No doubt their expeditions were also far more generously funded than the 'Beris crews', supported by the massive US outdoor market and its wealthy brands.

Later still when I began embarking on polar expeditions I spent time in Norway learning from unsung heroes of modern exploration, people like the late Rolf Bae, Robert Caspersen and Ronny Finsås. Again I noticed a much more sophisticated and calculated planning process to training and logistics than the typical tough but incompetent British style. Nobody ever seemed to lose fingers to frostbite on Norwegian trips and they did by far the most hard-core expeditions in the polar realm, whereas a lost toe almost seemed like a badge of honour to some Brits on trips that Norwegians consider casual trade routes, such as crossing Greenland or the normal South Pole ski route.

With a short stint working with my dad building climbing walls, including the impressive main wall at Kendal, I managed to just about claim to have made a living out of climbing and avoid returning to full-time education.

Late in 1997, with the miserable prospect of another long Welsh winter looming, I received a phone call that was to answer my prayers and change my life.

'I'm the marketing manager for Berghaus. We'd like you to join our sponsored team. We can offer you an initial £5,000 annual retainer; if you prove your worth it will increase,' said the mystery voice.

It was not by chance that I received that call. I had been pro-actively working towards my dream of climbing professionally, winning competitions, doing lots of hard routes and creating potentially valuable marketing assets in the form of inspirational photographs. Which is why, during some anonymous meeting at the Berghaus offices in Sunderland, whilst discussing the next year's marketing strategy to help them sell more jackets, somebody who had probably seen my Rare Lichen front cover mentioned my name, which led to that transformative phone call.

Had the conclusion of that meeting been to focus budgets on billboard advertising, that phone call might not have come and I might have missed my window of opportunity. Try as we might we are not entirely in control of our own destinies, but you have to be in it to win it. I was about to start earning a salary from climbing and enter a world of opportunity of my own creation.

The year 1998 was my coming of age. I said goodbye and thanked Martin and moved out of Tal-y-bont and into a wonderful house, usually a holiday let, in Llanberis. The last house on the road leading up Snowdon towards Cloggy, which I shared with Tim, his girlfriend, Jo, Chris Hope and a girl called Alison, who were all at Bangor Uni.

Tim managed to pass his exams and graduate with a degree, then got a job as a sales rep for DMM. The job came with a shiny new, racing-red, Alfa Romeo 955, a classic piece of beautiful Italian motor engineering that would almost cost Tim his driving licence but was a blast to hoon around in. We still climbed together a lot but he was often on the road, touring outdoor shops, touting DMM carabiners – and collecting speeding tickets.

One night after a few beers in The Heights, when the cursed Welsh weather had been spoiling our fun for weeks, Tim realised it had stopped raining and with his undiminishable enthusiasm declared that we should go to climb Right Wall, right now. He downed the rest of his pint and sprang to his feet.

'Right! Let's go and grab some head torches – who's in?' said Tim.

Right Wall on Dinas Cromlech is a classic E5 6a he had soloed the previous year. Chris Wentworth and I were game and we sped up the pass and marched up the steep hill to the crag.

Tim quickly dispatched the route by the light of his head torch. We enjoyed a fiercely competitive rivalry, and not to be outdone I first seconded Right Wall in my Tennies along with Chris in climbing shoes, then decided to up the ante by climbing the neighbouring but significantly harder Lord of the Flies, E6 6a. It had a big reputation but I had done it before so felt confident I could outdo Tim at this silly climb-by-night game. Though in coming years on bigger climbs I would realise climbing in the dark is a crucial skill on some ascents. Perhaps our boisterous games weren't so silly after all?

Halfway through the crux sequence my head torch stopped working and I was forced to down climb the hard moves by the meagre light of the moon to a rest where I could pull up Chris's torch. I finished the pitch, including the long runout at the top. Chris and Tim followed, the latter resentfully conceding that round of our ongoing game of one-upmanship to me. This tomfoolery became local legend and set the tone for much of Tim and my adventures together.

I had met a contemporary climber, Patrick 'Patch' Hammond. He was the same age as me, climbed at the same standard, was into the same style and enjoyed partying as much as Tim and me. He lived with his parents in the upper-middle-class neighbourhood of Rhos-on-Sea, where he was studying for his A levels. His dad, Tony, was a successful gold prospector and they owned a popular tourist attraction, some of the oldest-known human mines on the Great Orme near Llandudno.

With Tim often on the road, Patch became my regular partner and we climbed together loads in the first half of 1998. With the skills I'd learned from Noel but now with a stronger new partner, we onsighted many hard, multi-pitch routes in the steep zawns of Gogarth. Often it required rappelling in from the top to reach the routes. The rock is sometimes very loose and though only up to 300 feet tall, rising directly out of the sea Gogarth has the feel and character of a much bigger cliff.

Our other favourite haunt was the fast-drying slate of the Dinorwic quarries. The climbing style of slate could not be more different from Gogarth. The faces tend to be under vertical, enabling you to use holds that are literally the size of matchsticks. It offers very few gear placements that when available are often tiny RPs. There are occasional spaced bolts, an ethic unique to slate climbing that creates very long runouts with potential for huge but not necessarily dangerous falls.

We worked our way through many of the hardest slate routes, mastering the art of slab climbing.

These contrasting but complementary styles of Gogarth and slate climbing that we had spent so much time practising would soon prove to be invaluable when put to test on the mighty face of El Capitan later that year.

In summer 1998 I suffered my first serious fall and minor injury on my first attempt to lead an unclimbed route on Dinas Mot. It was an old project that Adam Wainwright had tried but found too difficult: a hairline crack up the steep, compact face, located several easy pitches up the massive, multi-faceted buttress.

I tried it many times on top rope, eventually unlocking a way to climb the moves and do it clean, but it was by far the hardest climbing I had come across on a trad route. Years earlier Adam had placed a piton in the thin crack below the crux that should've rendered the route safe. Though I didn't feel at my best, the piton gave me the confidence to try it on lead. I fell from the hard moves with my feet level with the piton that transpired to be part of a notorious, faulty stainless steel batch produced a decade earlier and it snapped. I hurtled down the face, smashing onto the ledge that Patch stood on 20 feet below before tumbling the same distance again down steep slabs before the rope snapped taught. Patch suffered vicious rope burns to his hands holding my factor-two fall that had created drastic forces when I, the leader, fell below the belay anchor; I had severely sprained my ankle. It could've been much worse but was an effective shot across the bow that probably averted a more serious incident elsewhere and tempered my gung-ho attitude. Slightly. For a while.

In July 1998 I went on my first international climbing road trip. It was to Norway with a strong team that included renowned alpinist Andy Cave and the sport climber Neil Gresham, who had recently turned to trad, making the third ascent of Johnny's famous route Indian Face. He was also a sales rep for DMM and as Tim Emmett had been demoted to a slower car following his collection of speeding tickets, we travelled in the beloved Alfa.

At the time there was a ferry from North Shields to Stavanger, where we went to visit a young friend of Andy's, Trym Saeland, to explore an area with a vast amount of unclimbed granite cliffs, little known outside Norway, called Rogaland. We loaded a roof box on the Alfa full with beers and a case of fine single malt whisky as gifts for our hosts, which Andy had assured us was valuable currency in the extortionately taxed, oil-rich, socialist state of Norway. We all stayed with Trym in his tiny studio apartment, where we completely filled the entire floor space, bedded down in our sleeping bags.

We were heartily welcomed into the close-knit Stavanger climbing community and I was introduced to characters who proved influential in later years, including Sindre Bo, Rolf Bae and Robert Caspersen. Unfortunately the trip was a washout: it rained heavily every day bar one of our two-week trip. Thankfully a couple of the crags in the region were so overhanging they stayed reasonably dry and we were able to do some climbing. I had just turned eighteen and was as cocksure and hungry to prove myself as they come. The others were all a decade older and far more mature. My catchphrase for that Norway trip was 'I'll climb anything you can in my trainers' and I did a good job of supporting my claim, favouring those specialist approach shoes that are good for climbing but disguised as regular trainers.

The ethical debate as to where it was appropriate to place bolts for sport climbing or withhold them to maintain adventure values was a hot topic in Rogaland at the time. As well as climbing many routes in my trainers, I did some of their hardest bolted routes using trad gear in my climbing shoes, just to prove a point.

The highlight of our trip was a couple of days in the jaw-dropping Jøssingfjord, which we nicknamed the Fierce Fjord, where Neil and I added the second free route, following Norway's strongest climber of the time Caspersen's first, to an absurdly overhanging 500-foot wall that forms a prominent silhouette at the head of the fjord called the Profileveggen ('profile wall' in Norwegian). We called our route Firefox, which was their name for a joint, and given E7 6c or Norwegian grade VIII was up there with the hardest multi-pitch routes in Norway at the time.

Our subdued, stereotypically conformist but extremely friendly Norwegian hosts weren't quite sure what make of my arrogant, energetic youthful self. We had a farewell party in the Stavanger climbers' pub Cementen on the picturesque docks of their oil-rich city, where I made a complete fool of myself due to my acute alcohol intolerance, blowing my shot of a dream end to the trip by going home with a blonde beauty and instead falling, or being thrown (I'm not sure which), into the harbour. After this they seemed to conclude I was OK.

On the last morning as we said our goodbyes (snatched between violent fits of vomiting amidst my desperate hangover from the previous night's partying), Rolf, the wildest of their crew, with whom I had most bonded, took me to one side.

'I have a gift for you, Leo,' he said, presenting me with a book. 'We should go here one day, it is the wildest place of all.' He smiled knowingly.

It was Ivar Erik Tollefsen's coffee-table photobook of the first climbing expedition, one he had led to the astounding otherworldly peaks of Queen Maud Land in the Norwegian sector of Antarctica where he and Caspersen had made the first ascent of the mighty Ulvetanna ('the wolf's fang'). It was *the* most astonishing mountain I had ever seen and inspired a life dream that I would dare in a later chapter of life.

After an overnight crossing the ferry arrived back into North Shields passenger port. We disembarked in the Alfa and drove onto the A1 heading south. We were on our way to the wedding of a mutual close friend, held at a castle on the way back to Wales. As we sped down the dual carriageway the imposing, recently unveiled Anthony Gormley sculpture the *Angel of the North* came into view. A 60-foot-tall human figure with 180-foot-wide wings wrought from rust-brown cast iron.

'Wow, look at that thing, I wonder if it's climbable?' Neil pondered.

I had just about recovered my self-esteem following my toxic hangover and responded, 'Ha, I'll climb that. I'll do it in my trainers!'

The car swerved onto the exit ramp, drifting tyres screeched around the roundabout and we slammed to halt in the lay-by beneath the *Angel*.

'Go on then, you cocky little shit!' Neil had had enough of my arrogance and intended to call my bluff.

'All right then!'

I stepped out of the car, walked the short way to the base of the sculpture and without pause shimmied my way up the iron fins that formed the body, onto the wing, then surmounted the over-hanging head to stand on top.

'Nah, nah!' I mocked from the highly conspicuous position.

'Stick your arms out,' shouted Adam, who was snapping a photo.

On the way down I casually strolled out along one of the narrow wings to the tip. It was 5 p.m. on a Monday and the A1 was full of rush-hour traffic that I noticed were braking dangerously to rubberneck at my display.

Suddenly the screech of sirens wailed over the hum of the traffic. Half a dozen police cars with blue flashing lights pulled into the lay-by beside the Alfa. I bolted back along the wing and slid down the fins like a fireman's pole in seconds, reaching the ground before the cops had made it to the base. I took off my jacket, calmed my breath and, trying to look as relaxed as possible, began to stroll casually towards the Alfa. I made it past the first two cops, who were running, helmeted and aggravated, towards the *Angel*. I held my nerve and kept walking until a plump, kind-mannered boy in blue accosted me.

'Excuse me, sir, I believe that was you up there and I am arresting you for a breach of the peace,' he said in his Mackem – not to be confused with Geordie – accent in the politest fashion the predicament could allow.

I was handcuffed, piled into the back of his car, driven to Washington Police Station, literally a mile from Berghaus's head office, and locked up in a cell. The others had kept their distance at the scene of the crime then left so as not to be late for our friend's nuptials. I had a roached packet of Rizla papers in my pocket which I was paranoid would lead the cops to investigate further should they discover them during my strip search so I promptly ate them. A challenging task without the aid of a drink. The same plump copper opened the door and escorted me to the interview room.

'I'm sorry, marra, but we'z got 'bout an hundred 999 calls from folks on t'A1 an' had to follow up,' he apologised.

They emptied my recently decriminalised pockets and set about taking my fingerprints.

'How way, man! I darn't think they'll 'ave this!' he said, attempting to make an ink impression from my granite-ravaged fingertips that left nothing more than a featureless smudge on the page.

I was left to sweat for another couple of hours before he returned and walked me to the entrance of the station.

'Am right sorry 'bout this, pal. We'll not be pressing charges, it'll not go on yer record and you'z free to go. The lads all think yer a cracker, and if I ever sees ya in the pub, I buys ya a pint, mate,' said the nicest policeman I've ever met as he released me.

I jumped in a taxi and arrived just in time for the reception party, full of old friends from the climbing world who were highly entertained by my brief incarceration.

Back in North Wales, I enjoyed the rest of summer with Tim, Patch and others, climbing classic test pieces onsight and seeking out ever more difficult and dangerous first ascents on the remaining unclimbed scraps of rock in the Llanberis Pass, unaware that soon my horizons were to be blown wide open and my perception shifted so far that I would never again feel the same way about those precious little crags and that special place that had been so formative. In September 1998, shortly after my eighteenth birthday, I made my first trip to the Yosemite Valley in California and nothing would ever look quite the same again.

PART TWO
Wild Times

El Capitan, SE Buttress
Yosemite, California
37.7307° N, 119.6320° W
El Niño, E7 6c, 3200 ft.

Porch

Cyclops
Eye

The Black
Dihedral

The Black
Cave

Big Sur Ledge

Calaveras Ledges

Galapagos

The Black Dike

The Footstool

Shanté Lomprey

9.

The Boy in the Valley

El Niño, Yosemite

'Nature provides the set, the ambition of your imagination creates the scene.'

Leo Houlding

The precipice below seemed to go on for infinity. A strong draught blew directly up the face of the void making the frayed end of the rope twitch and dance just a few body lengths below. It felt so wrong as I weighted the rope, my stomach knotted by nerves, tension racking my muscles and making me move awkwardly as I stepped over the edge. This was against everything I'd ever learned; this was how people died. I paused, took a deep breath, and then rappelled off the end of the rope and began to fall into the abyss.

A second later I was propelled sideways with breathtaking acceleration just feet from the wall, which flew past in a blur as I continued to gain speed before slowing down to a complete stop at the apex of the swing and dropping and accelerating back in to the next pendulum.

'Hell yeah!!!' I screamed in ecstasy, already sporting a bad Californian twang as the oscillations of the porch swing began to slow.

El Capitan is a sheer cliff 2,800 feet tall – three times the height of the Eiffel Tower. At the very highest point of the steepest wall there is a perfectly flat bench, easily accessible from above, where you can dangle your feet above that abyss. If you drop a stone from 'the Porch', it will not hit anything until it hits the ground twenty seconds later. It is one of the largest vertical drops on Earth.

The Yosemite Valley is a place of indescribable beauty. From the moment I discovered my passion for climbing, Pike had fired my imagination with tales of this fantastical place and his Ansel Adams photobook had inspired but not prepared me for Mother Nature's masterpiece.

Blessed with Californian blue skies 250 days per year, with trees taller than most British crags and cascading waterfalls that pour from walls of fairy-tale grandeur, Yosemite is in a class all of its own. I have travelled to many places lauded as 'like Yosemite' but have yet to come across anywhere that is even close. As the great Scottish naturalist John Muir said: 'It is by far the grandest of all the special temples of Nature I was ever permitted to enter.'

I would have to agree.

'But no temple made with hands can compare with Yosemite,' he continued. 'Every rock in its walls seems to glow with life . . . as if into this one mountain mansion Nature had gathered her choicest treasures.'

To think when he said that nobody had yet rock climbed there, let alone BASE jumped!

The outstanding natural beauty of Yosemite is equalled only by its wonder as an adventure playground. It is almost as though it were created for those with the skills and desire to explore and enjoy it to the limits of their imagination. Each season is clearly defined: snow-covered in winter, the deciduous trees bare; the mighty waterfalls at their peak in spring, the meadows awash with colourful flowers; the long, stiflingly hot days of summer; and my favourite, the fall, when the leaves come alive with a thousand shades of brown, yellow and crimson and the temperatures cool for hard climbing. The distinct scent of Yosemite, the sap of pine trees baked by the hot dry sun, is my all-time favourite.

There is another, less magical side to Yosemite. Though the park covers an area of over 1,000 square miles, the vast majority of the 4 million tourists that visit each year are concentrated in the six square miles of the valley floor. Most of them visit during the summer and at weekends. This creates a strange combination of national park meets theme park. Never-Never Land meets Disneyland. Deer, racoons and even bears, though technically wild, roam almost tame amongst the crowds. Ground squirrels shaped like Jabba the Hutt resemble many of the tourists that illegally feed them.

Mother Nature was on particularly fine form the day she sent the glaciers that carved such great walls from hard granite. But it is not only the walls and weather that make the Valley such an important place in climbing culture and an influential part of my life: it is the eclectic cast of dirtbag characters and world's best climbers that seasonally, every spring and fall, call Yosemite home – the Stone Monkeys.

One of these Stone Monkeys, an outlandish character called Scott Burke, invited me to his camp at the top of the Nose. Scott had been one of the top Valley climbers through the late 1980s and 1990s but never quite made it into the A team. Not very tall but ripped like a bodybuilder, he had a perm of dark hair, a slightly maniacal grin and a penchant for eighties-style day-glo attire and sunglasses. In fact he seemed to have stalled in that decade and although extremely friendly and psyched to the point of psychotic, already in his mid-forties he seemed to be straining to hang on to his youth, reluctant to accept that living in a tent might not be the best way to spend the next decade and that try and train as he might, his best climbing days were behind him.

Scott had laid siege to the Nose in a crusade to claim the second free ascent. Lynn Hill made the visionary, first free ascent of the Nose in 1993, and then repeated the feat in a single day in 1995. An ascent that to this day can be lauded as one of the most influential and outstanding in climbing history, and that created a blueprint, setting the bar extremely high for the El Cap free revolution that was about to begin.

After 261 days spent on the wall over the period of a decade, Scott would eventually claim the second free ascent. He used a top rope on the great roof, one of the crux pitches and his continuous ascent took almost a week making his achievement far less impressive than

Lynn's but a personal triumph of perseverance. It was during his long campaign that he enticed me to carry a huge load up the strenuous East Ledges to his long-established camp on the summit of El Capitan, right at the top of the Nose, with tempting tales of this epic Porch swing as reward.

The Porch swing was my very first taste of El Capitan and of big-wall climbing right at the beginning of my first big trip. It was September 1998, I was a cheeky, skinny eighteen-year-old, but I had already served my hard trad apprenticeship back in North Wales and I was bursting with motivation, hungry to prove myself on a grander, international scale and possessed of an insatiable appetite for dangerous fun.

That same season Dan Osman, a famous, larger-than-life American climber, had rigged the world's biggest rope jump from another Yosemite feature called the Leaning Tower. Over multiple weeks he had led a crew to build a record-setting 1,100-foot jump with normal dynamic climbing ropes knotted together. They made dozens of jumps from the complex rig. I had met him briefly on the top of the Lost Arrow Spire. He buzzed with energy as he described the rig and the sensation of the fall.

I was enthralled by this idea and decided to take the Porch swing a step further. Instead of walking along the rim of the cliff to create a swing, I would exit from the anchor point, creating a much more terrifying fall.

I lowered myself over the edge of the Porch attached to one end of a 200-foot rope with the other end secured to the diving board right next to me. Then, I let go to plummet for full rope length down the face, like a simulation of a giant lead fall. It was way more intense than the swing, my stomach lifted through my chest, I was unable to breath as my legs pedalled through the air. The dynamic rope stretched like a bungy cord before propelling me back into the air and finally I came to rest swinging, spinning and shrieking with exhilaration. Remarkably I did that jump another three times. I don't think I would do it now! Dan Osman died later that season pushing it further on the Leaning Tower jump. And

Scott Burke never did find a future for himself, succumbing to addiction. An alarming number of those Monkeys were to die prematurely, perhaps unsurprisingly given the accepted tolerance for risk, the pace and intensity of life amongst our tribe.

A month later, half a mile above the ground, clinging on to first-joint finger pockets in old piton scars, my feet level with my head on the lip of a house-sized horizontal roof called the Black Cave, I was struck by a moment of intense awe. This was without question the most insanely exposed and awesome position in which I had yet to find myself. 'Fierce with exposure' is how Royal Robbins described that same spot after the first ascent of the North America Wall in 1964.

The scale of this wall, its aesthetic perfection, the play of light across its face and the majesty of its place in the landscape was beyond imagination. This was the most powerful sensation I'd ever experienced. I felt exhilarated, alive, in love. I took a deep breath. The countdown had begun; I knew I had just minutes until my arms would tire too much to hold on any longer. This was it, the crux of the whole climb, the whole trip, success or failure down to the next few moves.

With the confidence of youth I attacked the desperate fingertip traverse along a thin rail with complete commitment and no fear of the potential big fall into the void (after my experience on the Porch swing). Moments later, with forearms bulging I found myself on the security of a small ledge having succeeded in climbing the last and hardest section of this giant climb, El Niño, my first El Cap route, on my first go.

'Hell yeah, Leo!' yelled our friend Ian Parnell who happened to be camping on a neighbouring route and was taking photos.

'Nice work, mate, no turning back now!' Patch yelled as he set off seconding the pitch.

Retreat was no longer an option, we could not descend the Black Cave and carried no bivi gear so we had to move light, fast and free and reach the top that day. Ahead lay another 1,000 feet of sustained, hard climbing and complex route-finding to the summit.

Patch and I had arrived in Yosemite by Greyhound bus from

San Francisco equipped with a few summers' experience of hard traditional climbing on the small but serious outcrops of North Wales, a rack sufficient for single pitch ascents and ambitions beyond our abilities.

To the casual observer Camp 4 is unremarkable. A basic campground with two toilets and a single water tap to serve 200 campers. Yet Camp 4, set amongst giant boulders and soaring pines, is hallowed ground to climbers.

As we walked through Camp 4 in that September of 1998 the energy was palpable. Ropes, haul bags and piles of climbing gear hung everywhere amongst the plethora of colourful tents.

It was here that the greats of the golden era of the 1960s, Warren Harding, Royal Robbins, Yvon Chouinard, had conceived and geared up for the first ascents of the seemingly impossible walls. Then came the Stonemasters of the 1970s and 1980s, Jim Bridwell, John Bachar, Ron Kauk, who began to explore ever more subtle and difficult aid lines up the biggest faces whilst also developing and pushing free-climbing standards on the smaller walls and these very boulders. Like shrines to climbing disciples. At the far end of Camp 4 was the Yosemite Search and Rescue Team (YOSAR), crewed by climbers who are allowed to live full-time in tent cabins in exchange for being permanently on call to rescue stricken climbers or, more often, lost tourists. Scott Burke had been one of them.

Slack-lines were strung between trees all around camp. Like tightropes but rigged from dynamic webbing that stretched, wobbled and bounced. It felt impossible to stand on the line but there were people walking them with ease, doing tricks and even surfing them, masterfully controlling a violent swing. On warm evenings around campfires, with guitars playing and beers flowing, you could hear tales of derring-do recounted in a dozen languages. I immediately felt at home.

Patch and I had come brimming with confidence in our climbing prowess but we were woefully underprepared for the strenuous cracks that embody much of Yosemite climbing and were utterly overwhelmed by the immensity of the big walls, with El Capitan the undisputed queen.

On first sight it takes some time to compute her sheer size. It is not until you spot a climber, a small speck of colour high in the sky, that you begin to comprehend the true scale. The buttress of the Nose stretches down vertically for 2,920 feet. Just 300 feet short of the tallest peak in England but, like Scafell Pike, 3,209 feet cleaved in half to leave a vertical cliff from sea to summit the size of a mountain. The obscene scale quickly crushed our burgeoning self-confidence, the hard routes on which we prided ourselves were closer to 30 metres than 30 rope lengths.

Unfamiliar with any of the skills, gear or tricks required to climb routes ten times the size of any we had previously attempted, we shrank away from the grand prize of El Cap and focused on the boulders and crags more akin to our native rocks as we immersed ourselves into the thriving counterculture of the Yosemite climbers.

The Stone Monkeys were a loose troop of impoverished, itinerant climbers living out of cars, caves and tents who each spring and fall would congregate in the Valley to push the standards of Yosemite climbing throughout the 2000s. As park regulations have tightened and the scene has continued to evolve with climbing entering the mainstream, the time has come to be defined as the Stone Monkey era.

The first Monkey I met was Cedar Wright. With a mop of big hair, thick glasses, an awkward stance, a high-pitched, loud voice and a wide, squinting grin, his appearance didn't fit that of the ninja I'd seen surfing the slackline but it was indeed him. He also turned out to be a record-setting big-wall speed climber and member of YOSAR. He was exceptionally welcoming and friendly to us enthusiastic fresh arrivals and we quickly became friends.

Dean Potter was transitioning from his days on YOSAR to becoming the Yosemite legend that would be remembered, already making his reputation with his progressive style of blisteringly fast

ascents of classic walls, sometimes linking multiple huge formations and often climbing without a rope. Dean was a huge guy, 6
foot 5 with hands like bunches of bananas, an intense stare and a
powerful presence. He had established a new clutch of hard, high
boulder problems around Camp 4 and had recently discovered
entire new areas of boulders around the Valley. He was also a
slackline master specialising in high lines rigged above precipitous
gaps that he would sometimes defy death to walk without a leash.
He wasn't as outwardly friendly as Cedar and seemed to skulk
around the edges of the scene whilst also clearly being the silver-
back of the troop.

José Pereyra was from Venezuela but lived in the USA. Half a
generation older than most of the Monkeys, he had recently left a
position as a mathematician at Salt Lake University to live in his car
and commit to climbing. He was small, wiry and long-armed, had
a thick Hispanic accent, a broad smile and always sported very cool
YSL shades with a perfectly matched straw hat. He possessed an
infectious positivity and mystical aura, like he knew something
most people didn't. He too was a first-rate speed climber and partner
to Dean, Cedar and others on fast ascents of huge El Cap routes. He
had an ironic reputation for moving in a very considered, apparently
slow fashion but, using new wave speed-climbing techniques, could
efficiently maintain that pace without pause for many rope lengths,
enabling him to set records.

There was one other Monkey I met that first trip, although it
wasn't until years later that we would come to share an intense
partnership and the wildest of adventures: a quiet, unassuming
badass, as strong and gifted as any of us, called Sean 'Stanley' Leary.
He had inherited from his grandfather a run-down old trailer on a
prize lot right by the River Merced in El Portal, a village just outside the entrance to the park about a forty-minute drive from Camp
4. As a result he tended to go home at night. This and his somewhat
reserved nature meant it was many years until we became great
friends.

There were many other Stone Monkeys in the loosely defined

troop. Some would return season after season for over a decade, some would only live the dirtbag dream temporarily, but we all shared a wonderful time in that magical valley, living our dreams.

Camp 4 felt like some kind of nirvana; the reality more than lived up to its myth. I had found my place and my people and was immediately adopted by a new dirtbag family. I was Peter Pan with the Lost Boys in Never-Never Land and I didn't want to grow up. Some of my new siblings would become Valley legends, my dearest friends and greatest partners, but were then just beginning to write their chapters on the sacred stones.

Although far stricter than bygone decades, park regulations were still pretty loose. We quickly figured out how to fly below the radar, to avoid the ranger-danger like Captain Hook and live free, both conceptually and financially. We were shown the sweetest 'out of bounds' bivi sites, learned how to sneak into the 'all you can eat' restaurant to feast for free every night on terrible food, that on Sundays weekend warriors abandoned a week's worth of groceries in bear boxes, and that tourists were happy to let us minesweep their breakfasts in the café where unlimited bad coffee was served for free.

At the time my nickname was 'Springer' as before poorly maintained ankles and knees began to object I was very fond of dynamic climbing, jumping between holds, features or even different boulders. Patch and I explored new ways of enjoying the well-trodden boulders around Camp 4, leaping across gaps or onto faces, movements that now feature alongside classic boulder problems in the newest bouldering guidebook.

It was during one of these dynamic explorations that I first met Alex and Thomas Huber. They were back in camp recuperating from their efforts on a new free route on El Cap they dubbed 'El Niño' in preparation for their ascent from the ground. They were both burly, muscled alpine guides from Bavaria, in their mid-thirties with long hair and big beards. Alex was more muscled and had established several of the world's first 9a sport climbs; he was one of the strongest climbers in the world. Together they have formed one of the most prolific big-wall free-climbing partnerships of all time, in Yosemite, the Alps and the greater ranges. They were as entertained as they were flabbergasted by my leaping problems, struggling to do the easiest jumps. They were also stereotypically Germanic and would celebrate their triumphant climbs by proudly donning their authentic lederhosen, the tight leather breeches, flowery waistcoats and felt hats appearing somewhat out of place amongst the ripped jeans and T-shirt-clad dirtbags. Despite our national idiosyncrasies we quickly developed a rapport and became firm friends. Gradually over the course of the next few weeks, as much by talking and hanging out with these Stone Monkeys as by climbing with them, the grandiose face became sufficiently demystified that Patch and I began to surmount the psychological barrier to even attempting to free climb El Capitan.

El Niño was the fourth free route on El Capitan and the world's greatest cliff had seen only a handful of completely free ascents in 1998. Alex and Thomas explained that unlike the other free routes, the Nose, the Salathé Wall and its easier variation Freerider that are mostly crack climbs, all the hard sections of El Niño were face climbing, a discipline at which Patch and I excelled. They encouraged us to give it a try. Patch had already climbed Freerider with Ben Bransby, narrowly missing out on a completely free ascent.

As our time in the Valley began to draw short, thanks to our new friends we were able to adjust our mindsets and come to terms with the vast scale of El Cap. We chose to view its climbs as multi-day, vertical camping trips, on which all your water must be carried and where one climb leads directly into another for up to a week. We decided to try El Niño but we lacked some vital, expensive big-walling equipment. We were informed it was usual for the first winter storm to arrive before the end of October and we would need to be equipped to sit out serious weather on the wall. It was already the last week of the month.

We needed a port-a-ledge with a rainfly, a giant haul bag and synthetic sleeping bags before we could make a safe attempt. Being trapped on the side of El Capitan in bad weather is a serious proposition. Rain runs off the bare granite ground of the summit, quickly forming massive waterfalls and runoff streaks that cascade down the lines of natural weakness in the cliff – often the same lines that climbs follow. If you are unfortunate enough to have set up your port-a-ledge camp in such a flow it is literally like camping in a waterfall. Everything becomes soaked, which is why you need synthetic sleeping bags that maintain their insulative properties when wet, as opposed to down, which does not. If you don't have this gear and end up requiring a rescue then you must foot the US$15,000 bill, something Patch and I weren't willing or able to do.

That very evening, in the Yosemite lodge bar, I met Kevin Thaw for the first time. A talented climber from the north of England who'd migrated to California years earlier, I knew of him from friends we shared back in the UK. Tall and athletic but prematurely grey, with the strangest Burnley-meets-Berkeley accent, he instantly extended his friendship as if we were old pals.

Kevin promptly introduced us to his old mate and climbing partner Conrad Anker. Conrad was a chisel-jawed, blond-haired, blue-eyed Californian who had grown up near Yosemite. A full generation ahead of me, he was already one of the most famous climbers in the US and living the dream of full-time professional climbing with serious financial support from the likes of The North Face and *National Geographic*. He had climbed great walls and peaks all over the world, and was in fact the very next day heading to spend a season guiding on Mount Vinson in Antarctica.

Over a pitcher of Samuel Adams, we explained how we hoped to climb El Niño but lacked the gear. Without hesitation Conrad, who had aid climbed the line and suggested its free potential to the Hubers, kindly offered to lend us everything we needed as he would be in Antarctica for the next two months. He had it all in the back of his truck right there in the parking lot. Had Patch and I not managed to quickly acquire those crucial pieces of equipment, we would not have attempted El Niño. Conrad's generosity provided me with a golden opportunity, one that would radically alter the course of my life for good.

1998 was the beginning of the end of the analog era. Shortly before leaving Wales I had registered my first email address – *fiercewarrior* – on Patch's parents' computer; they were the only folk I knew who had one. Back then I only knew one person with a mobile phone. The internet was a new concept yet to take over our lives and social media was not a recognised term. There was no cell phone signal in Yosemite. The only way to communicate with parents and friends back home was to send postcards or to call from outdoor payphones. The only way to arrange climbing plans was face to face or via notes pinned to the noticeboard in Camp 4.

After securing Conrad's gear I had gone to sleep quite conspicuously under a boulder next to somebody else's tent in the centre of camp. I was in a bright-yellow, high-quality down sleeping bag that my parents had bought me for my sixteenth birthday. I knew that my dad was planning to be in California for a week around that time but he wasn't sure if he'd make it to Yosemite and we hadn't made any plans to meet.

'I recognise that bag – Leo, is that you?' Dad said, having literally stumbled across me in the dark as he wandered through Camp 4 on the off-chance he'd find me. It was serendipity that he did, and the next day he was able to cast his son off on the adventure of a lifetime. One that we had begun together eight years earlier on the outcrops of the Lakes. He helped Patch and me carry loads to the base of El Niño and even joined us up the easy, first pitch that leads onto the top of the Footstool, a pedestal below the real start of the route from where the climbing immediately becomes hard.

The first three pitches are all rated 5.13, a cutting-edge standard. They were however very similar in character to the slate slabs on which I'd climbed so much and they suited my style. Towards the end of the first pitch there was a very long runout between bolts. I was progressing well, moving confidently over hard terrain, when I reached to clip a quickdraw onto the bolt then pulled up the rope to clip in and become safe. With a loop of slack in my hand, about to clip the rope, my foot slipped and I looked at a 60-foot fall down the slab. I might've been OK but equally it could have easily ended our attempt with an injury. Somehow, I stayed on the wall. I replaced my foot and in panic looked at the quickdraw. I began to pull up the rope again to clip. Then looked down at the 60-foot drop, then up at 2,900 feet of wall above. *You don't want to break your ankle on the first pitch, you fool! There are many more harder pitches above*, I said to myself before grabbing the quickdraw, clipping in the rope and lowering down to the ground. A rational decision that has haunted me ever since. After a quick rest I climbed back up and finished the pitch on the next go. On the second pitch, the first move is very hard right off the belay. I pulled on the first bolt to clean and inspect the holds then climbed that first go. The third pitch, one of the hardest of the entire climb, I also did first go.

Over the course of the next four days I continued to climb the remaining twenty-nine pitches, including many more 5.13s, all the way to the top without falling off. Other than that minor discrepancy, I had free climbed El Capitan onsight, which ranked my El Niño ascent as one of the cleanest of all time, as it remains to this day.

After the initial hard pitches, a day of less-demanding climbing was followed by an exhausting day hauling the heavy bags a thousand feet up the wall and fighting to erect the port-a-ledge and attach the fly, something we should've practised on the ground, for our first night on the wall. Our lack of big-wall knowledge and experience was clear; the logistics proved to be more demanding than the leading. As predicted, a savage twenty-four-hour storm ravaged our camp, but well equipped with Conrad's kit we weathered it, and even enjoyed watching the waterfalls cascading around us and being engulfed in spectacular cloud formations, only to be astonished by how quickly and completely everything dried up and fine, stable weather returned.

It was the following evening whilst lounging in the final rays of the day's golden light on the Big Sur, a ledge the size of a dinner table more than a thousand feet above the ground, halfway up the mighty southeast face, that my epiphany came. I had found new meaning and purpose in life. The black and grey diorite intrusions into the massive face of El Capitan and the golden granite form a distinctive geological map of North America. Many of the climbs and features on this face derive their names from this map: Pacific Ocean Wall, Atlantic Ocean Wall, Lost in America and the climb we were attempting, El Niño, the free variation to the historic North America Wall. I watched the shadows creep and stretch across the steep-sided Valley, progressively creating an entirely different view with the passing of time. The steady flow of giant American trucks on the loop road far below looked like toys, the people in the sublime meadow of yellow grass and ancient redwoods, like ants.

Patch, hanging free in space, spinning like a spider on a silk thread, slid slowly down our rope, the width of a finger, from above towards me. A pair of ravens, birds that can live for sixty years, swooped by making their unusual, distinctive croak. There is an iconic photo of Royal Robbins, Yvon Chouinard, Chuck Pratt and Tom Frost all hanging in hammocks under the Black Cave, the precise point from which Patch was descending, taken during their historic first ascent of the North America Wall in 1964.

I contemplated that those very ravens would have been young birds back then and may well have observed that first foray onto this side of their mighty cliff, and in the intervening thirty-five years of their lives could have witnessed the entire history of El Cap climbing. Starting with those golden-age pioneers who had spent ten days boldly forging their way, developing gear and techniques as they went up that impossibly huge face via the line of least resistance, heavily reliant on artificial aids to assist upwards progress. Those big black crows would then have watched visionary aid lines, imagined by the likes of Jim Bridwell, being forced up the blankest sections of the wall, and seen him and others race up the multi-day test pieces from the previous generation in a single day.

And now, in 1998, here were two teenagers from the UK, with no experience of climbing walls of this scale, attempting to find a path that they could climb without using any artificial aids, using only their own fingers and toes to navigate a free-climbable passage from the ground to the top.

It was our fourth night on the wall. We had already climbed the longest route of our lives and were barely over halfway. We had endured a serious but spectacular storm and climbed more consecutive hard, high-quality pitches than ever before. This was undoubtedly the best climb and greatest adventure I'd ever been on by several orders of magnitude. As the sun's warmth left me on the Big Sur and Middle Cathedral burned pink in alpine glow on the opposite side of the Valley, I realised I had never felt more content. That this – camping in a vertical wilderness, exploring terrain rarely if ever touched by human hand, pushing physical and psychological limits, expressing passion against nature's most fantastic creations, free climbing big walls – was the coolest adventure ever, and that I was willing to commit my life to it.

We decided to abandon the gear on the Big Sur ledge and to climb the next, hard section of the route unhindered by heavy kit. A circuitous line led far to the left then diagonally right back up to the Black Cave. Our hope was that with our two thin ropes tied together we would be able to rappel in a straight line down the overhanging face and somehow get back to our camp.

It was a gamble, but one that paid off. It was one of my best ever days of climbing, firing hard pitch after hard pitch, moving fast and free, light and lucky, adrift in an ocean of granite right in the centre of El Cap. Dangling in space near the end of two very thin dynamic ropes tied together that bounced unnervingly, I had to rappel well below the Big Sur until I finally regained contact with the wall and was able to free climb back to the safety of our camp.

All that lay between us and easier ground was one more hard section, the immense horizontal overhang of the Black Cave. Patch ascended the 300 feet of bouncy ropes first. An arduous, tiring and time-consuming process.

'Do you have the chalk bag?' he shouted when I was halfway up, already out of breath and sweating. I did not. On the small polished holds in the heat of the Californian sun, chalk was an essential aid to free climbing. Reluctantly I rappelled back down to camp and fashioned a huge makeshift chalk bag from a stuff sack and filled it with two whole blocks of chalk before frustratedly reclimbing the ropes.

Finally, I was ready to face the Black Cave, the pitch I was most worried about, overhangs not being my preferred style. To my relief the complex features through the huge overhang proved similar to the steep sea zawns of Gogarth and soon I found myself hanging on by my fingertips from the lip of the cave. And I was struck by that moment of awe. Patch seconded the Black Cave and set off up the next easier pitch only to become lost and spend two hours reaching the next belay. I became extremely frustrated by this delay, as I hung uncomfortably watching our daylight slip away. To my relief the remaining hard pitches were of world-class quality and went quickly, without incident. I completed the last hard section as darkness fell. The summit still seemed far away and I could not for the life of me see an easy path through the compact face above as the 'topo' – our route map – described.

Patch went up into the darkness, climbing by headlamp. I feared a cold, uncomfortable night.

'Sweet! They've marked the way for us!' Patch happily called down. Sure enough the fastidious Huber brothers, pre-empting climbing these pitches in the dark themselves, had drawn arrows in chalk every 10 feet to mark the way through deceptive and unlikely route finding for the last few hundred feet to the summit. Their chalk ticks marking holds throughout the climb had drastically helped me to climb to the route onsight. Though we had scoffed at the tape labels with which they had marked gear placements lower down, we were deeply grateful to Alex and Thomas for these waymarkers and very soon we were on the top.

'That was the most amazing climb ever!' I exclaimed to Patch. 'Thirty of the most amazing climbs all on top of each other! I don't think I'm going to be able to look at small routes in the same way ever again.'

My horizons had been reset, my perspective upturned and my ambition unbridled. Indeed, I never could again motivate myself for single-pitch climbs, especially dangerous ones, in the way I had before. It no longer seemed worth the risk for some inane little *arête* in the Llanberis Pass or a desperate sequence a few feet away from an easy climb on a Lakeland crag, not when there were climbs like this out there.

I wanted to travel the world and to climb big walls.

10

The Passage to Freedom

For the next three years I lived the dream of climbing full-time, travelling the world on trips and expeditions. I climbed all over Europe, from Norway to the Czech Republic, visited California multiple times, went to Asia, and Australia, made exploratory trips to remote walls in Chile, Peru, Mozambique and South Africa, as well as climbing hard trad routes all over the British Isles.

Between trips I rented cheap rooms in friends' houses around North Wales or sofa-surfed. I didn't own a car or even hold a driving licence. In fact I didn't own much other than my climbing gear, most of which had been given to me by sponsors. My wardrobe comprised almost entirely of Berghaus freebies. The modest retainer they paid me was just sufficient to fund the life of a wandering climbing bum. Much of the year I lived contentedly in a tent in spectacular climbing areas, many of which were national parks and areas of outstanding natural beauty. I ate simple food, drank cheap beer, wanted for little, climbed a lot, climbed hard and partied even harder at every opportunity.

I was young, free, single, had no bills, no debt, much time and had found my purpose in life: to climb big cliffs in far-off lands, seek ever more extreme adventure and enjoy each day as though it were my last. Throughout that period by far my biggest outgoings were flight tickets. I became a master at smuggling my grossly overweight luggage aboard.

My El Niño ascent was big news in the international climbing scene and launched me from up-and-coming to well on my way. I started to build a profile in the wider media too with features in newspapers, Sunday supplements, mainstream magazines and TV appearances. The first major TV project I was involved with was an episode of a BBC2 series called *Wild Climbs* in 1999. Andy Cave and I travelled to a historic sandstone climbing area called Teplice in the Czech Republic, renowned for its strict ethics and dangerous climbs. Arriving in Prague, we met the production crew, including Brian Hall and Keith Partridge, who I would later work with extensively on many exciting productions all over the world.

We went for dinner and then Cavey and I went out for a drink. At my behest it turned into a wild night and we ended up utterly leathered in a club with girls dancing topless on the bar as somebody set themselves on fire doing flaming shots and had to be extinguished in the middle of the dance floor. I didn't know that shooting started next day, so it's no surprise the film starts with me sticking my head out of the widow of a minibus to vomit down its side.

Remarkably, this proved to be the start of a reasonably successful career in television. Over the next twenty years I would be involved in front of the camera in around a hundred different productions, including hosting several of my own mainstream TV series.

I spent the winters of 1999 and 2000 living in Chamonix. I had intended to spend those seasons doing the classical Alpine apprenticeship, learning how to climb ice and big Alpine faces in winter. I did climb a dozen or so of the classics but soon discovered my skinny frame suffered miserably in the cold, that I wasn't fond of climbing with tools in clumsy boots and that riding powder and the Chamonix nightlife were far more fun than shivering on north faces. Looking back, I wish I had spent more time climbing the high mountains by day and less time drinking and dancing to techno in dingy clubs by night, chasing big lines instead of Scandinavian seasonaires. But I had a lot of fun, made a lot of friends and discovered a passion for snowboarding and skiing to rival my love of climbing.

What just about kept me on track or at least close to it during those years was my love of rock climbing, in particular my newly discovered drive for free climbing big walls. To climb at a high standard in a place like Yosemite required lots of practice and to keep in reasonable shape, so I managed to temper the late nights and large living in order to still be able to do hard routes.

I returned to Yosemite in the fall of 1999 and again in 2000. Patch had started university in Leeds so I went alone, confident I would be able to find one of my new Stone Monkey friends to partner with. No longer intimidated by the monstrous scale of El Cap and with eyes opened to what was possible on El Niño, I wanted to write my own chapter on the stone and make a first free ascent on the world's greatest cliff. There are big features and entire ledge systems on El Niño that are virtually invisible from below other than at very specific times of day when shadows reveal their existence. Other sections that even up close look impossible can be overcome, albeit with great difficulty, by the slightest Braille trail of matchstick edges, hairline cracks and textured diorite intrusions.

I set my sights on the biggest, steepest, blankest section of El Cap, The Dawn Wall, undertaking a ground-up siege of the massive, featureless face, intent on finding a Passage to Freedom. This would eventually become the name of my incomplete route. But it proved more difficult than I anticipated to find a reliable partner.

The climbing was hard right off the ground and it took a lot of time, first to aid climb an existing route, then to try to find free-climbable features that connected with others over many hundreds of metres before finally making a free ascent of each pitch. The lack of a committed partner really hindered progress. Originally I set off up the aid route Mescalito, but four pitches up I came upon a section I could not figure out how to free, so I retreated and explored another option further left around the line of New Dawn.

I fixed ropes for a thousand feet up to the palatial Lay Lady Ledge, a tiered flat terrace big enough to casually remove harnesses, and in between finding a free line and making the first free ascent of a dozen hard pitches I encouraged many people to visit my airy wall camp. I enjoyed sharing the wonder of the wall with people who would never have dared attempt to climb El Cap themselves. There were some who had never worn a harness before who were literally taught the ropes on the way up. Dozens of people came to visit, including a young Beth Rodden, who would later become a superstar, Kevin Thaw and Jason 'Singer' Smith, with whom I would later share major adventures. José Pereyra was another. He had become bored of speed climbing the same handful of trad routes increasingly quickly, a popular style at the time, and when he saw the quality of the climbing and fun I was having piecing the jigsaw together, he was motivated to get involved. With José's help, gradually we found all the pieces of the puzzle. At what appeared to be an insurmountable dead end, it was José who first managed an impressive, no points of contact, 8-foot side-ways double dyno to successfully reach another system. There were two very hard pitches that took me many attempts to successfully lead.

When the first winter storms arrived and the season drew to a close we had managed to reach El Cap Spire about halfway up the wall and I had climbed it all free, other than for one move of aid. To overcome a few metres of blank rock, instead of drilling three of four rivets, the standard practice for aid first ascents, I had bolted the badge from Tim Emmett's old Alfa Romeo onto the wall, engraved with the motto 'Music, friendship, good times and hard climb'. Therefore I only had to denature the rock with one hole and dynamic moves from natural features before and after the badge made for much more fun than pulling on quickdraws. We vowed to return and complete the climb the next autumn.

Back in the UK, at a party in the house Patch shared in Leeds with a strong crew of mutual climbing friends and techno fans, I first met Jason Pickles. He was to prove a pivotal partner, my right-hand man and first lieutenant when I would later earn the nickname 'Captain Faff' on some of my wildest adventures. We would almost die together on half a dozen occasions, surviving to be best men at each other's weddings.

The parties in Leeds weren't typical student-house gatherings with a few bottles of wine and a stereo. They were full-on raves in the dilapidated but spacious house complete with decks, ludicrously overpowered sound systems, light displays and smoke machines, attended by well over a hundred hardcore party people who would put the same effort into getting ready as they would to go out clubbing.

Jason, more commonly known as Jas, shared my self-destructive penchant to be the last man standing, and like me never accepted that first prize was the worst comedown. We weren't the only ones in the competition and sometimes the partying would last for days. My twenty-first birthday party would have made the Happy Mondays proud.

Jason was from Todmorden, a Yorkshire mill town with a rough reputation. Five years older than me, he had curly brown hair, hazel eyes, poor teeth and a muscular build. He was opinionated, well-informed, loved reading newspapers cover to cover, be it the *Telegraph* or the *Sunday Sport*, and was not afraid to get stuck in if things kicked off. He was from the right side of a rough town and though he had hung around with plenty of 'wrong 'uns' in his youth – joy-riders, drug dealers, petty criminals and people who brawled for fun – he had managed to keep himself out trouble with the help of loving parents and thanks to discovering climbing in his teens.

He had got out of Tod to attend university, where he read Politics, but loyally stayed in touch with some of his old pals – those that joined the military, others that never left the pub, even those that overdosed or served time.

He was a strong climber and had recently discovered Yosemite and caught the Valley bug. I liked his opposing characteristics of intelligence and brutishness: a Barnsley fan who could quote Chomsky and was equally content to debate current affairs or watch topless darts. We shared a love of travel, adventure, hard living and hard climbing.

A day or two after the big party, we had gone climbing on

Yorkshire grit with the others from the house. I was on good form despite the excesses and lack of sleep and onsighted three classic grit E7s, the benchmark standard of the day, and a bunch of other hard dangerous routes in a couple of days between heavy rain showers and clouds of smoke. I think Jas was impressed and we arranged to partner in Yosemite in the fall of 2000 for another attempt to force The Passage to Freedom to the top.

A week before we were due to depart I had a stupid accident bouldering at a grit crag called Slipstones, trying a massive double dyno that I'd already done in my trainers. I didn't make it, landed hard on the edge of the crash pad, badly spraining my left ankle. Jas and some other mates had to carry me down the lengthy walk to the car. My ankle swelled like a grapefruit. I should've gone to hospital. Instead we went to the pub and, reluctant to postpone my Yosemite trip, I went anyway, spending the first couple of weeks hobbling around Camp 4 and El Cap Meadow unable to climb.

I had been approached by the esteemed *GQ* magazine to feature in a model shoot and had arranged for a high-fashion crew from New York to meet Jas and I in Camp 4. It was a huge juxtaposition, the immaculate, perfumed city dwellers from the world of haute couture dressing us in designer labels and photographing grime-engrained, stinking 'Stone Monkeys in their natural habitat'. The flamboyant, renowned photographer actually created some really beautiful images and the lengthy published feature was very respectful towards us and really very good. Until the oncoming decline of print publishing, *GQ* was a major trendsetter. Alongside the proliferation of urban indoor walls, I suspect such publicity contributed to climbing's transition from a fringe, anarchic subculture practised by grizzly mountain men to a mainstream, trendy activity for hipsters and ultimately an Olympic sport.

We ate on their bill in the luxurious and expensive Ahwahnee Hotel, a corner of the Valley Stone Monkeys would rarely be seen in, and after hanging out for a few days we made friends, despite being from worlds apart. I would go on to meet with a couple of them in London and Barcelona, attending glamorous parties full of models and doing a short stint of lucrative modelling work before I decided that big-city life and the ultra-materialistic and superficial world of fashion was not for me and I returned to being a dirtbag in the wilderness and we lost touch. Irritatingly, showing off my jumps around the boulders during the shoot I hurt my ankle again, setting me back another couple of weeks.

Finally, after a month of drinking King Cobra malt liquor, smoking Camel no filters and socialising, with my ankle heavily taped I felt I could climb, though nowhere near my limit. Jas and I teamed up with José and Ammon McNeely, one of the best aid climbers and wildest characters on the scene. Known as the El Cap Pirate, he always flew a Jolly Roger from his haul bags that invariably contained dozens of beers, and after drinking a couple (which was by lunchtime every day) he liked to speak in character.

'Arrr, mi hearties, what say ye we storm that there castle and pillage the wall of all its treasurrrre!'

His pirate persona was no act – Ammon was the toughest, most reckless and fearless of all the Monkeys, and for that matter of anybody I've ever met. He fell foul of the draconian ranger law frequently, ultimately serving stints in federal jail for relatively minor infractions, and repeatedly suffered serious accidents that would have stopped most in their tracks but barely slowed him down. Even when he eventually lost his lower leg in a BASE jumping accident, he continued to climb, jump and sail the seven seas of El Cap. He was also a loyal, happy and dependable friend to many.

We had climbed the terrain I had freed the previous year up to Lay Lady Ledge and again fixed ropes to the ground. The upper half of the wall was steeper, less featured and looked harder than the lower half.

We hauled supplies for two weeks for our team of four, including all the water and Ammon's booze – some 180 kgs of liquid and at least the same again of equipment and food. Learning how to move and manage such vast loads over long distances up the steep wall and how to live on a cliff for multiple weeks would prove invaluable in years to come when the kind conditions of California would be replaced by the hostilities of the Arctic, Amazon or Antarctica.

Before we cast off to set sail up the ocean of granite above, we hosted a proper party on Lay Lady Ledge, something I'd wanted to do since first laying eyes on El Capitan. On top of all the gear for the forthcoming ascent we had hauled up a charcoal barbecue on which we cooked huge steaks, a whole chicken and a sheaf of corncobs. We had a mini keg of beer, boxes of wine and full bar complete with a cool box for ice and mixers, Seabreeze (vodka, cranberry and orange juice) being my preferred drink at the time.

A dozen people climbed up our ropes. Mostly guys but a few girls too', reflecting the gender balance in Yosemite back then, including a stunning, strong, blonde girl from the Czech Republic called Blanka with whom I would later share a brief relationship. I had procured an obscenely loud, battery-powered speaker system for my MiniDisc player (state of the art technology at the time). Lay Lady Ledge is in a big corner at the foot of the massive pillar that forms El Cap Spire on the Nose and the entire southeast buttress of the wall is concave, an amphitheatre that when the sound system was cranked up amplified the banging beats of Groove Armada, Layo & Bushwhacka!, Paul Oakenfold and more savage techno like C. J. Bolland and Richie Hawtin to all the climbers on the wall, whether they liked it or not, and across the whole Valley.

We set off fireworks and burned toilet rolls that unravelled down the wall in flaring flames. José was a big fan of organic hallucinogens and had procured a large bag of *Psilocybe mexicana*, magic mushrooms. Like we were on a giant podium, we danced, laughed and made merry for two days and nights. Although it is a very large ledge and we all enjoyed more than a few drinks, the overt danger of the massive drop below kept everybody keenly aware not to overdo it and there were no incidents or near misses.

After the party we cast off our fixed lines, moved camp a few pitches higher to El Cap Spire and set to work uncovering the next Passage to Freedom.

My first photoshoot, age 10. Shepherd's Crag, Borrowdale, Lake District. Already learnt the top-rope around the corner trick! I fell in love with climbing immediately. July, '90.

(left to right) Angel of the North, first ascent. Only time I've ever been arrested (no charge)! Aug, '98./ Trauma E9 7a, Dinas Mot, Llanberis Pass, North Wales. First ascent. July, '99./Old Man of Hoy, Ken Tilford, me, Dad. My first adventure climb; a life defining experience. Sept, '90./Satin, E3 6b, Stanage, Peak District, gritstone. First climbed by my hero and mentor Johnny Dawes. Nov, '01.

(left to right) The Prophet, Screamer pitch, E9 7a, El Capitan, Yosemite. My early attempts were the closest to the edge I've ever pushed. Oct, '01./The Prophet, Devil's Dyno, E9 7a. An 8 feet sideways jump unlocked my dream of a first free ascent on El Cap. Oct, '10./Patch Hammond, me, Thomas & Alex Huber. My one-fall climb of El Nino remains one of El Cap's finest ascents. Oct, '98.

(top) Cerro Torre, Patagonia. Kevin Thaw on the approach before my accident on a rare sunny day./(bottom) Moments after crushing my talus bone on Cerro Torre. A bad accident that ultimately had good implications. It took three days to get down to the town, El Chaltén. A mix of crawling, being carried and by horse. All Feb, '02.

(left to right) BASE jump from Kjerag, Norway. Danger and excitement are two sides of the same coin. July, '05./Conrad Anker & I as Mallory & Irvine – N. Col, 7,000 metres, Everest – filming IMAX movie *The Wildest Dream*. June, '07./Conrad & I near 8,000 metres, N. E. Ridge Everest. Highest drama shoot in history. It was -25°C with 50 mph wind. June, '07.

(left to right) Mount Asgard N. W. face. Skydived in, climbed it and BASE jumped off. My first major expedition was life changing./Onsight free climbing on a massive remote wall in the Arctic. The stuff of dreams and nightmares!/We weren't prepared for winter conditions in August on Asgard. I suffered here for ten nights./Inuksuk, E7 6c, Asgard, We failed to free climb it but reaching the top after such a fight felt like a success. All Aug, '09.

(left to right) Aid is a very different game to free climbing. Not my forte!/Seconds later I fell 50 feet shredding my fingers./Wingsuit BASE jump from Asgard. Me airborne and Stanley exiting./ Me, Jason Pickles, Chris Rabone, Ian Burton, Sean 'Stanley' Leary, Alastair Lee and Carlos Suarez. You can't buy that look in our eyes, it must be hard earned. All Aug, '09.

The Prophet, A1 Beauty, E9 7a. Perfect desperation. With Jason Pickles on our eventual free ascent nine years after our first attempt; I pushed to my absolute limit but succeeded. Oct, '10.

Unfortunately, after five days of complex rope shenanigans, utilising Ammon's aid skills, massive pendulums and exhausting what seemed like every possible option, I reluctantly accepted defeat. Though I had managed to free climb long sections, and big horizontal traverses in different areas, I couldn't find a continuous line that linked them all together. The wonder of free climbing is that it requires Mother Nature's cooperation – she must provide something to hold on to. If she does there is a certain magic, as if it were made to be climbed. But the vast area of rock I had explored yielded no such possibility. I was keen to continue to the top with a few pitches of aid through the really blank section to reach the more distinct features above, big corners and flying grooves that gave the impression of more free-climbable terrain for many more pitches. Jas and Ammon were indifferent but for some reason José was adamant it was free or not to be. He wasn't willing to embrace the massive workload ahead if we wouldn't end up with a free route. I really didn't want to bail again, I desperately wanted to top out one way or another. José suggested Jas and I blast up the Nose speed style whilst he and Ammon descended with all the kit. Neither Jas nor I had climbed El Cap in a day and had virtually no proper aid or speed-climbing experience. But we agreed this was a good plan.

We began to sort the kit we felt we needed. Two ropes, loads of rack, a rucksack containing warm jackets and waterproofs, a couple of litres of water each, some food and our trainers. All the stuff you would take on typical days climbing in the mountains.

'Oh my god, guys, why don't you just take a port-a-ledge!' laughed José when he saw the weighty pile. 'You are speed climbing, you have to go light to move fast. One rope, one set of cams, maybe a few small wires. No bag. No trainers. Carry one litre of water between you, a windproof on your harness and an energy bar in your pocket. Nothing more. You have to commit to the wall. We're already halfway up, it should only take you a few hours,' he said as he ravaged our stash, grinning like a Cheshire cat.

Jas and I looked at our drastically reduced load with concern.

Certainly it would be far less burdensome to climb with, but there was less gear than we would carry on a 30-foot grit route and we were about to do 1,500 feet of full-on crack climbing, including all the hardest pitches of the Nose, and then had a massive hike to descend. But José was the expert and I very much looked to him as my mentor so we didn't argue.

We said our goodbyes and I set off up the Texas Flake and across the famous King Swing pendulum. I am naturally a fast climber, but also an ingrained free climber. To speed climb, anything goes; you have to do whatever is quickest. If the climbing is easy for you then free climbing is fastest, but if there is a hard move or you're getting tired you must start to pull on gear. When it gets harder you crack out the aiders (webbing ladders) and resort to full on aid. It is a totally different mindset and did not come naturally to me.

Jas climbs at a more normal, much slower pace and also hadn't got his head around this strange new style. Neither of us had ever been shown the clever tricks that drastically increase the rate of ascent, such as leading in blocks instead of alternate leads, short fixing (pulling up extra rope at a belay and beginning the next pitch rope solo) or back cleaning (frequently descending short distances to retrieve gear vital for the next section). Our climbing shoes were tight-fitted for hard climbing, not loose and comfy for speed, and were soon crippling.

I also had a level of contempt for speed climbing, which is a form of aid climbing. To me it simply felt like cheating. Aid climbers routinely carry hammers, chisels and hand drills, which seemed to me to remove much of the magic of climbing. With these tools you *will* get to the top one way or another. Speed records were all the rage at the time. José held the record on the Salathé Wall, climbing the 3,200-foot route with Dean Potter in an incredible 6 hours 30 minutes. The long-standing Nose record held by Peter Croft and Hans Florine was an astonishing 4 hours 20 minutes. At the turn of the millennium, competition was heating up, more sponsorship money was flooding into the sport, people were making names for themselves and winning contracts setting records, and occasionally dubious tactics were being employed to decrease times. Extra bolts were appearing in crucial spots, people climbed the same route over and over again to shave minutes and would leave gear, sometimes lots of it, in key places to accelerate their next lap.

I wasn't into these poor ethics. I felt style and ethics were integral to climbing, more important even than success and certainly more so than records. My style was superior, free climbing from the ground up, with minimal aid. Jas and I were not speed climbing, we were free climbing with rests, and were not moving very fast at all.

Cellphone signal had not yet arrived in Yosemite and we had no communications on the wall. Accustomed to perpetual California-blue skies, we had not checked the weather forecast since leaving Camp 4 almost two weeks earlier, nor considered it might rain when we parted company with all our clothing that morning.

Dark clouds gathered, the wind picked up and temperatures dropped as we slowed to a crawl on the harder upper pitches. We were desperately short of hardware, making what should've been safe climbing feel dangerous, and we were becoming severely de-hydrated. I took over all the leading. Eventually, with cramping elbows and crippled toes, we dragged ourselves onto the summit, exhausted and humbled. It had taken ten hours and the sun was low over the horizon. Thankfully I knew the way down and we set off barefoot, unable to stand our torturously tight shoes any longer. As we hobbled down the long East Ledges descent a flash of lightning and massive clap of thunder accompanied the first drops of rain.

We followed the vague trail that tunnelled down through the manzanita and scrub oak as the rain intensified and darkness fell. We had no head torches, just a single LED keyring José had lent us for emergencies. Leaving the bushes, the open slabs began to get steeper and form a kind of gully with the precipitous face of El Cap below and another web-patterned cliff known as the Spider Wall above.

By now it was a full-blown storm. Torrents of rain were whipped by a vicious gale, the thunder and lightning became more constant.

Still exposed on the top of the cliff, soaked and shivering, Jas, who had never been up there before, looked scared.

'Don't worry, mate, we nearly at the raps. We'll be in the bar in an hour,' I mistakenly reassured him.

Moments later, as if I'd tempted fate, a wall of water flushed down the gully like a scene in a disaster movie. The huge quantity of rainwater accumulated on the bare granite summit of El Cap flash-flooded the gully we were descending.

A massive flash of lightning that seemed to last for many seconds was accompanied immediately by deafening thunder and illuminated a terrifying spectacle. The Spider Wall had vanished behind a cascading waterfall half a kilometre wide. The path we had walked down seconds earlier was the main channel of a raging river almost waist deep. Fist-sized boulders washed by the torrent rained down on all sides. All the water congregated not far below and there was no way we could descend any further to reach the rappels. I was astonished how fast our predicament had deteriorated. Within a couple of minutes it had become a survival situation.

We were standing on a glacier-polished smooth slab, 20 feet away from the edge of a thousand-foot cliff, attached to nothing, with rushing, rapidly deepening water all around. The metal climbing equipment buzzed like a transformer. Jas's hair began to stand on end, charged by the static electricity that saturated the atmosphere.

'Fuck! What should we do?' screamed Jas over the tempest, white with fear.

'Give me the rack, we'll have to rope up and climb back up the slabs. Hopefully we can find some shelter in the manzanita,' I replied.

Something I've learned about myself is that I tend to thrive the more serious things get. A powerful survival instinct takes hold. Fear subsides, a clarity of mind enables decisive action and access to unknown reserves of strength. Perversely, I actually quite enjoy facing life-or-death situations, perhaps the reason I've always pursued dangerous pastimes and gnarly expeditions.

Like with the battle joy that soldiers speak of, everything becomes simple and clear. There is no past or future, everything is present. There is no time to think, only act. The ultimate state of flow.

'Don't tie in or put me on belay until I get to that tree. If I get washed over the edge, no need for you to join me,' I said before charging up the deadly terrain like a man possessed.

To reach the tiny tree I had to leap across a torrent that would likely have taken me over the edge had I not made it. I tied it off with a sling and clipped it to the rope. At least now we were secured to the mountain. Jas put me on belay and I carried on fighting up the smooth slabs that are normally avoided even when dry, as the paths of least resistance were the main channels of the flash flood.

In a blur that could've been ten minutes or an hour I reached safer, but still exposed terrain. I was spent from the battle. Jas had regained his nerve and took over the lead until he reached the scrub. We crawled deep into the sharp bushes and curled up next to a log that provided meagre shelter from the tempest. Shivering hypothermically, we cuddled one another like children, taking it in turns to be Big Spoon and Little Spoon, rolling around each other when the current position became unbearably cold. Although not quite wearing shorts and T-shirts, our thin pants and summer tops offered only a little more protection. Jas was wearing the windproof, our only extra layer, everything else had been abandoned at José's insistence that morning, which seemed a lifetime ago. The lowest point of the night for me was when Jas realised the windproof had a hood which he could put up that would stop the icy water running down his neck. I was livid.

'Cover my ear!' I insisted in retaliation.

The storm raged all through the desperately long night, finally abating with the first light of dawn. Strangely it often appears the coldest part of an open bivi is as the sun rises. Just as you begin to think it will warm up it gets colder. An hour later the warmth of the sun began to take hold. The cloudless Californian blue skies had returned and our surroundings glistened with two feet of fresh snow. It took us ages to untangle ourselves from the rope we'd cocooned ourselves in with hands swollen and pruned like we'd been soaked in a bath all night. We almost had to cut it.

I have no idea how we managed not to succumb to hypothermia that night. I'm sure we would have if the storm had not been so short-lived, lasting just twelve intense hours, and would have either needed to be rescued or would have died.

'Fuck! I can't feel my legs,' said Jas in panic, collapsing as he tried to stand.

I couldn't help but laugh as he wobbled around like a turtle on its back. We had survived, the sun was out and we were safe. I massaged his legs back to life and like drowned rats we recounted the nightmarish scenes.

'Let's give it a couple of hours for the snow to melt off and then head back down,' I said.

'No fucking way. I'm not going back down there, Springer,' said Jas, sounding traumatised.

'Don't worry, it'll be fine now. Sun's out, storm's passed. We'll be down in—'

'NO! You don't understand. I am not going back down there.' Jas cut me off. I realised he really was traumatised.

So instead we began the long ascent back to the top of the Nose. We met a pair of Spanish climbers who had topped out the night before. They were fully equipped with sleeping bags, warm clothes, rain gear and had found shelter in a small cave and still claimed to have feared for their lives. When they saw us dressed for a summer's stroll, looking like drowned rats, they were astonished we had survived. An 8-mile hike through deep snow in tight climbing shoes led us back to down to the Valley via the Yosemite Falls trail. We arrived back in Camp 4 just as our friends from the search and rescue team were rallying to come and find us.

'Good timing. I was starting to get a little worried!' laughed José, clearly happy to see us. 'I wasn't expecting you guys to climb so slow. I need to teach you a few tricks, Leo!' He winked.

Over the following couple of seasons he did. I embraced different styles of climbing with less arrogance, accepting you must learn the rules before you start to break them. The next year I climbed the Nose with Singer in under six hours. Over time, I mastered speed climbing, claimed a few of my own records and added useful skills to my growing repertoire.

Of all the epics I've endured, I don't think any have been worse or closer to the edge. It was an entirely avoidable disaster caused by incompetence and overconfidence, mostly on my behalf. Had we checked the weather forecast, climbed a bit faster, brought a bit more clothing, headed directly down the falls trail or even just started half an hour earlier, we would've been on the rappels before the flash flood hit.

Yet looking back, that night was one of the most powerful, formative and memorable of my life. Jas and I bonded in a way that only those who have shared such an epic can. We learned valuable lessons that would be indispensable on much more serious adventures in the future. But most of all I realised that I had enjoyed it. Though I would never have intentionally put myself into such a death-defying situation, when faced with one, that rush of battle joy was unlike anything else, unleashing a warrior instinct too fierce for normal life. I began to develop a taste for the gnarlier things in life.

In 2015 the American Tommy Caldwell, perhaps the greatest big-wall free climber of all time, would solidify his reputation by claiming the first free ascent of the Dawn Wall, largely following the line of Mescalito, using his superior strength and ability to complete the dream I had once shared. He also employed, on a scale not seen before, tactics previously regarded as dubious and unsporting, fixing the whole wall, installing multiple long-term camps, adding dozens of bolts to existing aid routes and spending hundreds of days over seven years effectively removing the adventure from the ascent, turning El Cap into a sport route, enabling him to perform at the very limit of what has been achieved. His creation is in my opinion the hardest climb in the world. In the age of Instagram, his final, successful seventeen-day ascent with Kevin Jorgeson went viral, watched live by millions, even receiving praise and honours from the sitting President Obama and was immortalised in the theatrically released and highly acclaimed movie *The Dawn Wall*.

In 2020, accompanied by Alex Honnold of *Free Solo* fame, Tommy Caldwell also completed The Passage to Freedom, respectfully retaining my name. Again they employed heavyweight, top-down tactics over multiple seasons and found a major variation involving huge traverses, climbing several pitches of the Nose to avoid the blank section that had ended my attempts. The upper section had indeed been free climbable. I would like to try their route in the future.

Shanté Lamprey

II.

Patagonian Disaster

My dad was uncharacteristically apprehensive as we said our good-byes at Manchester Airport.

'Make sure you look after him, won't you? I don't know why, but I've been worried about him going on this Patagonia trip,' he said to Andy Cave after dropping me off.

Cavey cannily managed to dodge an answer. Having shared a few adventures together already, including the Norway trip when I got arrested for climbing the *Angel of the North* and that wild night in Prague, he was wisely unwilling to take on such responsibility.

Andy was closer to my dad's age than mine. A Peak District-based certified UIAA mountain guide and strong rock climber, originally from Barnsley with a broad Yorkshire accent, he had started life 'down t'pit' as a coal miner, discovering climbing during the downtime caused by the miners' strikes of the early 1980s. 'Billy Elliot goes mountaineering,' we liked to taunt him. Wiry, with an intelligent face and thoughtful demeanour, having racked-up a shining resumé of impressive mountain ascents, he was someone I greatly respected and trusted.

This was to be my longest ever trip and biggest adventure by far. In truth I was not sure I would ever return permanently to the UK. I was already considering relocating to California or perhaps to base myself year-round in the Alpine mecca of Chamonix. For the meantime I would cram in as many trips and expeditions as I could, following the optimum climbing seasons in an endless summer of adventure.

There are two equally world-class climbing areas in Patagonia, both dramatic collections of sharp granite towers on a colossal scale, subgroups of the mighty Andes mountain range that forms the spine of Patagonia and runs for most of the length of South America. The Fitz Roy and Cerro Torre group in Los Glaciares National Park, above the lively mountain town of El Chaltén in Argentina, is the more accessible and frequently visited. Torres del Paine National Park in Chile is a two-hour drive from the closest town and the long walk to base camps gives it more of a remote-expedition feel.

The climbs we were to attempt would be mainly rock, but the mountainous nature of Patagonia meant we would encounter hazardous sections of snow, ice and glacial terrain as well as notoriously severe weather. Though I had four Yosemite seasons and lots of rock-climbing experience, I'd only done a handful of true alpine ascents and was glad to be partnered with Andy. We were departing for Santiago, Chile, on our way to climb in the savage Torres del Paine. I would then go on from there to meet Yosemite friends in El Chaltén to try the ferocious Cerro Torre. After that I'd go directly to Venezuela with José Pereyra on an expedition to climb the unique Cerro Autana, a *tepui*, or table-top mountain, protruding from deep in the Amazon rainforest.

The granite spires of the South, Central and North Towers of Paine rate amongst the most spectacular and challenging of any summits on Earth. The Central Tower is only 9,462 feet but what it lacks in altitude it makes up for in ferocity. The east face is amongst the world's tallest vertical cliffs at 4,000 feet tall and is ravaged by brutal winds that make the summits some of the hardest to reach.

We were a team of six. Dave Hesselden, a reliable, reserved character, talented winter climber and long-time alpine partner of Cavey, had recently returned to the UK after a decade spent building a successful rope-access company in Hong Kong. Dave would be climbing with Simon Nadin, from Buxton, Derbyshire, formerly known as the 'Buxton Stick Man'. Also quiet, Simon had a decade earlier been amongst the best climbers in the world, having won the 1989 climbing World Cup, the televised competition that had inspired me to start climbing. He was no longer stick-like. Family and his work as a fireman had replaced climbing as priorities in life but his pedigree meant he could still rival most on steep terrain.

At the eleventh hour we were joined by two more of Cavey's friends. They had been planning a kayaking expedition to Pakistan that had been cancelled following the US coalition invasion of Afghanistan in the wake of 9/11. Neil Harvey and Ross Purdy were both well-rounded outdoorsmen from the Lake District. White-water kayaking was their main passion but both had at one time been avid climbers. They were very conscious of the high standard of the other team members, but Cavey had assured them that there were some less severe objectives in Paine and they would enjoy the expedition. They turned out to be a hoot and Ross would come to be a dear friend and later godfather to our children. At twenty-one, I was fifteen years younger than the rest of the team and had deep respect for all of them. The wisdom I gained from the time we spent together had a profound impact on the choices I would make in the aftermath of Cerro Torre.

The climbing we did together was also fun. We arrived at the frontier town of Puerto Natales, rapidly being transformed into a tourism hub by the Chilean government. We shopped for supplies to support ourselves for twenty days in a remote base camp in the rarely visited Bader Valley below the then-unclimbed south face of the South Tower of Paine. Next day a bus would take us to the park entrance, where we would meet with local gaucho outfitters, authentic Patagonian cowboys who would transport our gear by horse a day's trek to base camp.

Naturally I made sure the team went clubbing the night before, but somehow we managed to make it back to the hostel, grab our gear and still catch the bus, though without sleep. Two bumpy hours later and we were blearily overseeing the loading of horses before beginning the long hike to the Cuernos trekking hostel on the shore of Lago Nordenskjöld at the entrance to the Bader Valley on the far side of the park. From here we would leave the trail and head up the formidable hill of stunted forest leading to the mouth of the valley where we would establish a base camp. As it was already late in the day we discussed spending the night in the hostel but ended up pushing on to recover the gear cached by our gauchos.

Feeling less hung-over than my older companions, I soon left them behind and eventually found myself on the wrong side of a deep canyon looking across at the gear. There was no way to cross, not without risking death, so I descended to find the others. But by the time I reached the hostel again, it was dark and I hadn't seen them. I concluded we must've taken different routes past the rock buttress and that once they realised the error they too would return to the hostel. I gave my passport to the custodian and explained my friends would be arriving shortly with the money to pay for the beer I ordered.

A couple of hours later an utterly exhausted-looking Dave stumbled into the bar and almost wept with delight when he saw me.

'We thought you'd tried to jump the canyon and were dead,' he explained.

Having realised they were on the wrong side of the gorge they had descended and then continued directly to the cache without stopping at the hostel, assuming I was ahead. When they discovered I wasn't there, Dave had come back down while the others pitched camp. They had arranged a signal of torch flashes to let them know all was well and we could see the lights of their camp high up the distant hillside. Dave flashed his light six times, they responded with six flashes. Unfortunately, there had been a miscommunication. The signal for 'all is well' was three flashes. Six flashes meant 'he's not here, start searching.'

As Dave and I passed out in the comfortable beds of the hostel the others split into teams to begin searching. In the middle of the night Andy and Simon came to the hostel to request help. Somehow the custodian failed to realise that I was the twenty-one-year-old, blond Englishman they were searching for and he valiantly radioed for help. A helicopter was scrambled for the next day.

The following morning the search teams reconvened at the hostel ready to initiate a full-scale search and rescue operation. Only then did they discover a well-rested Dave and I contentedly eating breakfast. Luckily no one took it badly.

The horses had dropped our kit just below the treeline at the entrance to the valley and we pitched our three tents, dug a toilet pit and constructed a mess area from fallen timbers and plastic sheeting we had bought in town, settling into our new home. Andy and I decided on a fine-looking objective on the east *arête* of Cerro Mascara. A Spanish team had sieged the line with a lot of aid over eight days the year before so we decided to climb it free, climbing the first two pitches and then returning to our little tent for the night with ropes in place for a one-day push to the top. After a day's bad weather spent listening to Cavey slurp porridge, we climbed back up the ropes and freed the rest of the route without major incident. On the top, in front of an epic backdrop of jagged peaks and giant walls, a condor swooped by, the gargantuan bird in perfect proportion to the landscape. With winds strengthening, we slipped down the ropes into the shelter of the wall and returned to base camp.

Simon and Dave had climbed a new route and were happy. Ross and Neil had undertaken a hilarious epic but despite having not reached a summit they were also happy. They had done enough expeditions to know that summits are simply fleeting destinations and that journeys are what count. We spent another week exploring the valley but the weather didn't allow another climb before it was to time to pack up.

Back in Puerto Natales I met my friend Javier Sepulveda. We had known each other in Yosemite but became good friends partying in London, where he worked writing code for the BBC. His family were exiles of the Pinochet regime and though Chilean he had been raised in the UK. Excitable and energetic, Jav arrived driving a beat-up old Toyota Hilux with his usual wide smile. Simon and I said goodbye to Andy and the rest of the team, setting off to drive 500 kilometers on unsurfaced roads across the Patagonian steppe to Argentina and the town of El Chaltén.

After two days' driving, the sublime skyline of the Fitz Roy–Cerro Torre group grew on the horizon. El Chaltén was still a small town in 2002. The road there was still unpaved, the internet had not yet arrived and though adventure tourism had begun, it was only in its infancy. The place had a wild Argentine hippy vibe, like Camp 4 except we felt welcome there. Lots of young Argentines had come for the austral summer months, pitching their tents on the free campground, and plenty of international climbers who were also on long trips, including many I knew from Yosemite. Immediately I loved it. A financial crisis in Argentina, not uncommon, also meant that our dollars went a lot further.

The notorious bad weather that plagues Patagonian climbing is often very localised, meaning a tempest can be savaging the summits but just a few miles away and a few thousand feet lower in El Chaltén it could be summery. In 2002 it was still common practice for climbers to base themselves a few hours' hike from town beneath the peaks in historic rudimentary huts built by previous expeditions, hoping and waiting for a weather window.

The arrival of the internet and accurate forecasts in 2004 meant climbers could wait down in El Chaltén, and in an effort to preserve and restore the pristine nature of the wilderness, the climbers' huts were dismantled. Now climbers base themselves in the comfort of town, monitoring the weather online and enjoying great bouldering and sports climbing along with the welcoming, festive atmosphere of a seasonal tourist town.

The fact we could see the mountains when we arrived back in early February 2002 was a good sign. Sometimes they are obscured by cloud for weeks. We headed straight to the mountains. Simon was keen to go on a solo photography mission whilst Jav and I had decided to try a twenty-pitch route, Claro de Luna, on the west face of Saint Exupéry, considered to be one of the more amenable climbs on one of the smaller peaks in the Fitz Roy chain.

Reaching the west side of Saint Exupéry was a demanding hike on a poor trail through treacherous areas of landslip but we tagged along with a couple of Americans who knew the way. The approach continued gently upwards on a dry glacier over unstable moraine bands for five miles to a sandy wash and a jaw-dropping bivi site between iconic Cerro Torre and the shark's tooth of Fitz Roy. From here a final 2,500 feet of steep talus led to another bivi site near the start of Claro de Luna. We pitched our tiny tent on a patch of sand sheltered by a giant boulder.

We had shared a rope in Yosemite and though Jav was a solid climber this was a much more intimidating situation. We climbed pitch after pitch on amazing rock, all the while nervously looking to the west in fear of the lenticular clouds that signal a change in the weather. Not knowing when a front might come added a massive element of commitment to climbing such a long route. There is a rawness to those peaks, like they are freshly made. They are alive and evolving. Avalanches rip loudly through the night; rock falls leave dust traces like smoke from artillery shells. The climbing was first rate but there were plenty of sharp edges to cut ropes and fridge-sized loose blocks to negotiate. One such block dislodged by a climber tragically killed his partner on the same route some years later.

'It's getting pretty late and the wind's picking up,' Jav said. He seemed tired. 'Do you think we should turn around?'

'We're almost there, mate, we might never get another chance.'

The wind was howling when we finally made the summit at dusk. Jav was looking knackered as we began rappelling into the darkness. By the time we were halfway down he was falling asleep, slumping in his harness at the belays. Though descending ropes is far less time-consuming and difficult than climbing, it nevertheless requires great care and concentration. The tiniest mistake can have fatal consequences and severe fatigue greatly increases the danger.

I was getting worried we had bitten off more than we could chew as the rappels seemed to go on for ever, but the weather didn't deteriorate too much and in the first rays of dawn we finally reached the ground. Jav looked like he'd been on a night out clubbing as he staggered over the talus, virtually cross-eyed. I felt thankful to have shared such an epic adventure with my friend but was perhaps naive as to the real severity of our surroundings.

From a distance, Cerro Torre cuts a daunting silhouette, a ferocious fang capped by a giant snow mushroom, ravaged by hurricane-force winds and often obscured by bad weather for weeks at a time. It becomes no less daunting on closer inspection. In fact, it grows steeper, taller and more intimidating the closer you get. But there is an undeniable appeal to that menacing tower, such beauty in its savage form and its almost unattainable summit, so alluring in its difficulty. In 2001 there were only two ways to reach the very summit, though there were over twenty different routes that leave the ground. For the final summit pyramid they all funnel into either the spectacular snow and ice flutings on the west side or, until it was removed in 2013, a bolt ladder drilled up the headwall of the east face.

I had gotten to know Kevin Thaw in Yosemite. Although he was in his mid-thirties, his life had shared a similar trajectory to mine. From grey moors above Manchester in the north of England his passion for climbing had led him to the Alps, then to Yosemite, where he'd decided California suited him better and he stayed. In ten years living out west he had climbed dozens of hard El Capitan aid routes, was a top-class free climber and made himself a part of the blissful California climbing scene. He seemed to know everybody and was close friends with Conrad Anker, Dan Osman and many of the top climbers of the era. He had eventually been granted a green card under the 'aliens of extraordinary ability' scheme. His skills also earned him a place on the prestigious North Face athlete team, making impressive trips to gnarly peaks in the Himalayas, Alaska and multiple trips to Patagonia.

Tall and athletic but prematurely grey, Kevin lived off a diet of M&Ms, Skittles and roll-up cigarettes. He didn't train or climb that much and seemed to have lost some of his fire for Yosemite when we first began to hang out. Yet when it came to walking uphill with a heavy pack he was able to keep an astonishing pace and could climb to an impressive standard off the couch. And if his passion for California seemed to be waning, Patagonia had apparently plugged the gap. He was psyched for Cerro Torre.

The third member of our climbing team was a complex character called Alan Mullin, a rough Scotsman, in his early thirties, shorter than average and of medium build with an intense, slightly psychotic stare that belied the mental health issues that would ultimately lead to him taking his own life years later. He had discovered a passion and talent for Scottish winter climbing late in life, after leaving the army. Scottish winter climbing often involves climbing in bad weather, the small mountains punching well beyond their weight in the suffering division. Though I have dabbled over the years, I have never been taken by climbing with tools and have always disliked the cold, leading me to have climbed much more on the other side of the world in sunny California than just up the road in Scotland. Having never held ice axes until he was twenty-five, Alan progressed with alarming speed and within just a few winters was climbing some of the hardest routes, soloing some of them and establishing his own top-level, very dangerous test pieces.

Kev and I had climbed with Alan during a winter meet at Glenmore Lodge, Scotland in 2001. Fine conditions had led to a fun day on a challenging route but I had not gelled with Alan. I got a dark vibe, that climbing for him was some kind of battle, against the mountain, against himself and against others. He was always guarded and seemed like he had something to prove. He appeared to thrive on fear but not in a healthy way, like he wanted to get hurt. I've always felt driven by positive energy, a love of having fun in high places with great friends. Though I too had something to prove, otherwise why would I be attempting such a desperate and coveted route on my first trip to the region? But I wanted have a laugh whilst doing it.

I was surprised that in 2001 Kevin and Alan had partnered up to climb Fitz Roy via a new route on the massive west face. Kevin had obviously been impressed by Alan's appetite for suffering and though Alan lacked any experience of big rock climbs or alpine summits, he proved to be a capable partner as they completed their impressive climb, though bad weather meant they narrowly missed tagging the true summit. Kevin led and freed the whole route while Alan fought his way up the rope behind, carrying most of the gear. Kevin's unfazed, unexcited demeanour just about balanced Alan's unnerving, ill-at-ease manner. Which was good as we were about to attempt one of the most coveted and controversial climbs in the history of mountaineering: the infamous Maestri–Egger route on Cerro Torre.

The route, first up the east face then the north, is named for the famous climbers who purportedly climbed it in 1959, the Italian Cesare Maestri and Austrian Toni Egger. They undoubtedly reached a point about a quarter of the way up because a stash of their gear was found there, but not a trace of them above that point exists despite Maestri claiming to have placed some bolts. Toni Egger, according to Maestri, died on their descent from the summit, but doubts about his story surfaced not long after the ascent and have never really gone away. Forensic research by expert climbing historians suggests that Maestri found solace in creating a triumph from a tragedy. It is widely considered Maestri's 1959 claimed ascent is a lie. The first irrefutable ascent was made in 2005.

So when Kev, Alan and I arrived at the base of the east face in February 2002 we were standing at the foot of what was still one of the greatest unclimbed prizes in the mountaineering world. Several teams had made it high on the north face above the col between Cerro Torre and Torre Egger (named after Toni), but none had reached the top. Kevin certainly possessed the appropriate experience for such an attempt, though Alan and I did not. I suppose Kevin felt with my high-level rock skills, Alan's ice prowess and his own pedigree in both, under his direction our three-way partnership had the ingredients for success.

We were to attempt the route light, with supplies for three days, fast and free, using our two ropes only for protection, each of us leading blocks of pitches: one block to the snow patch, then another to the col where we would bivi. The north face is hard to see from any direction and back then photos of it were hard to come by, though Kevin had procured one with the lines and high points of previous attempts marked. Kevin and I would share blocks, taking the most logical line up the rock and, hopefully, Alan would prove our secret weapon on the final block of mixed climbing through the snow mushroom to the summit. We then intended to descend the frequently climbed Compressor route on the southeast ridge. All our gear and supplies were packed into two big, heavy packs and a smaller leader's load. Only the leader would climb, with the two others jumaring up the rope with the heavy bags.

I was unashamedly intimidated by the colossal pyramid, in particular the snow mushroom that capped the summit, which would occasionally shed truckloads of frozen debris down the face. Whilst we geared up one such load exploded on the glacier just a couple of hundred metres from where we were sitting. Alarmed, I looked at Kevin; he barely looked up from rolling his cigarette.

'Don't worry, it's much more active over there,' he said calmly.

Kevin and I then played the customary game of paper, scissors, stone to decide who would lead the first block.

'Stone blunts scissors,' I crowed. 'I win.'

'Do you want the first block?' Kevin asked.

I looked up. The massive, snow-capped pyramid loomed ominously and infinitely above. It was hard to imagine a more threatening, intimidating and menacing mountain. But in that hostility there was an undeniable allure, something beautiful in its savage form, temptation in its unattainability. And, of course, the vain attraction of the virgin line, to be the first to succeed where so many had tried and failed. Sun reflected off streaks of water that ran down the compact granite and channelled into streams down lines of weakness. High on the north face, snow plastered to the wall by the wind glistened. And as it slowly warmed it also threatened to collapse down our line at any moment. I glanced towards the prominent southeast ridge, such a striking line, its sharp edge far less exposed to falling ordinance offering a much safer and more enticing objective. No doubt that was one reason it was the most popular way to the summit. That and the hundreds of bolts the Italian climber Maestri had drilled, desecrating such perfection to force an unnaturally easy route up one of the world's hardest mountains when his 1959 ascent fell into question.

That was not what we had come for. We had come in search of

glory, in the uncertainty of the dangerous line above, for the first ascent of the north face. We would rise to the challenge. The thought stirred a sort of narcissistic courage. I put aside the last of my doubt.

'I'll take the first block,' I said and reached for the gear. Minutes later I had fought my way across the *bergschrund* and begun to climb.

The familiar process of climbing forced me to focus on the immediate challenge and banished any lingering fear of what lay ahead. No point worrying about the next 4,000 feet if you can't do the next move. I felt wholly in tune with what I was doing and as strong and fit as I had been at any point in my life. We moved fast and efficiently, covering a couple of hundred metres of serious terrain in just a few hours. Our objective started to seem less absurd, more attainable. But then it got steeper and harder. I led wearing a backpack that seriously hindered my efforts. I removed it and left it clipped to a runner for Kev to manage. Load lightened, I pushed on up increasingly difficult terrain. At a tiny ledge I arranged a cluster of gear to make a belay and fixed the ropes for Kev and Al.

I heard the familiar 'swoosh' sound made by large masses of snow parting company with the ominous white summit mushrooms. Only this sounded louder, closer. A small chunk of ice hit my helmet. Then another. And another. There was nowhere to hide as increasingly large blocks of ice pummelled my head and unprotected back. I regretted jettisoning my pack. Once again I was gripped by fear as I hung impotent at the mercy of the mountain, praying the bombardment would cease and not escalate. Then it stopped. Kevin arrived within minutes.

'Nothing to worry about, it's just a bit of slough.' As usual he seemed completely unfazed.

There remained just one steep section between us and our first target: the triangular snow patch. There I would relinquish the lead to Kev. Less difficult terrain should then lead all the way to the col more than halfway up the mountain, where we planned to sleep. Above the col lay the dubious delights of the unclimbed north face, the real bulk of our challenge. Yet right now that was a problem for the future. All I had to do was find the best way to climb just one more rope length. I ruled out traversing to a large corner some way to my right as a waterfall cascaded down it. I didn't relish the thought of getting soaked and freezing for the rest of the climb. I saw another option directly above: an immaculate face of gold split by a laser-thin crack. Though it was not more than 40 feet before the angle eased and the holds seemed more plentiful, it nonetheless looked extremely hard.

At home in the UK, or even up on El Cap, those 40 feet would form a prize challenge to climb free. But up there, on that austere mountain? Fifteen miles from the end of the road in that wind-swept wilderness at the far end of southern Argentina? Where there are no rescue services and no helicopters flying? Prudence dictated these factors should be considered. The drastic consequences of an accident in this kind of setting had to be weighed in the balance. This was no place to take chances.

So the wise thing to do would have been to let go of my aspirations to free climb and resort to a few moves of aid. A few pitons hammered into the thin crack would certainly have led me quickly and safely to the snow patch. Soon, and for some years after, I would wish that was what I had done. Then I spotted a rope hanging down right by the crack. I had seen it earlier but it hadn't interfered with our climb until that point. It was in good condition and led all the way from the col down to the glacier, anchored intermittently. We understood it had been abandoned the previous season by a Swiss team who had attempted this route in an out-dated, inferior style, laying siege to Cerro Torre with thousands of metres of fixed rope like this one, intent on reaching the top by any means, valuing the outcome over the process, the summit over the style. And yet despite lowering the bar in this way, they had still not succeeded.

In those days I was not disposed towards prudence or wisdom. I was talented and hungry. The false sense of security offered by the abandoned rope was too strong. Tentatively I set off free climbing up that desperate crack. I left the belay and made some difficult, flamboyant moves, and as I climbed I inserted into the crack a pair of tiny brass wedges, the very smallest and most marginal protection carried by a climber, no thicker than a pound coin swaged to wire more appropriate for jewellery.

I continued with increasing difficulty and danger, up the blank face beside the crack, lured upwards by the thought that should it become too hard I could at any point grab the abandoned rope, until I reached a spot just a few feet away from much easier ground. But I could see the next move would be the hardest. I considered attaching myself to the Swiss rope before I committed, rendering my situation completely safe but effectively annulling the ethical validity of our ascent.

So with foolish bravado I denied myself its security and threw all my might into a desperate sideways move climbers call a 'rock over', my right foot level by my hands, big toe perched on an edge half the width of a pencil, the fingernails of my left hand gripping a hold as thin as a matchstick, and then pushing rightwards with all my strength. Suddenly, just as my right hand was about to grab a good hold, my foot exploded off the pencil edge and I fell.

Immediately a sickening pain erupted from my right foot to grip my whole body from bowel to brain. The foot felt like it had been clobbered with a sledgehammer. As I fell I grabbed the abandoned fixed rope directly in front of me, but all the force I had generated for the move had now compounded with gravity and however hard I squeezed I couldn't stop myself. I could feel the rope burning into my fingers and my knuckles being ripped apart as they grated down the coarse granite face.

I screamed. I had broken my ankle before I had even stopped falling, plummeting for about 60 feet before the tiny brass nuts stopped me. I came to rest far below Kev and Alan but with a surge of adrenaline I scrambled to reach them with tension from the rope. My eyes were bloodshot, my fingers a shredded mess of flesh and blood, burnt almost to the bone. My right foot pointed in the wrong direction and was already horribly swollen. It was the most severe pain I'd ever experienced. It pulsed from deep inside my ankle, making me retch and cry. I knew it was serious. Kev and Alan knew that too. I mumbled about going down alone and apologised to them profusely for ruining our chance. They kindly reassured me that our objective was no longer to climb Cerro Torre but to get me safely down and out of there before the next storm. Suddenly it dawned on me that, now unable to walk, I was going to find this challenging.

'Take a couple of these, mate, they'll help,' Alan said, looking shaken as he handed me a bottle of pills from his pocket. Unbeknownst to Kevin or me, Alan had been addicted to tramadol, a powerful synthetic opioid, since his discharge from the army years earlier, following an accident that resulted in chronic back pain. The ensuing descent would be no less epic but undoubtedly more tolerable thanks to Alan's stash.

First we had to get off the wall. Ironically the abandoned fixed rope that had encouraged my mistake and indirectly caused the accident made retreat to the base of the wall significantly easier. Though my hands were in a terrible state, we decided the best course of action would be for Kevin and Alan to descend with all the gear and I would rappel myself. Gripping the rope to control my descent was agony where I'd already suffered severe rope burns on my fingers was agony, but that paled to insignificance at the slightest nudge to my right foot. I slid unceremoniously down the cliff, trying to protect my ruined ankle.

By the time we reached the glacier the tramadol had taken the edge off the pain but removing my rock-climbing shoe revealed a grotesquely swollen ankle. Even with the liner removed, I still only just managed to force it into my alpine boot.

Roped together with Kevin leading the way, I began crawling down the glacier. The snow had softened significantly since our approach that morning and thanks to the steep gradient I was able to slide down with relative ease, although at one point I did fall neck-deep into a crevasse. Alan was struggling to maintain his composure. I remember telling *him* to calm down and take some deep breaths, that everything would be OK!

As I crawled along another avalanche swept down from the snow mushroom right over the area where we had been planning to sleep. Had I not fallen it was where we would have been right at that moment. This wasn't the light slough we'd encountered earlier. The face almost disappeared for a while in the cloud of debris. I took some solace in the thought that perhaps my mistake had in fact saved us from a much worse fate. In January 2022 precisely the same occurrence took the life of a renowned climber sleeping on that very col whilst descending from successfully climbing a new route on the north face.

Around 1 a.m. we reached Norwegos camp. A pair of Argentine climbers who had retreated from their attempt on the Compressor route selflessly offered their help. Early next morning they set off to town to raise the alarm and rally people to assist in a rescue.

On the other side of the Torre Valley, in Campemento Polacos, where Javier and I had stayed, were my Yosemite friends José Pereyra and Roberta Nunes. They had seen our headlamps slowly descending the glacier in the night and concluded all was not well. So José hiked across and arrived before we left Norwegos. I was feeling pretty sorry for myself but he had not lost his wide grin. He possessed a deep, mystical aura, and was somebody whom I greatly admired and respected as a mentor and friend.

'Well, it looks like I'm going to have to find somebody else to lead the hard pitches on Autana,' he said. We both knew I wouldn't be joining our upcoming trip to Venezuela. 'Don't worry, Leo. It all happens for a reason. It will be OK in the end. We just have to get you down this enormous talus field and back to town first.' He chuckled. I think he was a *brujo*, as they say in Spanish, a spiritual teacher. His presence and light-heartedness made me feel less in despair at my predicament.

Kevin is a strong guy, easily able to carry my then-lean frame on his back. But the steep scree of rocks ranging from tennis balls to car-sized boulders shifted underfoot and he stumbled frequently, and each slip proved unbearably painful. So I cut pieces from my foam sleeping mat, taped them to my knees for padding and with the aid of a walking pole and gloves to protect my damaged hands began painfully crawling down the treacherous talus field. Another dose of Alan's tramadol helped take the edge off things.

It took hours, but once again the steep gradient assisted my efforts. The worst part was the final flat section leading to the ice of the Torre Glacier. No longer working with gravity, I struggled over ridgelines of glacial moraine until eventually I made it to the open terrain of the glacier where Kevin was once again able to carry me.

The first people to respond to the call for help were a pair of older Russian climbers, Alex and Tim, whom I had befriended in base camp. Apparently they had left camp within ten minutes of our Argentine friends reaching them, raising the alarm. They and Kevin took it in turns to piggyback me for miles down the glacier with the ones not carrying me shouldering all the gear with Alan and José.

Gradually other climbers of various nationalities who had nobly abandoned their own plans to help a fallen comrade began to arrive, until just before dark the chief park warden came with a stretcher. More than twenty people responded to the call for help, rotating as stretcher-bearers until finally, in the middle of the night, we made it to the cable crossing back to Campamento Bridwell and my tent.

Next morning the town doctor arrived in camp with a horse. By now my ankle was the size of a grapefruit and had turned a nasty purple-black.

'I don't think it's too bad?' I said to her unconvincingly.

'No, it is bad, your season is over and you need to get to a hospital. You may need surgery.' She had that Argentine directness but she meant it compassionately.

The most painful part of the whole retreat was the horse ride to town. Lower limb fractures and serious injuries should be elevated, ideally above the level of the heart, which proved impossible riding a horse. The jolting movement combined with my foot repeatedly brushing through branches of scrub was almost unbearable. The

X-ray machine was broken at the small clinic in El Chaltén and an ambulance was arranged to take me to hospital in El Calafate, four hours away along a dirt road.

Throughout the whole evacuation the weather had been exceptionally good. I was racked with guilt towards my partners, especially Kevin – he had long dreamed of attempting the Maestri–Egger and I had ruined his opportunity. Had the weather deteriorated to its usual Patagonia ferocity my retreat would have been a true epic. But basking in windless sunshine throughout, it felt more like a humiliating failure. Kevin offered to accompany me to hospital but I flatly refused, insisting that he and Alan stay and try to climb something in my absence. Unfortunately that was the final weather window of the season and they didn't get to climb anything.

The hospital in El Calafate was grim, like something from a bygone era, ancient cast-iron beds and the sickening smell of disinfectant. Nobody except the consultant spoke any English and his was basic though better than my extremely rudimentary Spanish. Far more grim was the result of the X-ray. I had severely crushed my talus bone and would require major reconstructive surgery. He advised returning to the UK for the procedure but I would first need to spend up to a week confined to bed with my foot elevated to reduce the swelling before it was safe to fly.

I didn't have travel insurance, nor did I, or my parents, have sufficient funds for a new flight home; my return ticket was only valid from Punta Arenas in Chile. The final insult to injury came on my discharge five days later. The hospital was unable to provide me with any crutches. Alone, with three big holdalls and a crushed talus bone in an open cast, I once again set off crawling, this time along the pavement to the bus station. I had to rely on the kindness of strangers to help with my bags and more of Alan's tramadol to help me endure travelling overland by bus on shaky, unsurfaced roads for two days. I finally flew back to Manchester where my dad picked me up, precisely where he had dropped me off with his prophetic expression of concern six weeks earlier.

12.

My Right Foot

Ten days after the accident I was nil by mouth in Carlisle Royal Infirmary preparing to go into theatre. The damage was clear in the X-ray. It looked like somebody had smashed my talus with a hammer.

'How long until I can climb again?' was the first question I asked the surgeon.

'Son, you don't seem to understand the severity of your injury. You'll be lucky to walk properly again, let alone climb,' said Mr Ions bluntly. 'You have a severe compression fracture of the talus, sometimes called aviator's ankle as it was a common injury for fighter pilots following crash landings during the war. We are going to take a bone graft from your hip and put a screw along the length of the talus. If the surgery is successful and the graft is accepted you will have to be non-weight-bearing on crutches for three months and partial-weight-bearing for another three. During that period you must treat your foot like fine china. If the graft is rejected we will look at ankle fusion. If avascular necrosis occurs, amputation of the foot can be the best course of action.'

Amputation! I was stunned.

'Even if the surgery is successful, during six months on crutches you will experience severe muscle atrophy and osteoporosis of the other bones in your right leg. It will be another six months of rehabilitation until the extent of recovery is clear. You are young, fit and healthy, which is a benefit. With luck you should ultimately regain full strength although full mobility is unlikely.'

I thought I had broken my ankle and was looking at two or

three months out of action. Now the best-case scenario was a year out, and the worst, crippled for life.

The talus is the uppermost bone in the foot, crucial for all ankle movement; its upper ball joint connects the complex arrangement of small footbones to the large, lower-leg tibia and fibular. It has a notoriously poor, indirect blood supply, meaning it takes much longer to repair than almost all other bones in the body. A severe fracture may not heal at all and can cause the death and ultimately collapse of the bone leading to constant, intense pain due to nerve exposure and can result in amputation of the foot.

The dream I had been living had imploded into a nightmare because of one minuscule bad decision. I ran the scene over and over in my mind. What had I been thinking! Why hadn't I just clipped into the Swiss rope? Or pulled on a few bloody pieces of gear? Who cares about such arbitrary concepts as free climbing when the consequences are so severe? I'd had my fair share of minor injuries and been on the scene of a few more serious climbing accidents, but I had never really considered that it might happen to me, and that if it did how negatively life-altering it could be.

Although I was racked by regret, I never even considered quitting. Climbing and adventure had already become such a fundamental part of my identity. All my friends were climbers, all my future plans revolved around climbing and wild adventures. It had given me purpose, a perspective on the world that I felt was enlightened, shown me wonderful places I never imagined existed, introduced me to people and a lifestyle that valued experience and nature above possessions and inspired a deep passion that seemed to me to be the very meaning of life.

When I came around from the anaesthetic and saw the vicious, 10-cm-long wound that had been cut deep into my ankle, the severity of my injury finally dawned on me.

I moved back into my old bedroom in Violet Bank. The musty smell of damp saturated the air as I lay in my childhood bed, unable to walk, looking at the woodchip peeling off the walls, the mould colonising my once-beloved climbing wall, my foot throbbing with nauseatingly deep pain. The prospect of my future had become an incomparably bleaker picture than the world of opportunity that had lay ahead as I stood beneath Cerro Torre just a fortnight earlier.

Mum and Dad had separated and divorced in the years I had been gone. Carla had left home and now Dad rattled around the big, cold house alone and depressed. This was no longer the family home full of love and joy that I remembered so fondly.

My mum, Lindsey, had given birth to my sister, Carla, when she was nineteen. She had spent her entire adult life as a devoted, loving parent, taking jobs that she didn't enjoy and didn't challenge her intellectually in order to pay the bills, with precious little time or money for herself.

She was always far more sociable and outgoing than Dad, who was quite antisocial, hated pubs and preferred the solitude of the hills. Though Mum enjoyed the outdoors, it has always been at the milder end of the spectrum. She tried climbing a couple of times but quickly concluded it wasn't for her.

Shortly after Carla had left home Mum graduated from the Open University with the degree she had long desired in Psychology. Having given her children the best start she possibly could, her parental responsibilities were fulfilled and after twenty-four years of marriage, she wanted to begin a new life that was her own.

I had been based in Llanberis, obsessed with climbing and travelling constantly throughout that period. I had seen very little of Mum or Dad and felt strangely distant, perhaps intentionally disconnected from the family break-up.

It was much harder for Carla, who lived in the local town and saw them both regularly. She and Mum are quite similar and naturally close. Mum soon found new love and remarried.

Dad was heartbroken when Mum left and struggled with his mental health for a couple of years. We have always been very close, no doubt in part thanks to our shared passion for climbing. His suffering made it difficult for me to accept Mum's remarriage.

The first weeks I spent hobbling around the empty house on

crutches in constant pain were without doubt the low point of my life. Carla had bought a house with her long-term boyfriend, Mum had remarried and was building a new life, Dad had recently met somebody and began to spend more and more time developing his new relationship.

I felt lonely, broken and was teetering on the edge of despair when by chance I met a guy who had experienced the awful complication of avascular necrosis of the talus. Five years earlier he too had smashed his talus in a climbing accident and was still on crutches, his foot horribly swollen and black. The slightest foot movement caused agony to his exposed nerve, he couldn't even swim. He said the pain was becoming unbearable but he couldn't accept the idea of amputation.

'Your surgery has been successful. The graft has been accepted, clear indications of new bone growth. Your prognosis is positive. You have been very lucky, young man,' said Mr Ions, examining the X-ray at my check-up not long after I'd met that poor crippled chap.

It was a eureka moment. Until that point I had been feeling anything but lucky. Now I realised that a year out of action was nothing compared to continual suffering or a life without a foot, that though not being able to climb was bad, never being able to walk was far worse. I *had* been lucky and with a conscious effort I decided to change my mindset. Depression and self-pity would waste energy and vital life-force that I needed for bone growth and healing. I would try to maintain a positive disposition, focusing on physio and rehab.

My primary concern was to recover as completely as possible so as to be able to enjoy climbing and my life of adventure once more. It didn't matter how long it took.

Prior to my accident I had been of no fixed abode for much of the last few years of near-constant travel, my stuff was stashed in various people's garages and my mail was being sent to several different addresses around North Wales. I had also not been submitting tax returns, nor was I on any electoral register, or on the books of any dentist or doctor's surgery. In short, my affairs were not in order. I had been far too busy travelling and having fun.

I decided to be proactive with my convalescence, to get my affairs in order and use the forced time out of action to lay a solid foundation for the next chapters of my life.

I had received one piece of very good news. I was in the middle of a three-year sponsorship contract with Berghaus when the accident happened. There was a clause, standard in professional sport endorsements, that stated if I was unable to perform my obligations for three months the company retained the right to terminate the agreement. I told them how serious it was from hospital. Promptly they had responded informing me that they would honour the remainder of the contract no questions asked and would review the situation at the end of term and wished me a full and speedy recovery.

Their financial support during that difficult time was invaluable. When approached by other brands since I have stayed loyal, grateful to Berghaus for standing by me during my lowest period, and I still work with them today.

During the Paine expedition there had been much downtime due to bad weather. I had relentlessly questioned my older team mates, who were all interesting people who lived in nice houses in nice places and seemed to have financially stable, fulfilling lives and yet still found time for expeditions.

I was particularly curious about Ross Purdy. Twenty years my senior, slightly shorter than average with a barrel chest, Ross was a jolly chap, always smiling, joking and taking the piss. Although he was a talented builder, he didn't seem to work much. He was into mountain biking, caving, climbing and other adventure sport but white-water kayaking was his main passion. He seemed to have been on an extraordinary number of kayak expeditions, spending many seasons on rivers in exotic places, having grown up the son of a parish vicar in Wythenshawe, a deprived area of Manchester.

He now lived in a spectacular cottage in the South Lakes with

30 acres. I was intrigued as to how a river bum who worked as little and played as much as possible had come to enjoy such an affluent life. Was his partner from money? Had he won the pools?

'No, lad, I bought a house when I was twenty-five. I rented out the rooms and it cost me less than renting a place.' This was in Didsbury, which wasn't as nice as it is now. 'That and I don't waste money on fast cars and fancy things. Unless I need them for my sports.'

This had been a common theme amongst the whole team. They had all invested in property early in life and all seemed to have reaped substantial returns. I quizzed Ross as to why he had settled in the Lakes and not California or the Alps.

'Home is home, youth. It's all good and well living the life when you're having fun, but when the chips are down, living abroad isn't all it's cracked up to be. The weather might be shit but the Lakes is a great place to live and you can't beat the British sense of humour.'

Back in Violet Bank, nursing my ankle, I decided I would try to get a mortgage and buy a house.

It was 2002, the UK economy was booming and house prices had just begun their meteoric rise. Financial regulation was at its all-time loosest with credit being virtually thrown at anybody who wanted it. I declared myself to HMRC, paid a nominal amount of back-dated tax as I hadn't actually earned very much, registered to vote, made sure all my bank statements, National Insurance and all that other boring stuff showed the same address and eventually, armed with a file full of accounts and a letter of employment from Berghaus, managed to convince the portly manager of the Penrith branch of Midland Bank, recently incorporated into HSBC, of my eligibility to borrow and was awarded a 125 per cent mortgage in principle up to £100K. Yes, 125 per cent – they were willing to lend more than a house was worth, entering into negative equity immediately upon purchase, such was the buoyancy of the housing market! I didn't have any savings nor much disposable income, but I began searching for a house from my childhood bedroom on the internet, a novel concept in 2002.

I decided I wanted to experience living in city for a while and thought that lodgers would be easier to find somewhere with lots of people and in particular students. Sheffield is the undisputed capital city of British climbing. I knew the city and had lots of friends there. After being gazumped on a couple of properties with all sales going to sealed bids in the frenzied market, I doubled down and put in an offer 20 per cent over the asking price on a three-bedroom end-terrace in Heeley that I hadn't even viewed, not too far from the gentrified area of Nether Edge where I used to visit Johnny. The offer was accepted, leaving me just enough funds to furnish the house. I got the keys in November 2002.

Immediately following my Cerro Torre accident I received an enquiry from a chap called Ed Stobart, who worked for Chris Evans' production company, Ginger TV. He was interested in making an episode about me for a BBC2 series called *Extreme Lives*. He had heard about my accident and thought that following my recovery over the course of a year to see if I would make it back to the top of my game might make for interesting viewing. There was hardly any fee involved; the premise of the series was simply to follow people who lived any sort extreme life doing their thing. I knew the exposure would be good for my profile and provide some value for my sponsors so I agreed on the basis that I really would be doing my thing.

Ed proved good company and over the course of the following year we shared some memorable experiences. He filmed me before I left Violet Bank and soon after moving into Slate Street, the first climb I did after getting off crutches, during which I stress-fractured a weakened bone in my foot, and at the legendary closing party at Space in Ibiza before representing Berghaus a few hours later at an outdoor trade fair, where I immediately bumped into Sir Chris Bonington.

We also undertook a couple of bigger shoots, including, with Jason, an ascent of the Leaning Tower in Yosemite, a mini big wall that we had made the first free ascent of, followed by the fastest speed ascent the year before. I figured active rehab was the best way to get strong again and jumaring would be great conditioning for my right leg.

I stayed in Yosemite after Ed and Jas left. José was there, recovering from a knee injury. Javier, my Chilean friend, was around too and my friend Harry Pennels, soon to be my tenant in Sheffield. They were desperate to climb El Cap but lacked the confidence and skills to try. We teamed up along with Blanka, the strong Czech girl, and a friend of Jav's from South Africa called Louis. Six people is a large team for a big-wall climb, bearing in mind you have to bring all the water.

We made a party-style ascent of the North America Wall, a climb that shared much terrain with El Niño. We were up there for over a week and once again brought a full bar and the deafening speakers. José and I did not lead a pitch but managed the proceedings and allowed our less experienced friends to do all the fun stuff whilst we discussed quantum mechanics and psychotropics, and he inspired me with more tales of the amazing *tepuis* of his native Venezuela.

'Autana was really something, man. You missed out. It is special even amongst *tepuis*. You have to face a lot of hardship, a lot of challenge just to get to the wall. Mosquitoes, mud, snakes, spiders, scorpions! But the jungle is alive, it is life, you can feel it! And then the wall is hard. Really hard. Vertical jungle, killer bees, vampire bats and real climbing. Really good climbing. Then the Cave, oh man, el Cuevo de Autana is another thing! Like a cathedral in the mountains, the walls covered with quartz crystal that shimmers like diamonds. You will love it. You have to go!'

He carried on excitedly: 'And the yopo! Oh, the yopo! It really blew my mind.'

'What's yopo?' I asked.

'Ha ha ha! What is yopo! Well, it's a plant. But it's a kind of magic. A really powerful hallucinogen, much more than mushrooms or peyote. The Piaroa people believe it is sacred; they use it for vision quests, to find their spirit animals. We partook in a yopo ceremony with their shaman. It is powerful – I saw things, learned things.

'But your accident. You should not worry. It all happens for a reason, my friend. Sometimes that reason is not clear for some time. I think you are going to be OK, in fact I think you will go far.' He told me this with the authority of his former life as a university lecturer.

We climbed in capsule style, a common tactic for remote walls in gnarly places. Instead of moving all the gear up pitch by pitch and establishing a new camp every night as is the usual way on El Cap, the lead team climb for the day and then return to the same camp leaving ropes fixed to the high point. It requires more rope than the standard style and is slower but it is suited to heavyweight ascents and means you can keep camps in safer places on more dangerous walls. On this climb it meant we could party for days on end from comfortable camps without having to constantly go through the arduous process of packing up gear and hauling bags every day. We set up a huge rope jump from underneath the Black Cave. José spent more than an hour standing on the edge of the port-a-ledge, trying to pluck up the courage to jump, which he eventually did, his poncho flying like a cape as he fell.

José and I used the ascent to experiment with complex rigging and haul systems. We talked things through together but he left me to set everything up on my own – tricks and techniques that I would use to great effect on future expeditions. We only had three camps during the ascent and, more remarkably, brought the massive amount of gear – some seven huge haul bags and three port-a-ledges – up the whole wall in just four giant hauls using unorthodox systems.

When we reached the summit we tied all the ropes together including the very thin 6mm tag line and lowered all the gear to the ground from a tree, then dropped the rope saving a huge amount of work.

'I think you can safely call yourself a big-wall climber now, Leo!' he said to me. Over five seasons in Yosemite I had learned so much from José and the other Monkeys. The more I knew, the more I wanted to learn and test that knowledge to push the limits.

That was to be the last time I would see José. He died on 3 January 2003 in a big fall after dislodging a loose rock whilst climbing a new route in El Potrero Chico, Mexico. He was forty. A couple of weeks earlier he had sent me a message: 'Come to Mexico, Leo! This place is very special. Perhaps the place I will stay.'

José was the first of my close friends to die prematurely. I had looked to him as both a climbing mentor and a spiritual teacher. I felt his loss acutely.

For the final shoot in the BBC film that would be called *Extreme Lives: My Right Foot* we had discussed returning to Cerro Torre, but though my foot was healing well, I was not nearly fit enough nor ready for a rematch. Following José's death I felt an urge to visit El Potrero Chico, the place where he had spent his final days, to meet the people he had been hanging out with and see where he died. Ed Stobart joined me with a crew including my friends Brian Hall and Keith Partridge. Timmy O'Neil, another Stone Monkey and close friend of both José and mine, joined me and together over two days we climbed a long route with a big reputation called El Sendero Luminoso, the Shining Path, on the same face where José had died.

Precisely one year after my accident on Cerro Torre I managed to onsight the whole climb with difficulties up to 5.12+, which was a respectable standard. I was back. José was gone. The film was broadcast in a prime Sunday-night slot on BBC2 and was watched by many millions. I found some of the scenes very cringe worthy, questioning why I had agreed to film a scene in a nightclub, but it was well received and undoubtedly helped further both my career as a climber and in TV.

I returned to try the same route on Cerro Torre with Kevin on long trips in 2004 and 2005 but both seasons were thwarted by unfavourable conditions for that climb. In 2004, accompanied by Cedar Wright, we spent six weeks in base camp and were granted only a single climbable day. The weather was much better in 2005 but too warm for that line on snow-capped Cerro Torre, the high temperatures causing frequent avalanches. Instead we made the first free ascent of the iconic, 1,400-metre-tall north pillar of neighbouring Cerro Fitz Roy. Caught in one of Patagonia's infamous storms on the descent, we completed more than fifty rappels in hurricane-force gusts. Eventually we stumbled into base camp, suffering from audio hallucinations after fifty-six hours of continuous action with no sleep. All those long weekends of partying were finally proving their worth! Although it was a neighbouring peak, climbing Fitz Roy with Kevin provided closure to my Cerro Torre episode. I had survived, recovered, grown and returned to summit one of the mountains that had almost killed me. I would still like to climb Cerro Torre but, tired of the constant bad weather, have not returned since with so many other places to explore.

My accident on Cerro Torre and José's sudden death made me re-evaluate my life, especially my relationships. Shortly before departing for Patagonia I had nipped into Rock + Run, a climbing shop in Ambleside, to buy some chalk on my way to a crag in Langdale. An errand that would change my life. Behind the counter was an exquisitely beautiful girl, tall with sun-kissed skin, long blonde hair and wearing flared hipsters and a crop trop.

'Hi, can I help you?' she said.

Yes, you can, I thought.

I knew some of the other guys who worked in the shop and they quickly introduced me to Jessica Corrie.

It transpired she had just returned from an extended surf trip to southeast Asia, having graduated in Neuroscience from Edinburgh University the previous summer. Her parents had a second home in Little Langdale, a small cottage not far from Ambleside, where she was living for a short while before heading to Colorado to spend a winter snowboarding, then to Hawaii, where her brother lived, for another summer of surfing.

Though I had always thought it a romantic myth, it was love at first sight, at least for me. Not only was she jaw-droppingly pretty, she also possessed a subtle, self-assured confidence, a relaxed demeanour, kind smile and clever, compassionate eyes. She clearly had a passion for adventure sports and although she played it down, was also an experienced climber. I asked if I could borrow a bouldering pad but the shop didn't have one they could lend me.

'I've got one you can use. It's in the cottage just before the pub. Door's open,' said Jess.

I found the chocolate-box cottage easily. It felt weird letting myself into a stranger's home and helping myself to her gear. It was a charming little place with a wobbly roof, a clematis climbing the whitewashed wall and rose bushes around the perimeter in one of the very nicest valleys of the central Lakes. Though it appeared tiny from the outside, it was quite the Tardis inside. Low ceilings, thick walls, small windows, ancient beams and odd-shaped doors that led to more rooms than seemed feasible. It would later become our family's second home. When I returned the crash pad later that afternoon, I left a note attached to it with my phone number, asking her to drop me a line if she'd like to go out climbing or for a drink. To my joy, the next day she did!

The following weekend was the Kendal Mountain Festival, only in its third year but already well on the way to becoming the definitive annual tribal gathering of the UK mountain sports community. Already becoming well known in the outdoor world, I had been invited to be the patron of the festival and that year, 2001, I was presenting in the big theatre. I enquired if Jess would be attending the festival and if she would like to meet for a drink? She came to my show and afterwards we got to know each other a little better amongst the chaotic, lively bar scene and danced energetically to electronic music at an infamous party.

As patron and a guest of the festival I had a room in a nice hotel called the Stone Cross Manor. At that time it was customary for the organisers and VIP guests to keep the residents' bar open until the early hours, long after every other licensed premise in Kendal was closed. Jess came and amongst the drunken mayhem of the after-party we snuck off to my room. It hosted a magnificent four-poster bed. As Jess and I got to know each other even better there was a knock at the first-floor window. A very drunken Tim Emmett had climbed up the porch and traversed across the window ledges to my room and was perched, grinning like a maniac through the glass. I quickly closed the curtains and apologised to Jess, who thought it very amusing. We began a brief but intense love affair.

I had never had a serious girlfriend and didn't really want one. I was happy being single, travelling the world, meeting new people and sharing experiences without any responsibility or commitment. But Jess stirred a deeper emotion. For the first time I could imagine sharing my life with somebody, with her. But she had plans to spend the next year in the US and I was already committed to at least three months of back-to-back expeditions in South America. We decided not to try to maintain a long-distance relationship, could see other people, but made tentative plans to meet in Yosemite the following autumn.

However, in September 2002 Jess's father, Jackson Corrie, a lifelong climber then in his late sixties, suffered a climbing accident at a gritstone outcrop in Staffordshire called Ramshaw Rocks. He had hit the ground from 20 feet up, landed on his feet, fallen backwards and severely struck the rear of his head on a rock. He was in a coma, his brain was damaged and it wasn't clear whether he would survive or to what extent he might recover.

Jess returned home from Hawaii early to be with him in hospital. Gradually he recovered but had suffered irrevocable brain damage, and though able to function and live independently, his personality changed and he was never quite the same man as before. She arrived back in the UK and we met briefly before I departed for Yosemite. The mutual attraction was intense, the lengthy separation serving to verify how strongly we felt about each other.

Though we had communicated very little in the previous nine months, she had often been on my mind. I had had a few brief flings with other girls in that period, which had only led me to realise just how special Jess was and how much I cared for her. A voice deep inside told me I'd found a keeper and if I got another chance I mustn't lose her.

The deep soul-searching and life-questioning following my

accident and José's death had made me realise that there was more to life than climbing.

'I've always quite liked the idea of living fast and dying young,' I said.

The look of horror on Jess's face caught me off guard.

'NO! There's so much more, life is long and full of stages. Don't waste all the rest of them going too fast at the start.'

I wasn't looking for love, it caught me unawares. I thought that El Capitan, high exposure, great adventures in epic landscapes was the love I sought. But Jess made me realise that all that wonder would be squandered were it not shared. That any life, no matter how intense and rich, would be more fulfilled if it could be enjoyed with a soulmate. A voice inside my head told me she was the one.

Jess had mentioned to her parents before leaving for the US that she thought becoming a GP might be a good career as she could earn sufficient money working just a couple of days a week and find work somewhere with a small economy such as the Lakes. In her absence her dad had submitted applications to several medical schools complete with forged signatures. To her surprise, whilst she was in Hawaii she received acceptance offers to study Medicine in both Exeter, close to Cornwall's surf, and Sheffield universities.

I told her I had just bought a house in Sheffield. She moved in as soon as I got the keys. For the first few weeks we slept on the crash pad I had borrowed from her on the floor in the living room whilst, with help from my dad and the leftover cash from the mortgage, we updated and furnished the property. Five years later we married in a fairy-tale ceremony in the Cathedral Quarry, a spectacular cave close to the cottage in Little Langdale in the Lakes.

Before starting work on the house we had a massive house-warming party. It happened to fall on the same day as the final of an international climbing competition held in Sheffield. The house was a small, two-up two-down terrace with loft conversion, so when over 250 revellers showed up things got a bit out of control. The house was literally rammed and overflowed with people who spilled out onto the street accompanied by earth-shaking bass and high-tempo techno. I set off a massive firework repeater out of the velux roof window, just as the police showed up. Somebody broke the toilet, water under high pressure flooded the tiny bathroom, and soon after that the dining-room ceiling collapsed. The officer was unbelievably cool.

'Try to keep the door shut and turn the bass down a bit. No more fireworks, eh? And maybe don't do it again next weekend,' he said with a wink. I liked Sheffield.

Serious accidents are explicit moments in life where everything instantly changes. Where the infinite myriad of previous opportunities and possibilities is suddenly completely reset, presenting an entirely different set of choices and possible outcomes. These moments occur to all of us, thousands of times a day, every single decision taken and act performed becoming the foundation for everything that will follow. So much of life is repetition and gradual change that we rarely notice the key moments that chart our ultimate heading. On reflection, certain pivotal events do stand out in memory, none more so than traumatic experiences where everything that happened before and everything that happened afterwards can be distinctly categorised.

Life-changing accidents are rarely perceived as positive events at the time. Usually they involve severe pain, termination of existing goals, an extended period of convalescence and sometimes permanent physical impediments. However, with the passing of time these drastic alterations of course can easily be identified as those pivotal life moments that lead us to where are and who we become.

Were it not for my accident I would almost certainly not have got my act together to get on the property ladder so early in life and that would ultimately lead to a level of financial security my parents never enjoyed and a nice house in the Lakes. I would never have crossed paths with Ed Stobart, who a few years later would secure me my own big-budget TV show, *Take Me to the Edge*, where I would spend six months travelling the world introducing five 'normal' people from the UK to the delights of amazing adventures. I earned more from that one job than from the first ten years of my climbing career, paying off my mortgage before I was thirty.

Though Jess and I might still have ended up together, our relationship leading to marriage and children would certainly not have played out as it did. Most importantly – I kind of had it coming, I was pushing too hard, too frequently and in the wrong ways at the wrong times. I was lucky it was my talus and not my neck. I had found the edge. Ever since that fall I have been more cautious, more calculated. I'm sure it has helped to keep me alive. Especially considering what was to come next.

13.

BASE Instincts

'The time is coming now,' said Dean Potter in his deep, baritone voice.

Nervously I checked my leg straps, adjusted my goggles and repeatedly reached down with my right hand to touch my pilot chute on the bottom of my container. Mustn't fumble that. Breathing deeply, bathed in the rose-pink light of the sun's final rays, the four of us took in the sublime vista. Dark shadow engulfed the Valley stretched out beneath us as the alpenglow crept up Half Dome's northwest face to where we stood atop the bare granite of the highest point of the Yosemite, feeling like kings.

'How's it looking down there, brother?' asked Stanley over the phone.

'All good, great night for a ride,' replied Bullwinkle.

We could just make out the clearing in the forest of Mirror Lake 5,000 feet below and see the flash of his head torch as he rode his bike to check the ground was clear.

'OK, I gonna count – Monkeys ready to charge?' said Ivo in his high-pitched eastern European accent.

'Ready!' we all replied in unison.

'OK – three, two, one, GO!' shouted Ivo.

I sprinted hard towards the drop, increasing my stride to place my right foot on the very edge of the huge cliff, and dived out into the void. Chest out, eyes on the horizon, arms stretched out in front, I feel weightless as I plummet. Slowly I spread my arms wide and down to my sides, straightening my legs as I gain speed. The familiar features of the Regular route accelerate through my field of view. I can see the others in my peripheral vision. The rush of the air becomes more powerful, I feel the pressure building against my bare hands and start to push against it, increasing my angle of attack, turning my body into a wing.

The momentum of my running exit transfers smoothly into a delta, then I start to track, my rate of forward motion increasing rapidly. Finding the subtle balance of tension and relaxation in my body required to generate the optimum vector, I hit the sweet spot and feel my velocity surge. Not much vertical cliff left, the ground is fast approaching. It's decision time – am I flying fast enough to outrun the aptly named death slabs? There is a flat section I've got to clear first then the slope runs at a steady 45 degrees for another 3,000 feet, all the way to the landing zone. Shit, the top of that tree's not far away . . . hold it, hold it . . . Yes, I'm clear.

Maintaining a constant altitude about 300 feet above ground level on the same trajectory as the slope I feel like Superman, flying faster than terminal velocity. Through the dusk I can see the terrain level out, so I grab my pilot chute and pitch from full track almost thirty seconds after my feet left the Earth. The parachute explodes open with a loud crack; it's a hard opening that hurts my neck but I'm on heading, drifting away from the mountain. Grabbing the steering toggles, I release the brake lines and look to check the canopy is properly pressurised and all the lines are clear. It's flying beautifully, not much altitude to spare, little bit of brake to extend the glide, clear the trees, ease off the brakes, pause, hard input on left toggle to gain some speed on the final turn, ease up and . . . flare! Touch down like a feather.

Check that everybody's made it down safely.

'ALL RIGHT!!!!!'

Don't shout! Still got to keep a low profile, armed rangers with night vision have been known to stake out the landing, like Captain Hook waiting to trap the Lost Boys. Adrenaline surges through my bloodstream, eyes bulging, skin tingling, body shaking with excitement. I want to do that again, now! Taking a running jump off Half Dome and out-flying the death slabs may possibly be *the* most amazing thing a human can do. It is too much fun, insatiable but deadly.

BASE is an acronym for Building, Antenna, Span (Bridge), Earth (Cliff), the objects from which it is possible to jump with a parachute, a term coined by the Californian grandfather of the sport Carl Boenish. I first encountered BASE jumping on a climbing trip in Norway with Cavey in 1999. We were climbing an impressive 1,000-metre-tall cliff called Kjerag that rises directly from the turquoise waters of the Lysefjord near Stavanger. We made a first free ascent of a route called the Shield over two days and while I was leading the overhanging headwall I heard a terrible noise.

'Rock fall, watch out!' screamed Andy, recognising the terrifying sound from his Himalayan climbs.

Panic-stricken, I held on tight, pulled myself close to the wall and looked up. A cluster of big silhouettes fell from the sky but they were far from the wall and posed no danger. It took a moment to register what I was seeing but as the shapes grew nearer then hurtled past I realised they were human. A mass suicide? Then I noticed one of them was somersaulting like an acrobat and the others seemed perfectly stable as they began to accelerate out over the fjord. I watched transfixed as they fell for what seemed like an unfeasibly long time. Just as it seemed from my vantage point that they were gong to hit the ground, five bursts of colour appeared far below. Hollers of ecstasy echoed upwards as they floated gracefully to Earth and landed on the small patch of grass where we had camped a day earlier.

An inversion flooded the fjord, engulfing us in mist. We climbed through the damp cold for hours, breaking through the fog into the midnight sun of Norway's summer a couple of pitches below the top. At the summit we basked in the warmth above a kingdom of cloud like Jack up the beanstalk. It was breathtaking.

A lone figure appeared carrying a small backpack. A typically Viking-looking Norwegian bloke. We chatted briefly, and Andy and I glowed with pride following our significant ascent. Then to my absolute disbelief the Viking waved goodbye and took a running jump off the cliff into the cloud.

'Oh my god! Did that really just happen? That was the coolest thing I've ever seen!' I yelled to Andy.

I vowed then and there to take a running jump off the same spot one day. I was going to learn how to BASE jump.

My next encounter with BASE jumping was less inspiring. A few months later I was back in Yosemite. Two years earlier a famous BASE jumper called Frank 'the Gambler' Gambali, a friend of Kevin's, had BASE jumped from El Capitan and landed in the meadow only to find the rangers staking him out. They gave chase and he jumped into the Merced River to escape. It was spring and the river was gushing with icy melt water. He drowned.

To object to the draconian rules that had prohibited BASE jumping in all US national parks since the early eighties and had led to Frank's death, a group of BASE jumpers had organised a protest jump from El Capitan. The media had turned up in force and Frank's mother was there too, fronting the campaign.

There were hundreds of people in the meadow, 'BASE is not a crime' banners were held high. A large landing area had been cordoned off for the jumpers to land. In between attempts on The Passage to Freedom, I was at the top of a tall tree with José. There was a festival atmosphere as we all watched the small dots hurl themselves from the diving board and the first jumpers landed safely to shake hands with the rangers. It had been agreed they would confiscate gear but the park would not press charges. The event was broadcast live to all the news networks.

The party ended abruptly and the protest backfired horribly when one of the jumpers, a sixty-year-old woman called Jan Davis, failed to open her parachute and crashed into the talus below the East Buttress. From the top of my tree I saw her flailing as she impacted the ground and died.

The inquest concluded that, knowing her gear would be confiscated, she had used an old rig with a different deployment system.

In the rush of freefall she had neglected to remember this and with just seconds to rectify the error failed to do so.

None of this put me off. The recommended way to enter BASE jumping is to start by making at least 200 skydives. You learn how to control your body in freefall, how to handle and land a canopy and some of the fundamentals of parachute design, packing and rigging. Then you make jumps from a hot-air balloon, or more commonly a bridge. It is airspeed and the apparent wind it creates that provide stability in freefall. With no air speed these zero velocity exits are very different to jumping from a plane. The first six seconds of a BASE jump is more akin to jumping from a cliff into water, your movement is dictated by the input carried from exit until you accelerate enough to provide sufficient airspeed with which to work. Bridges are safer than cliffs as, if you have an off-heading opening, there is nothing to hit. Once you gain some experience you can progress to cliffs. Every exit is different, and though there is no graded scale of severity there are widely accepted categories with safer, beginner's jumps at one end and extremely technical, low-margin flights at the other that are suicide for all but the most expert and current pilots.

A skydive rig contains a main canopy and a reserve. Experienced skydivers may use very small high-performance mains and even entry-level main canopies can be prone to rare failures. Reserves, however, almost never fail and must be repacked and inspected by a certified rigger every six months. BASE rigs only contain one canopy, very similar to a reserve, and are packed in a similar fashion although usually by the jumper themselves.

To allow time to recognise a problem, cut away the main and deploy the reserve in the case of a malfunction, the minimum deployment altitude of a main in skydiving is 2,500 feet. Since this is far higher than most BASE-jumpable objects there is no point in using a main, instead jumping directly to the far more reliable reserve-style BASE canopy.

Because skydiving requires an aircraft and aviation is subject to stringent laws and costly insurance, the sport is highly regulated, controlled, assessed and certified. By contrast, especially back then, BASE jumping had no rules, no governing body and no licence required. Any idiot was free to get hold of a rig and jump off a cliff. However, the extremely high consequence of a mistake and the overt risk so apparent in BASE, provide a good level of self-regulation.

Tim and I learned to skydive together in 2003 with the sole intent of starting to BASE jump and fly wingsuits. We undertook the Accelerated Free Fall (AFF) course – a series of eight jumps with instructors and about six hours of ground school. In less than a week we were qualified skydivers, having completed twenty jumps and gained our A-licences, which would allow us to jump anywhere in the world.

I was impressed with skydiving. The exhilaration of taking a small plane to 13,000 feet, opening the door, climbing out onto the wing with one of your best mates then tumbling through the sky for a minute before opening your parachute and spiralling it to Earth is something that everybody should experience. Tim and I would make hundreds of skydives together over the next years.

At the time BASE jumping was just starting to come out of the shadows. Equipment was no longer adapted skydive gear but had been developed and built specifically for object jumps. The pioneers had mastered techniques and best practices. An increasingly wide knowledge base was emerging and being shared, but it was still a niche activity practised by very few and hard to get into. The explosion in popularity would come towards the end of the decade with improvements in wingsuits along with the rise of GoPro and YouTube.

Although there were a handful of climbers who had BASE jumped previously, right around that time a whole bunch of us all came to the same realisation that the sports were an obvious complement to each other, and if performed carefully, BASE jumping could be practised safely, almost all accidents and fatalities being caused by pilot error, be that jumping in poor conditions, packing errors or mistakes in the air. The era of the flying Monkeys had begun and Yosemite, already the most epic natural playground, was about to get a whole lot more extreme.

On the drive from San Francisco to Yosemite you pass just south of a nondescript American strip town called Lodi. On the outskirts, sandwiched between two major highways and surrounded by vineyards, lies a small airport with two asphalt runways and half a dozen spacious aircraft hangars. In the large gravel parking lot, home to a selection of run-down vans and truck campers, is an old DC3 twin prop inscribed with the words 'Eat, Fly, Skydive'.

The Lodi parachute centre began operations in 1964 and is still owned by the eccentric Bill Dause, a small, wiry man with long grey hair and a major Napoleon complex who had at one time spent more time in freefall than anybody in history. He shared the initials and was rumoured by some to be B. D. Cooper, the infamous skydiving bandit who in 1973 held up a plane in mid-air and jumped with a million dollars of cash, never to be seen again.

Open seven days a week, 365 days a year, weather permitting, when I first visited Lodi in 2004 you could learn to skydive for $500, a quarter of the price of anywhere else. A tandem jump was $100, a jump ticket to 13,000 feet was $20 and you could do a hop and pop from 5,000 ft for an unbelievable $5 – cash only. It had one of the best skydiving aircraft fleets in the world, operating two powerful Super Twin Otters that could hold twenty-five jumpers each, a super-fast Beech 99 that could climb to 13,000 feet in nine minutes, and two little Cessna 206 single-engine planes. It was common for them to run up to thirty-five loads on a Saturday. Most drop zones have just one five-seater Cessna, run only at weekends for the summer months, and ten loads per day is considered exceptional. You could camp for free on the edge of the large grass landing zone, sleep in your car in the parking lot for as long as you liked, or if you became more of a regular you could stay in the staff hangar.

It was the only drop zone in North America not affiliated with the US parachute association. Bill owned everything himself, meaning he didn't have to lease anything from anybody and didn't need USPA insurance, allowing him to dictate how his drop zone ran, who could do what and how. And dictate he did, in a some-times tyrannical fashion as the captain of his own pirate ship, known to summarily fire staff for taking too long for lunch and ban jumpers for not packing fast enough to catch their allocated load. However, if he liked you, you were respectful and played by his rules, he could be kind and welcoming to all and would usually rehire and allow those banned to return when he was in a better mood.

By chance, Lodi happens to be exceptionally well geographically located for BASE jumping. Just a half-hour drive east there is a 500-foot-tall electricity pylon known as the Power Tower and there are three 2,000-foot radio masts called the Walnut Grove Antennas, both benefiting from surprisingly lax security. The Auburn Bridge spans a 700-foot drop an hour north. There are tall buildings in nearby Sacramento and skyscrapers in San Francisco, though secu-rity there is more of a problem. Then of course there is the Yosemite Valley two hours to the west, as if designed to be the ultimate BASE playground, made extra exciting by its prohibition and the omnipresent ranger-danger. Because of these objects and the loose regulation Lodi was a magnet for BASE-jumping skydivers.

Skydiving has its own ecosystem. At the bottom of the food chain are packers, who spend all day packing other peoples para-chutes, in Lodi for $5. Then there are the camera flyers, who usually film tandems and quickly turn around an edited video for them to take home for $100. At the top of the pecking order and earning good money are the highly skilled performance coaches and quali-fied tandem masters who jump with people strapped to them. There are also AFF instructors, pilots, aircraft engineers, parachute rig-gers, manifest and administration staff and others. Drop-zone life is an entire subculture with all kinds of waifs and strays coming and going, many people spending entire careers in these jobs. The influ-ence of Bill Dause's no frills, all jumps cowboy drop zone in the BASE-jumping world is comparable to that of Camp Four in climb-ing and located just a couple of hours' drive away.

It was the Lodi rigger Pete Swan who took me on my first BASE jump from the Power Tower with Dean and a few others. I had only done thirty skydives but convinced him to take me. On the top of the massive pylon he watched me put on my rig then asked if I was ready. I felt I was, but then he pointed out that my pilot chute bridle ran through my leg strap, meaning I would certainly have died if he hadn't checked.

This error corrected, I climbed over the railing and with the pilot chute in my hand jumped into the darkness. Instead of hopping off in the correct, head-high position, I plunged head first like a diver, released the pilot chute when almost upside down, causing a big swing and 90 degree off-heading opening. I landed safely and immediately decided to do a lot more skydives before my next BASE jump.

'Excuse me, mate, I heard you mention BASE. I live here in the Lakes and I'm pretty active, let me know if you'd like to get out?'

This was how Shaun Ellison introduced himself to me at the Kendal Mountain Festival in 2003. He was a confident, friendly guy with a nose that had clearly been broken multiple times and a taste for very fast cars. He had overheard me talking to somebody about my ambition to get into para-alpinism, a term recently coined by the French to describe climbing something and then BASE jumping off. Shaun was an experienced skydiver with over 1,000 jumps and an accomplished BASE jumper. Over beers I introduced him to Tim and immediately plans were hatched.

Shaun had done many jumps with his close friend Duane Thomas, a well-built, softly spoken Kiwi with over 500 BASE jumps. They had undertaken one of the very first BASE jumping expeditions to the Sam Ford Fjord in the frozen north of Baffin Island, home to many of the tallest cliffs in the world. Their expedition was a major accomplishment considering they all came from a skydiving background and none of them had any expedition or climbing experience.

Duane had seen an article in *National Geographic* about a remarkable cave in the Arabian desert of Oman called the Majlis al
Jinn – the meeting place of the genies. The subterranean cavern,
the second largest cave chamber on Earth by volume with a surface
area of eleven football pitches and the height of the Old Man of
Hoy, was only accessible via three sinkholes, tunnels in the roof of
the cave, and Duane had the crazy idea to be the first to BASE
jump into it. The only way out would be to pre-rig a long rope
and jumar up it. Shaun and Duane had taken Tim on his first
BASE jumps off a bridge in Belgium around the same time I'd
jumped the Power Tower.

In August 2004 Shaun, Duane, Tim and I teamed up for a
BASE/climbing tour in Europe. They would take us on our first
cliff jumps and continue to mentor us in BASE and we would
teach them to climb, with the idea of going to Oman together the
following winter. The first stop on the tour was Lauterbrunnen in
Switzerland, widely regarded as the European capital of BASE
jumping.

Beneath the fabled Eiger in the Bernese Oberland, the steep-sided
valley is flanked on both sides by overhanging cliffs from 1,000 to
2,000 feet tall, from which waterfalls cascade into the lush green
lowlands. Snow-capped 4,000-metre peaks and glaciers tower
above whilst quaint old chalets set amongst pastoral agriculture fill
the valley floor. A network of steep funicular railways and soaring
cable cars connect the valley to immaculate Alpine villages and
big mountains beyond, providing uniquely easy access to more
than a dozen exits within a half-hour walk. It is a picture of Swiss
perfection and engineering marvels, one of the few places where it
is possible to make four, five or even more cliff jumps per day with
ease. BASE jumpers like Alpinists, skiers and paragliders are not
only tolerated but welcomed to practise their extreme and dangerous sports within agreed parameters.

My first cliff jump was an exit known as the Yellow Edge. The
1,200-foot tall slightly overhung wall is a five- or six-second slider-
up jump with a friendly field in which to land. I was scared gearing

up – jumping from a cliff with a parachute is something I'd long dreamed of doing but was also against all my instincts as a climber. It was an awkward spot, a steep gravelly clearing amongst pine trees disconcertingly close the edge. Tim was bursting with energy as usual, whilst Shaun and Duane especially seemed incredibly calm and relaxed.

We drilled the plan, solid push on the exit, count to six, wait a bit longer, deploy, check heading, quickly correct if necessary, fly a rightward pattern to lose altitude and land in the designated field with the cut grass, so as not to damage the silage and upset the farmers.

'How do you know when to pull?' I asked. 'Surely you're gonna count really fast.'

'Don't worry! Ground rush is intense. Wait until you get scared then pull. After a few jumps, wait until you get scared and count to one. Or if you like to pull low like me, count to two,' said Duane.

I put my expensive carbon-fibre skydiving helmet on the ground to nervously fiddle with something that probably didn't need adjusting, and to my dismay watched it slowly roll towards then off the cliff. Without hesitation Duane handed me his. Duane jumped first, then me, Tim, and Shaun last. We all landed safely. Tim and I were as excited as we'd ever been. The weather forecast for the next day was bad and it didn't look like we'd be jumping in the morning so we went to celebrate a dream come true and get drunk in the BASE bar.

Tim and I were still coming to terms with the nerve-racking responsibility of packing our parachutes, an involved process with many steps and checks that must not be rushed as a small error can be fatal. Shaun patiently oversaw and helped us the next morning. Duane had already packed and was anxious to go as he was about to make his first wingsuit BASE jump. It was the very early days of wingsuit BASE jumping, a discipline that would explode in popularity a few years later and completely reinvent the sport, opening new exits, lines and possibilities that were hard to comprehend.

As we were about to witness, it would also usher in a deadly era that would claim the lives of hundreds of people, including too many of my close friends.

'What was that?' I said in alarm. 'I just saw something fly behind that chalet – oh shit, it looked like Duane!'

Shaun and Tim looked at me in disbelief. We were down in the valley near the landing area, looking up at the top of the tallest cliff to watch Duane jump. He had given us a one-minute call but we had not seen him go.

We ran around the building and to our horror saw Duane lying motionless, next to a crater in the grass a foot deep, his white wingsuit soaked red with blood. His canopy was out of the container but had not yet inflated when he impacted. Unaccustomed to the changed aero-dynamics and visual perception of wingsuit BASE he had over-delayed by a fraction of a second and paid the ultimate price.

Dealing with the aftermath of such trauma was terrible. Shaun had to escort Duane's wife back to London, whilst Tim and I dealt with body recovery and began the repatriation process. Packing up Duane's possessions in the hotel was eerie. Hours earlier he had kissed his wife goodbye and left to play in the mountains, planning multiple jumps that day, an intense few weeks of adventure and a lifetime of dreams and goals. Now they were a dead man's things, his wife would never see him again and two futures had been destroyed. Shaun, his close friend, would never BASE jump again. I had only done one cliff jump and already seen two people die. I decided to take a timeout from BASE.

For six months I tried to ignore the urge deep inside. My head told me this was a bad idea but in my heart I craved that intense level of excitement and had so many ideas and dreams that involved flying from cliffs. Temptation got the better of me and my next jump was the realisation of one of those dreams – El Capitan with Dean.

Though it is impossible to rationalise the risk versus reward analysis of BASE jumping, I felt then as I do now, that it is not entirely dissimilar to climbing, the extreme danger is what makes it so exciting, the proximity to death defining what it means to be alive. Crazy as it may sound, BASE jumping *can* be practised safely. I have friends who have done over 3,000 jumps and practise BASE almost every day. However, it is extremely unforgiving and requires the utmost diligence, caution and care to avoid incident. These are not traits common in those attracted to dangerous sports and therein lies the problem.

I have no doubt that witnessing Duane's death at the start of my BASE career made me profoundly more cautious and ultimately able to complete well over a hundred jumps without so much as a twisted ankle. Although there were more than a few near misses, and eventually another fatality encouraged me to hang up my wings for good.

I mainly focused on terminal velocity jumps from big walls, the Half Dome jump being the tallest at close to 5,000 feet from exit to opening, but I also did lower, slider-down jumps. The slider is a piece of mesh attached to lines that slow the pressurisation on jumps from taller objects with higher deployment speeds to reduce opening shock and avoid damaging the canopy. On lower, slower exits the slider is removed to enable faster pressurisation. My lowest jump was 200 feet from the Stealth rollercoaster at Thorpe Park near London for a TV show hosted by Ant and Dec in front of a live audience of 200 people. The test jump went perfectly and I landed right by Dec and high-fived him. The next morning conditions were suboptimal; the wind had picked up by the time everyone was in position. I should've called it but felt pressure to perform the stunt and jumped in a lull. A gust of wind came just as my parachute opened, causing an off-heading. I turned too aggressively in correction to avoid crashing into the metal structure, lost all my altitude and crash-landed into a spot the size of a garden shed surrounded by hideous steelwork and a barbed-wire-topped security fence. There was silence on set as everybody feared the worst. To my surprise I landed unharmed and quickly climbed the tall fence and punched the air in fake triumph. I got lucky. Again.

Television also gave me the chance to jump the famous Majlis al

Jinn in 2008. It was the final and by far the most serious stunt in my TV show *Take Me to the Edge* after a crazy six-month world tour that had seen me snowboard down the ash of an erupting volcano in the South Pacific, eat the heart of a cow I had freshly slaughtered, before taking Maasai warriors climbing in Kenya and getting drunk on potent rice-wine moonshine with Buddhist monks in the Himalayan kingdom of Bhutan. My television-safety friend Brian Hall was there, and Shaun Ellison too. It was a terrifying jump compounded by the pressure and complication of the cameras.

A round hole 30 feet across led through a tunnel 80 feet deep into the blackness of the cave. I had to wait at least a second and a half to clear the tunnel but would hit the ground at four, leaving a safe deployment window of just a second and a half. I'd already rappelled down into the cavern to check the landing, which was good, but it felt so wrong standing in the bright sun of the Arabian desert, poised to jump into the dark tomb.

I took a deep breath, leapt, fell through the tunnel and pitched. For an awful second I flew the canopy blind whilst my eyes adjusted to the massive change in light exposure. Flying a parachute inside a cave with walls on all sides was a strange and scary experience. I landed relieved, staring in awe at the shafts of light illuminating the massive chamber. *That was the scariest thing I've ever done. I will not do that again*, I told myself.

Except less than a month later I was standing once again on the edge of that hole, heart beating furiously. This time a massive twenty-three-person crew had joined me, with a crane and proper movie cameras to shoot a big-budget Range Rover commercial. The job had come in at the eleventh hour when the cave they had planned to jump into in Mexico had banned access. The stunt had already been pitched to the client and they were desperate to find another site. At such short notice, the only way to navigate the labyrinthine red tape of Omani bureaucracy was to use the same stunt team that had been granted permission just weeks earlier, so Brian, Shaun and the same in-country fixers were all back, together with

Tim, who would also jump, and we were able to command a king's ransom for the privilege.

Tim jumped first. Cameras were rolling and I was seconds away from following when the director yelled 'CUT!' I wanted it over with but a film reel had snapped and needed to be replaced, causing a half-hour delay. The wind was picking up by the minute as the heat of the sun intensified, creating all kinds of strange thermals and unpleasant air flows through the tunnel. Finally we were on and I was off into the blackness again. Tim gave me a massive hug when I landed and we shed a tear, remembering Duane and his dream to do what we had just done.

I also returned several times to Kjerag, the huge cliff in Norway where I had first encountered BASE jumping, and made a dozen or so jumps there. Sure enough, on one occasion I got the chance to jump through a cloud inversion just like the Viking I had seen while climbing with Cavey. Running off the cliff in the clear sun to fall into and through the layer of white mist and fly into the murky day beneath felt absurd. It was indeed the coolest thing ever.

Only of course it wasn't. That came on a beautiful June day in 2008, the biggest and best of my life on rock. That day my partner Stanley and I free climbed the route Freerider on El Capitan in eleven and a half hours, BASE jumped off the top, cycled up the Valley to the northwest face of Half Dome and free climbed that too before once again flying down to the Valley floor. This was something never done before – or since, for that matter – and it came at the end of the most intense eight weeks of my life, when I attained a level of fitness, strength and endurance that I've never equalled since. The volumes of precious knowledge, experience and wisdom I gained would benefit my adventures to come. But it was at times a traumatic process and taught me the value of the most important asset of all: your friends.

Combining BASE jumping and climbing was an obvious challenge and I had originally intended to partner with Yosemite legend Dean Potter to attempt an even more ambitious project with three elements: free climb and BASE jump from El Cap, Half

Dome and the third big wall in Yosemite, Mount Watkins. Dean had already done the double (no Watkins) with support partners and without BASE jumps in 2003 and had been working towards the futuristic triple ever since, making several aborted attempts. I think he had decided he needed a committed, strong and invested partner to share in this Herculean challenge instead of relying on subordinates for support. I was that partner. Dean had been pushing the limits of Yosemite climbing for a decade, nicknamed The Dark Wizard for his audacious free solos, leash-less highlines and progressive BASE jumps. He took me on my first El Cap jump and I respected him greatly.

But the timing was unfortunate. Dean's twelve-year marriage was unravelling and though we spent almost twenty-four hours a day together for a month, he never once spoke of it. After a couple of weeks, I noticed he had an anger, even a hatred deep inside. That dark energy seemed to be from where he drew extraordinary strength. I was the opposite, performing at my best when the vibe was positive. I wasn't bothered about setting records and dominating rocks or people. I just wanted to have a laugh with fun people in high places, pushing myself to see how far I could go.

One day he started shouting and yelling at me when we were climbing because I had done something trivial he disagreed with, placed a wire instead of a cam or clipped the rope wrong. I wasn't intimidated by him like most people and told him to go fuck himself and not to speak to me like that. He looked like he was going to punch me but then calmed down. We had a long chat that night. He apologised and explained he had stuff on his mind, suggesting he was about to get divorced. I could tell he craved the support, camaraderie and mostly the increased performance of a solid partnership, but he was known for falling out with those who shared great adventures with him.

Dean and I carried on climbing and flying together for another few weeks but it became more and more strained and less and less fun. I moved out of his place in the village of Yosemite West to get some space and I realised I was not enjoying being in his presence.

And I began to feel unsafe being tied to him simul-climbing, where you're moving together without a belay, the only way you can climb a route like Freerider fast. Needless to say, simul-climbing requires absolute trust in your partner.

Though we were getting closer to our ambition and with more time I could see it being possible, I felt the triple was out of reach with the few weeks I had remaining in the Valley. I thought we had a realistic chance of doing the climbs in a continuous push but not in a day. When I voiced this Dean became angry; for him, it was all or nothing. It felt like he was prepared to die to climb those three walls in twenty-four hours.

A week of bad weather rolled through. When it cleared and great conditions returned, I felt a sense of dread that I was going to have to go climbing with Dean again, and I realised it was time to call it quits. I had learned a great deal from him and felt bad not being able to see it through, but I couldn't handle being around his bad energy any more and wasn't willing to make the same level of safety compromises as he was.

In an awkward conversation I told him I didn't want to climb with him any more, that I was grateful for his hospitality and sharing his knowledge, but that I didn't think he was in a psychologically stable place and I didn't feel safe pushing so hard towards the limit with him. He didn't respond, just got in his car and drove away. We would never share another civil word. When I emailed him a couple of months later he replied with what was effectively a death threat that I felt justified my concerns and vindicated my actions.

Still, the break-up left me depressed and after six weeks away from Jess I was ready to go home. I was about to change my flight and bail two weeks early when my friend Bullwinkle suggested I team up with Stanley and try the double instead. I'd seen Stanley a few times when we were working on El Cap and had been surprised that Dean had lied to him about us having ropes in place, obviously suspicious of what Stanley was planning. When we met, it turned out he was psyched for the double and had been training for it. It seemed a shame to have invested so much time and energy and leave without trying something major. So Stanley and I teamed up and climbed Half Dome. Immediately we clicked. It was the opposite experience of climbing with Dean: laid-back, relaxed and heaps of fun. The contrast to the tense, stressful six weeks I had just spent climbing and living with Dean and his aggressive, dark drive could not have been starker.

Yet Stanley was also a complex character. Although I had known him for ten years and we had bouldered, slack-lined and BASE jumped plenty, we had never roped up and I didn't really know him that well. Because he lived in El Portal, just outside the park, and didn't like large groups he would go home every night and didn't hang out in Camp 4 that much. He was tall, lean and softly spoken with a slightly maniacal glint in his eye, but also incredibly kind and genuinely humble. He had adopted a stray dog he found half dead by the road in Mexico and loved Nexpa as much as any human. There was a nurse called Patty who worked at the Yosemite medical clinic and was part of the scene. She was deaf and Stanley had learned to sign so he could communicate with her. His gentle demeanour and permanent home in the Valley made him popular with women and he always seemed to have different good-looking girlfriends until he fell in love with a Brazilian climber called Roberta. I was a close friend of hers and they were a great couple but she was tragically killed in an accident whilst driving his truck in 2006. She died in his arms while he walked away with cuts and bruises. I don't think he ever fully recovered from the deep psychological wounds.

Stanley was as fast and fit as anybody, the unsung hero of the era. He regularly partnered with famous climbers to break records though rarely received much of the limelight. He and Dean held the Nose record for a while at 2 hours 34 minutes. Later, with Alex Honnold of *Free Solo* fame, he became one of very few to climb three El Cap routes in a day.

He was quite an introvert and never played the game of professional climbing, posing for photos and working the media. 'Spray' they call it in the States. He hated it. He wasn't sponsored and didn't get any gear for free. He worked rigging complex, high-speed cable camera systems at American football games and big events like the Olympics. The company was originally owned by an old-school Yosemite climber and because Stanley was a grafter and helped develop the system for ten years his boss looked after him. Stanley would earn $1,000 a day during football season, only needing to work a few months of the year. He lived for free in a property he had inherited in the best climbing area in the world and could self-fund expeditions to almost anywhere he chose. When the cable-cam company was sold the new owners halved his rate. By that time some Stone Monkeys, myself and Dean included, had become famous and earned healthy salaries from climbing. But Stanley had missed the boat and didn't seem to understand that sponsorship is a business relationship, that you have to create something of value. He just wanted to get paid to climb every day.

Freerider is the easiest free route on El Capitan yet it's still hard at 5.13. We employed techniques, radical for the time, to speed us up, including simul-climbing over half the route, even the notorious Monster Crack. This awkward, 6-inch-wide offwidth has ended the ambitions of many strong climbers to free El Cap. Now climbers use rope-capture devices between them whilst climbing simultaneously, hugely increasing the safety of that style. Back then climbing together was closer to soloing: a fall at the wrong moment would be unthinkable. Each climber's safety was totally dependent upon the other.

Things had gone so well that we were actually ahead of schedule when we reached the top. We couldn't BASE jump until dusk so we paused to enjoy the sunset on a comfortable ledge just below the top. It was a watershed moment. Although what we were doing was so intense and difficult, the vibe was so relaxed and enjoyable. We were having such a laugh. Our goal was immense but unimportant. It was just a destination to aim for along our extreme journey. We were powered by pure, positive energy, had found that elusive state of flow and were enjoying the ride.

El Cap is a very safe jump, tall, steep with a diving board exit and acres of meadow in which to land. However, it is high profile and carries a high security risk. It is highly prized even amongst skydivers with no desire to BASE jump anything else. The landing zone is right by the road and there are more busts by law enforcement here than anywhere else. BASE jumping is a serious offence in US national parks. The comedy of the Peter Pan and Captain Hook stand-off is completely lost on the rangers, who treat BASE jumping like terrorism and have been known to pull firearms on fleeing jumpers. The consequences are especially high for foreign nationals like myself. Not only will our $5,000-worth of gear be confiscated and a fine of $5,000 issued, but the Department of Homeland Security reserves the right to deport and refuse future entry to anyone convicted of a federal offence, and national parks are federal property. Every time I jumped in Yosemite I carried the fear that if I was busted I may never be allowed back to my beloved Never Land, or to any of the other world-class climbing areas in America.

That spring of 2008 was a transitional period in the once subdued, underground world of Yosemite's BASE scene. There were at least twenty of us who were highly active. I personally made twenty-three jumps on that trip. Sometimes there were six of us jumping together. Wingsuits were becoming popular and totally changing the game, opening access to new exits, flight lines and landing areas. Traditionally there were less than ten exits; within a decade there would over sixty. Multiple sites were being jumped every single day and that was just amongst the crew we knew, not accounting for all the outsiders. Total jumps number must've been well into the hundreds per month.

There were unwritten rules to maintain our low profile – don't day blaze, don't open too high and display long canopy rides, no loose talk or bragging about plans and exploits – but not everybody stuck to them and we were becoming too high profile. The park authorities had had enough and the rangers were out to put an end to the party, ramping up their efforts to catch the criminals in the act. As dusk fell and we prepared to jump we knew there could be trouble.

Our friend James Q. Martin dropped in to take some photos and Ivo met us on top to share the jump. We geared up unhurriedly and completed our final checks.

'Three, two, one, GO!' Ivo always liked to do the count.

The three of us took a running jump together, tracked hard for about twenty seconds and pulled low far from the wall, already across the road. As we lined up to land at the back of the meadow, my heart sank as the wailing sirens and blue flashing lights of half a dozen ranger cars sped towards the parking lot. Before we had even touched down the rangers were out of their cars and running. They must've been on a stake-out, watching the exit with a telescope from a covert vantage point.

'BASE jumpers, halt! We have you surrounded!' came a triumphant voice over a loudspeaker.

Shit! Of all the days for them to come after us! Luckily we had considered this eventuality and had a plan. Instead of running we lay down in the long grass and stayed very still. It was dark down in the Valley and we knew if we held our nerve we couldn't be seen. As the rangers charged forward, confident they were going to make a bust, a dozen of our Monkey friends who had been hanging in the meadow began running in different directions all carrying backpacks. The chase was on. Meanwhile we slowly and silently gathered our parachutes and commando-crawled along a slight depression to the river, where we carefully hid our gear.

Chaotic scenes unfolded as our friends were apprehended and searched but none carried any BASE gear and could not be arrested. We made our way along the meandering riverbank, keeping a close watch for danger. We crawled through a narrow drainage tunnel that led under the road and into the woods below El Capitan where we waited for what seemed an age until we plucked up enough courage to make our bold escape. With taped hands, covered in chalk and approaching the parking lot from the El Cap side of the road, we easily passed as climbers.

The flashing lights of the ranger vehicles illuminated a comical scene. There were dozens of armed officers emptying haul bags and searching cars. They had just seen three BASE jumpers land in the meadow and failed to bring them to justice. They were pissed. We strolled calmly out of the parking lot, avoiding eye contact with the uniformed law enforcement and our Stone Monkey accomplices, then hopped on our bikes and began the four-mile ride to the Half Dome trailhead. It had worked and we had got away, although we had lost three precious hours evading capture.

Stanley and I stormed up the death slabs to the base of Half Dome's northwest face and began climbing in the middle of the night. Just over four hours later we were on the top where Aaron, who had been pivotal in our escape from the meadow, met us with two more BASE rigs. Tired and stiff we completed the mission by diving together off Half Dome in the dawn light. We landed at the higher, more discreet landing zone and, not wanting to tempt fate, hid our gear. Over twenty-two hours we had completed two of the most iconic BASE jumps and both free climbed all fifty-eight pitches of two of the world's finest climbs, more than a mile of hard climbing. Sitting in the meadow after the double, high on our success and sleep deprivation, we discussed our dreams – where to take things, what to do next.

Over the following five years we shared many wild experiences and became close friends. In Stanley I had found the partner I had hoped Dean would be. As fit, fast, capable and experienced as anybody, but laid-back, humble and, best of all, fun to be around. The relationship cemented that day would form the foundation for the next phase of our lives, when we would take the techniques and tricks we had mastered in this sun-kissed playground to some of the most remote and savage arenas Earth has to offer.

PART THREE
Big Times

Chomolungma, Mt. Everest
Tibet, Himalayas
27.9881°N, 86.9250°E
8,848 m

Mount Everest
8,848 m

Second
Step

first
step

Mallory's
Body

Camp
IV

Camp
III

Camp II
7,600m

North
Col

Camp I
7,000m

Advanced
Base Camp
6,400m

12 miles

Base Camp
5,150 m

Shanté Lamprey

14.

The Wildest Dream

We walked in line, each in the footsteps of the one in front. All attached to the same bright-blue rope, moving slowly up the steep snow slope we edged towards the top of the world. Below, the view stretched for eternity, a cloud inversion flooded the valleys, the summits of five of the world's highest peaks floating like islands. It seemed like you could see the curvature of the Earth from our great elevation. Encased behind goggles and oxygen mask, buried beneath the hood of an all-in-one down suit, each in their own bubble high in the death zone, we looked and felt like spacemen exploring another planet.

Paranoid about my skinny frame succumbing to the cold, I had attached chemical heat patches to my base layer before we left Camp IV at 3 a.m. Being activated by oxygen, they had thus far failed to produce any heat in that rarefied air but now, approaching noon, it suddenly felt I had a hot water bottle down my top. It was 14 June, extremely late in the season for a summit push. In fact, we knew from satellite imagery that the monsoon was due to arrive that very afternoon and conditions on the top of Everest were unusually mild.

I knew that to stop would hold up the whole procession – we still had several crucial scenes to film and were on a tight schedule – so I kept going until finally I simply couldn't take it any more. I was massively overheating. I stopped, pulled off my huge mittens, tore down my hood and oxygen mask. Unzipping my down suit I stripped to my T-shirt, steam bellowing from me like a kettle as I ripped off the heat pads in mild panic.

'Well, that's not something you see every day,' chuckled Kevin Thaw.

Very quickly I cooled off and minus the heat patches and a mid-layer we continued our procession to the top of the world.

Months earlier I had received the kind of phone call that usually only happens in the movies.

'Hey, Leo, it's Conrad Anker. Do you want to climb Everest with me? It's for an IMAX movie about Mallory and Irvine. I'm Mallory, do you wanna be Irvine?'

Like many committed climbers I had come to view Mount Everest and the associated circus of high-altitude tourism with some contempt. It frustrated me when I told people I was a climber and they asked, 'Have you climbed Everest?' I knew full well that the climbing on Everest is more akin to a flight of stairs than the vertical walls of my domain. Even back then in 2007 the great majority of Everest summiteers were not really climbers but clients of guiding companies, many of whom had virtually no other mountaineering experience save perhaps for the other seven summits – a trend that has massively increased in the years since. But that contempt soon evaporated into childhood dreams when I got Conrad's call.

'Absolutely! When do we go?'

The story of Mallory and Irvine is the greatest mystery of mountaineering and one that had captivated me since childhood, years before I became a climber. On 8 June 1924, George Mallory, one of the most accomplished climbers of the time, accompanied by Sandy Irvine, a strong young athlete and gifted engineer, were last seen disappearing into the cloud, less than a thousand feet below the summit, high on the final ridge of Mount Everest. Did they reach the top almost thirty years before Edmund Hillary and Tenzing Norgay? Volumes have been written and careers dedicated to investigating this enthralling mystery.

In May 1999 Conrad was part of a major expedition that set out to try to find any evidence as to what might have happened. The upper reaches of Mount Everest were covered with far less snow than usual that spring following the particularly intense El Niño climatic phenomenon of 1998. At around 8,400 metres Conrad was part of team conducting a search when he wandered out of his allotted zone, intrigued by an unusual patch of white. Some distance from the standard North Ridge route, on an area of the mountain where almost nobody would ever tread and aided by the lack of snow, Conrad discovered the body of George Mallory, almost perfectly preserved for seventy-five years by the permanent sub-zero temperatures of high altitude. Mallory had sustained a compound fracture in his right leg, with a length of broken hemp rope still tied around his waist, clear evidence of a fall. His pockets contained a number of intriguing artefacts but, to the disappointment of many, not his camera, perhaps the only key that might finally reveal the truth. The discovery made headlines around the world, rekindling popular interest in the great mountaineering mystery.

One of those whose interest was stirred was Anthony Geffen, executive of a high-end production company called Atlantic Productions. He and Conrad had been discussing a film for years and Anthony had finally just about managed to secure the multimillion dollars of finance required for a major IMAX production.

Conrad had also secured the services of our old friend Kevin Thaw, who was slated for a summit bid on the behind-the-scenes production team. I had never been above 5,500 metres and had relatively little mountaineering experience. This was in part why I had been cast for the role of Sandy Irvine. He was equally new to high-altitude mountaineering, whereas Mallory, like Conrad, had a wealth of experience. This was something that we wanted to explore in the film.

It is widely considered that some people's genetics simply do not allow them to acclimatise well, no matter how fit, patient or experienced they may be. I was a little concerned I might be one of these people. With so many high-altitude tourists reaching the top, it would've been a blow as a professional climber not to make it.

There was also the factor of the overhyped but undeniable mortal risk of climbing Everest. I'd heard the unnerving but unverified statistics, such as one in ten Everest climbers die, or more certainly that every year there are around half a dozen fatalities and the year before our expedition eleven climbers perished. Kevin set my mind at ease.

'It's a package holiday. The Everest gong show is unlike any other climbing trip. It really is high-altitude tourism. You won't have to carry a load or pitch a tent. The outfitters' Sherpas do everything and we're going with Himex, the best show in town.'

To my astonishment, most of what he said was true.

'Because it's there.' Mallory's timeless, philosophical response to the question, 'Why climb Everest?' Nobody has yet crafted a more succinct reply. As well as being one of the top climbers of his day, Mallory was an intellectual and prolific writer. A deep thinker, he studied at Cambridge during the era of the Bloomsbury set, a loose group of writers, philosophers and artists such as Virginia Woolf and John Maynard Keynes. He socialised, corresponded and was even rumoured to have been a muse for several of them.

Mallory undertook three expeditions to Everest – a reconnaissance in 1921, an initial attempt in 1922 and the second ill-fated attempt in 1924. Throughout these expeditions, he and his wife, Ruth, corresponded frequently, creating a very personal, romantic and eloquent first-person account of their experiences and emotions. These letters were to provide the storyline and much of the dialogue for *The Wildest Dream*. There is a clear conflict in Mallory's writing: his desire to conquer Everest, to push the limits of human accomplishment, to gain the recognition and success he craved and had seen his Cambridge contemporaries enjoy, against the love for his wife, Ruth, the long absences from her and his three children and the simple domestic pleasures of rural England. It is a conflict I recognised and could empathise with.

Our expedition in 2007 did not set out to provide a final answer to the mystery but to explore the story both on the mountain and in the extensive historical archives. Conrad and I would be kitted out with precise replicas of the 1924 clothing and boots. The movie would be shot in large-format IMAX for the super-big screen and would be part documentary following our actual ascent and testing of the period gear on the mountain, part investigation and part dramatic recreation, some of which we would film high on the mountain with Conrad and I in character as Mallory and Irvine but with no dialogue. That would be added in voiceover by a prestigious Hollywood cast reading the letters written during the 1924 expedition. Liam Neeson was to be the narrator, his late wife, Natasha Richardson, the voice of Ruth, Ralph Fiennes as Mallory and Hugh Dancy as Irvine.

Prior to our expedition I immersed myself in the story of Mallory and Irvine. My mum reminded me that I had been captivated by the story at primary school and of the award-winning project I'd undertaken on the mystery. I read most of the dozen or more books written on the subject, my favourite and by far the most exhaustive being *Into the Silence* by Wade Davies. I also set out to climb some of the hardest routes Mallory established in the UK to try to gauge the standard at which he was operating.

Perhaps the single most critical question in the mystery is that of the Second Step, a formidable obstacle on the northeast ridge near the summit. Mallory and Irvine were last seen disappearing into the cloud by support climber and geologist Noel Odell from a position on the north-northeast ridge 3,000 feet below, not far from the site of modern-day Camp IV.

The route Mallory and Irvine attempted was not confirmed climbed until 1960, when a Chinese expedition comprising Wang Fuzhou, Qu Yinhua, and a Tibetan, Gongbu, became only the third expedition to reach the summit. Qu Yinhua, the leader, spent three hours overcoming the Second Step using aid-climbing techniques and suffered severe frostbite, losing several fingers and toes. The North Ridge wasn't climbed again until 1975 when another large Chinese expedition fixed a ladder to overcome the Second Step, which has remained in place to this day with another much longer ladder added by a commercial expedition in 2006. Every single ascent since has utilised the aid of these ladders to overcome the Second Step.

As well as real-world testing of the period kit high on the mountain, our other main objective was to temporarily remove the ladders from the Second Step, restoring what is without doubt by far the most difficult section of the entire route to the state in which Mallory and Irvine would've found it in 1924. We would then attempt to free climb the obstacle, the only way that Mallory could've reached the summit, to assess the difficulty and if we felt it would've been possible in Mallory's time.

Acclimatising at your own pace whilst staying healthy is the secret to success on Everest. That and the massive logistical support of the unbelievably strong Nepali climbers who do all the real work on the mountain. Though I had heard about the Everest circus and high-altitude tourism, I was quite shocked by the reality. Base camp was more like a small town, like some kind of high-end refugee camp, set amidst the spectacular desolation. Hundreds of colourful tents, home to thousands of people, spread across a flat, gravelly area just beyond the toe of the massive Rongbuk Glacier that poured down like a giant serpent from Everest's majestic north face. Well above the treeline, frozen for nine months of the year, little life exists in that dry, wind swept place. That season, base camp was split into two small towns, with the well-ordered, military-style Chinese camp half a kilometre from the more ramshackle collection of several dozen other expeditions.

Beijing was due to host the 2008 Olympic Games and as part of the celebrations China was planning to carry the burning Olympic torch to summit of Everest in the run-up to the games. In 2007 they were conducting a full dress rehearsal complete with 2008 branding, no doubt to ensure the televised torch ascent would be a success no matter what. Our expedition arrived a month later than all the other teams. This was intentional. We didn't want hundreds of other people around spoiling our shots on summit day.

The Himex base camp was meticulously well ordered and by far the most luxurious camp I'd ever imagined. We each had our own three-man tent. Yellow, rectangular box tents the size of railway carriages housed two spacious canteens, an extensive kitchen, a well-equipped studio tent complete with three-phase electric generators and a toilet block with hot showers. But the piece de resistance, apparently new for that season, was a huge, insulated geodesic dome with panoramic views of Everest. It was heated, carpeted, fully furnished with a bar, sound system and 60-inch TV – I was gob-smacked and impressed. More like glamping in the VIP area of Glastonbury than any expedition base camp I'd ever experienced before or since.

Himex, the Himalayan Experience, high-end guiding company, were not only hosting our entire expedition and movie production, they were also managing a Discovery Channel reality TV show called *Everest: Beyond the Limit*. Another production team of about ten people were following six clients, three guides and at least ten Sherpas who were already well into their acclimatisation cycles on the mountain and were currently all 20 kilometres away and 1,400 metres higher in advanced base camp.

Our first encounter with the complete 1920s kit Conrad and I would be wearing was to be filmed near base camp. It was with genuine excitement and anticipation that we opened the wooden crate. Although we hadn't committed to using the replica clothing to the summit, we were keen not only to test it but to use it as high as we deemed safe. Anthony's team had gone to great lengths to research and replicate as closely as possible the precise layers, materials, cuts and finishes of the 1924 kit. The base layer was a close-fitting, comfortable blend of silk and merino wool. Interestingly, merino wool made a major comeback as a base layer in the early 2000s, but I have always detested wool against my skin. However, it was the silk in the blend of our replicas that touched the skin and I found it far more agreeable.

Next were two collared silk shirts, a heavy felt vest, a fine Shetland wool jumper, the outer layer the iconic, beautifully tailored, belted trenchcoat made of gabardine, a tightly woven, windproof waxed cotton. The originals had been manufactured by Burberry in London, who still held the patterns in their archives. On my legs, the same silk/merino-blend long johns, several woollen layers of different thickness, and characterful plus-four gabardine breeches. The finishing touches were magnificent rabbit-fur mittens and a hat as used by First World War fighter pilots, an incredibly long woollen scarf and puttees, a kind of wraparound gaiter that sealed the boot to the lower leg. Everything was completely bespoke and though I had been for a couple of fittings this was the first time I had worn the whole outfit.

It was a cold and windy day and getting changed in the small replica tent had been chilly. But immediately it was clear that with as many as seven layers on top and five on the bottom the gear was not only warm but quite adjustable, the gabardine creating a very effective wind barrier. We set out to climb a small summit above base camp called Ri Ring. It would be good for acclimatisation and was also climbed by Mallory as it provides a commanding view up the labyrinthine Rongbuk Glacier to Everest's north face. Far from acclimatised and already higher than I'd ever been, I puffed and panted and very quickly began to overheat. I removed a couple of mid-layer, woollen jumpers and we continued.

An interesting attribute to the 1920s clothing was that everything was either button- or clasp-closing that could be tricky with cold, numb fingers, as zips were yet to be invented, as was elastic, meaning there was very little stretch in any of the layering. This had the unintentional benefit for the dramatic period recreation we were filming of forcing Conrad and I to move in quite a stiff, wooden fashion very reminiscent of the black-and-white moving pictures of the actual 1924 expedition.

The only issue with our replica gear was the boots. Though they looked outstanding, it quickly became apparent that unlike our positive first impressions of the clothing, these were not fit for purpose. They were greatly oversized to allow for up to four pairs of socks but as a result felt like clown boots, incredibly imprecise and uncomfortable. The soles were thin and without insulation but worse, within the hour, I began to slip repeatedly and upon inspection two of the metal cleats in the soles of one of my boots had fallen off leaving smooth leather, like dress shoes. None of the

1924 expedition members suffered any frostbite on their toes` nor did Mallory's body show any signs. I can only conclude that some oversight had been made in the research and construction of our replica boots.

There were two high-altitude cameramen on the team, Ken Sauls and Jimmy Chin. Both had summited Everest before. Ken was a burly mountain man who lived at 10,000 feet in the ski town of Silverton, Colorado. As well as being an accomplished skier, big-wall climber and mountaineer, he was a cinematographer and camera operator in the movie industry.

Jimmy was one of Conrad's closest friends. A first-generation Chinese-American, Jimmy was a world-class big-mountain skier, climber and alpinist who a decade earlier had discovered an even greater talent behind the camera. He was already regarded as one of the best climbing photographers and was developing skills that would eventually lead to an Academy Award as a movie-maker for his film *Free Solo*.

We visited the Rongbuk Monastery, just a few miles below base camp, to receive a blessing from the lama. With the rhythmic chanting of the monks, the fluttering of the prayer flags, the solemn faces of our Sherpa friends in the dazzling high-altitude sun, all set against the epic Everest backdrop, our Puja ceremony was deeply evocative . . . Until suddenly the nasty ringtone of a cheap Nokia phone ruined the atmosphere. Instinctively we all embarrassedly reached for our pockets. The surprise that there was cell-phone signal was eclipsed by the shock and humour of witnessing the lama halt his melodic prayers, reach into his robes and take the call!

There was something endearing about the practicality of this Buddhist ceremony. Nobody minded the interruption; along with ice axes, boots and other summit equipment, a couple of crates of beer were also blessed and after about half an hour the Sherpas all got very excited and started throwing flour around and painting it on each others' faces.

On 16 May, after ten days in base camp, we began the 23-kilometre hike to ABC (Advanced Base Camp) at 6,400 metres.

Once acclimatised, this is a day hike, but first time up it is worth spreading over two days with an interim camp. The second day took us through the spectacular ice pinnacles, where we donned the period attire to recreate another scene based on photographs from the 1924 expedition. I was feeling the strain of the altitude when I arrived at ABC – a scaled-down, less luxurious version of base camp in an even more desolate and hostile location, although still far more lavish and well serviced than any other expedition camp I've encountered.

The normal process of acclimatisation is to undertake a series of rotations, ascending increasingly higher up the mountain, sometimes to sleep, before descending to rest, recover and generate increased levels of oxygen-transporting haemoglobin in the blood, as well as allowing the organs to adjust to the decreased pressure.

Most expeditions spend a couple of nights at ABC before the real mountain terrain begins, and the fixed rope that leads continuously for 6 kilometres to the top, radically altering modern Everest ascents. I remember thinking how unnecessary it was on most of the low-angle terrain, although I would be deeply grateful for it later when descending in a blizzard.

A crevassed glacier crossing leads to a steep ascent up a 300-metre ice wall to reach Camp I on the North Col at 7,000 metres. It is usual to spend a fitful night plagued by headaches, shortness of breath and sickness here before descending to ABC. Another rotation is made with a night in Camp II at 7,600 metres before retreating all the way back to base camp for up to a week of rest and recuperation in the comfort of luxurious oxygen levels at 5,400 metres. However due to our late arrival and pressing filming schedule we would not be descending below ABC at 6,300 metres for the remainder of the expedition.

Filming a high-production-value movie is a time-consuming and complex process at sea level. Shooting in IMAX is even more exacting and in the extreme environment and cold of high altitude it was a truly desperate endeavour. We suffered a severe blow when Jimmy Chin received the devastating news that his mother was dying and he had to leave immediately. The other camera operator had no mountaineering experience and failed to acclimatise, leaving the expedition early on. This left Ken Sauls with the burden of being the only person able to operate the complex IMAX cameras high on the mountain.

At Camp III, just shy of 8,000 metres, on our final acclimatisation cycle, we undertook the highest period-drama shoot in history. Unfortunately, a storm blew through that afternoon, drastically complicating an already desperately challenging shoot. We were attempting to film Mallory and Irvine's final departure from camp on their summit bid with the actual North Ridge of Everest, where they disappeared, right there in frame.

The blizzard conditions wreaked havoc with the camera and lenses. Though up until this point Conrad and I had been greatly impressed with the replica gear, and other than the boots had been seriously discussing a summit bid using it, during this shoot we discovered its limitations. When moving and generating body heat, I have no doubt the layers of silk, wool and gabardine were capable of safely cladding a summiteer. However, when standing around for long periods in −25°C and 40mph of wind it was incomparably less warm than the modern down suits worn today. Conrad has an extremely high cold tolerance. I do not. We were about a fifteen-minute walk from Camp III, attempting this final, crucial dramatic scene and conditions were deteriorating. I knew I was getting dangerously cold and should change into my down suit but also that this really was our last chance for these critical shots.

Eventually, but not before it reached full blizzard conditions, we had enough footage and abandoned the shoot, retreating to the tents. My hands and feet were completely numb and had turned white and waxy – the beginning of frostbite. My lips were blue and I was shaking uncontrollably – the early stages of hypothermia. Mingar Dorji, my Sherpa tentmate, vigorously massaged my feet. I drank hot tea and gradually, in a cocoon of down feathers, I began to warm up. The next day I felt as fine as can be expected on the edge of the death zone and we descended all the way to ABC.

It was clear that we had all been pushing too hard and that it was no longer safe to use the period gear.

Our only cameraman, Ken, who had been working harder than anybody, had developed a hacking cough. It got worse over the next days of rest until Monica, the doctor, diagnosed bronchitis and advised him to descend to base camp immediately, meaning not only would he not be summiting but that we no longer had a camera operator for the summit push. Obviously this was a total disaster. It's not as if another high-altitude camera operator could be flown in. Even if there was somebody with the unique skillset available they would need a month to acclimatise and we had no more than a week.

A crisis meeting was held in ABC. Apparently, the whole production was insured and almost all of the millions in expenses could be reclaimed *if* the expedition was cancelled before our summit bid. Having invested two months into the project, finally acclimatised and with everything 100 per cent ready, high camps stocked, oxygen caches in place, a reasonable weather window, Kevin, Conrad and I secretly discussed a moonlight departure for a pirate summit should the plug get pulled. Thankfully Anthony, who had invested more than anybody, was desperately keen to avoid resorting to an insurance claim and a salvage plan was formed.

Two of the Himex guides, Kiwis Mark 'Woody' Woodward and Dean Staples, had already summited once leading the Discovery team and were fully acclimatised. They had not yet left and were willing to return to the summit following a basic crash course on how to operate the complex, heavy IMAX camera. It was a long shot, but obviously the summit-day footage was critical to the film and this was our only option.

By this point we were the only expedition remaining on the mountain north or south. After weeks and months preparing for that all-important summit day, it was remarkable how quickly people dispersed and departed once they'd made their bid for glory. ABC was completely abandoned. Other than that slightly

N. E. Ridge of Ulvetanna, E6 6b, 6,000 feet. Queen Maud Land, Antarctica. I saw a photo of this peak as a teenager and vowed to one day climb it. 15 years later we spent 19 days making the first ascent of the mile long N. E. Ridge. Jan, '13.

(top) Cerro Autana, Amazonas, Venezuela. The local Piaroan tribe believe it to be the stump of the tree of life./(bottom) Yopo Wall, E6 6b, 1,500 feet. Like the Yopo ceremony we battled through the darkness to reach the light. All Feb, '12.

(left to right) Stanley and Jas enjoying Autana. Jungle walls are so full of life and colour unlike high mountains or polar regions./Shaman Bolivar and his wife. His Yopo ceremony was the most terrifying and powerful encounter of my life./Cuevo de Autana. A Cathedral within the sacred cliff. The Autana expedition was transcendental. All Feb, '12.

(top) Ulvetanna Peak, Fenriskjeften Mountain (the fang in the wolf's jaw), Queen Maud Land, Antarctica. A place so remote it wasn't discovered by climbers until 1994! Dec, '12./(bottom) Sean 'Stanley' Leary, 23/08/76–13/03/14. The world's nicest psycho died wingsuit BASE proximity flying in Zion, Utah. An unsung hero of the Yosemite Stone Monkeys. I miss him. Aug, '09.

(left to right) I was very excited to finally arrive at Ulvetanna./Stanley & I in the ice cave we cut to weather storms beneath the wall./Jumaring up a mile high climb in the white desert./Day 15, high on the wall we were hit by serious weather. Thankfully we were ready./Jas, Chris, me, Al and Stanley a long way from home on the summit of Ulvetanna. Our last great climb together. All Jan, '13.

(left to right) Jean Burgun with 200 kg pulk snow-kiting towards the Spectre, Trans-Antarctic Mountains. Next level epic!/About to begin our journey to the end of the world, Jean & Mark Sedon express their gratitude./Nothing lives on the high Antarctic plateau. The Spectre Exped was my most ambitious and difficult trip so far./Kiting towards a parhelion we covered 2,000 kilometres./Me exhausted in brutal conditions on approach to Spectre. All Dec, '17.

(left to right) N. Ridge of Piz Badile, HS 4a, 3,000 feet. Freya climbed it by herself (age 7). Jackson (3) was mostly on his mum's back. July, '20./Jessica, my wife since '06, and Jackson (18 months) enjoy their first technical summit, Triglav 2,864 metres, Slovenia. Aug, '18./Family expeditions have brought a new dimension to life. Wind Rivers, Wyoming. Aug, '21./Jackson (4) on his first big climb 'by my own'. East ledges, Pingora Peak Cirque of Towers, Wind Rivers, Wyoming. Aug, '21.

(top) Jackson (age 3) near the top of N. Ridge Piz Badile. This photo went viral and was featured in dozens of newspapers worldwide. July, '20./(bottom) Freya (8) facing her fear with a smile on the shockingly exposed East Ridge of the Wolf's Head, 5.9, Cirque of Towers, Wind Rivers, Wyoming. Aug, '21.

weird feeling of an out-of-season tourist town, I much preferred it. The circus had left town and it began to feel more like a real climbing expedition. We had a lot to film high on the mountain above Camp III, but everything had been covered up to there, so we were able to take our time and enjoy the first three days of the ascent.

On 10 June we departed ABC. This time, after almost a month above 6,000 metres and all our acclimatisation cycles, the steep ice wall leading up to Camp I on the North Col felt almost easy. The long slog up the shoulder to Camp II also felt casual compared to previous rotations. Following the fixed rope there was no chance of getting lost and we were able to ascend at our own pace.

I was appalled by how much trash had been left behind by all the other people. Entire camps with supplies, food, oxygen bottles and gas canisters had simply been abandoned. This was not the mountain Mallory had set out to climb, nor did it bear any resemblance to the kind of climbing and adventure that I adore. The standard routes on Everest, and now those on all of the other 8,000-metre peaks as well as the Seven Summits and a handful of other commercial peaks, have become their own form of mountaineering. The great Doug Scott called it 'high-altitude tourism'. It is all about conquest and glory, money and ego, with little respect for the mountain, the environment or the hundreds of other 'mountaineers'.

A part of me had wanted to try to climb without oxygen. I know Conrad felt the same but we were not there for our own climbing ambitions. We had a job to do, we were there to make a movie and chose to put our ethics aside.

At Camp III I strapped on the mask and turned on the gas. On a low flow rate I slept much better than the previous night, but when we began to ascend the next day on a higher flow rate the real benefit of the artificial assistance became clear. Bottled oxygen made a drastic difference, effectively taking at least 1,000 metres off the altitude and making ascent far easier.

Just below Camp IV I was just thinking, *Well, this so-called death zone isn't that bad* – then I saw the first one. Initially I thought it was one of our team sitting alone in the snow right beside the rope. He was wearing the same bright-yellow boots as me but I didn't recognise his down suit. He was eerily still with his head slumped, and it dawned on me that this was not one of our team. I knew there were no other people on the mountain. At least none living. The path took me to within a metre of the corpse, and I couldn't resist my morbid fascination to look more closely. It was only the bare skin of his face, blackened and dry like old leather, and his ghoulish, contorted expression that revealed his lifelessness. The Brazilian flag sewn onto his suit revealed his identity. He had perished the year before and sat there still, frozen into the snow.

I felt so healthy and casual, the terrain so benign, I struggled to visualise this poor man's final moments. What had he thought? *I'll just rest here for a few minutes*? Was he totally delirious with exhaustion? Had people seen him and just walked past? Would they even have known he was dying?

Above I saw more, these ones more obviously bodies, lying face down or crumpled in the snow. I counted fifteen with my own eyes high on the mountain, a pair of them frozen like gargoyles either side the path. Sometimes, at the request of the deceased's families, Sherpa teams from other expeditions would try to move the more recent bodies away from the trail to a slightly less unceremonious grave. But after a couple of seasons many became too encased in the ice to be moved. It disturbed me. Was it really worth it? How had they got it so badly wrong? Any notions of a glorious death in the mountains were shattered by these grim waymakers. I had to simply ignore them and not dwell on melancholy thoughts.

We arrived at Camp IV before noon. Conrad and one crew set off to the spot where he had discovered Mallory's body in 1999. I went with another crew to the approximate vantage point of Odell's last sighting. The upper reaches definitely looked steeper and more technically challenging than what we had encountered so far.

Right above camp was the yellow band, an intrusion layer of

sandstone amidst the dark and light limestone that forms the majority of the exposed rock. A feature called the Exit Cracks leads steeply up this to the Northeast Ridge proper. The precipitous Kanchung Face falls for eternity to the east. An exposed ridge traverse leads to the First Step, a prominent but small vertical step in the ridge. Above, hazardous terrain that resembles a slated roof covered with snow is not technically demanding but a stumble or fall would have drastic consequences without fixed ropes. A feature called Mushroom Rock is guarded by an old body known as Green Boots. Then the formidable Second Step must be overcome, followed by the less challenging but still technical Third Step. Above lies the triangular snowfield, steep but not difficult, before a final cliff barrier forces the route off the ridge and onto the North Face that drops for 7,000 feet to the Rongbuk Glacier but leads with relative ease to the summit. All this must then be reversed to at least Camp IV to complete the summit day.

I shared a tent with Conrad that night. The years of planning, months of preparation and the six weeks we had spent on the expedition all came down to this – summit day. We were sharing the tents, sleeping bags and equipment that had already been used by the Discovery team. I was dismayed that half my sleeping bag was frozen solid with ice.

'No problem, just dry it out over the stove. Take your time and be careful not to melt it,' Conrad advised as if it were as normal as changing the bed sheets.

We brewed hot drinks, ate noodles and discussed our complex summit-day tactics. I was nervous, excited and raring to go.

We left camp at 3 a.m. It was cold but with only a light breeze. In the pitch darkness my world was reduced to the few square metres illuminated by my head torch, the great distance ahead and vast exposure out of sight and out of mind. I was struck by how easy it felt. Finally acclimatised, carrying a light load and with the massive advantage of bottled oxygen, I felt stronger than at any point during the trip.

We quickly ascended the Exit Cracks onto the exposed North

Ridge. For the first time since the North Col I had to use my hands for a few moves. Attached by jumar to the bright-blue fixed rope that had been put in place at the start of the season by Ang Phurba and his Sherpa crew, I scrambled up without pulling on it.

We traversed the ridge, along the 'slate roof' – the likely scene of Mallory's fall, judging from the position of his body. It seemed highly plausible that an easily made slip from there could result in a long, ragdoll fall to his ultimate resting place.

We continued past Green Boots and a couple of other macabre waymarkers to reach Mushroom Rock, where we were all to rendezvous and change oxygen cylinders. The camera team and fixing team went ahead to climb then remove the ladders from the Second Step.

The rose light of dawn drenched the ominous Kanchung Face below and the still-distant summit pyramid above; it seemed from our lofty perch we could see a hundred miles in every direction across the might of the Himalayas, north to the Tibetan plateau and south to the Nepali lowlands.

The First Step was a noticeable but easily surmountable obstacle and I suspect this was where Odell had last seen Mallory and Irvine.

The Second Step, the real crux of the mystery, is often described as a 90-foot cliff band. For 75 feet it is possible to scramble to where a snow patch ends in a final overhanging corner, caped by a boulder not more than 15 feet tall depending on the depth and solidity of the snow. It is nonetheless a formidable obstacle, by far the hardest on the whole route. Following the discovery of Mallory's body in 1999 Conrad had continued to the summit and attempted to free climb the Second Step. However the Chinese ladder is situated right in the way. Conrad stepped on one of the rungs of the ladder, negating his free ascent. He concluded that the only way to claim a truly free ascent would be to get rid of the ladder completely.

With the ladders removed and the mountain all to ourselves, the Second Step was restored to its 1920s state, though we had the massive advantage of modern clothing and climbing gear.

We scrambled up the easier terrain to the snow patch where I attached myself to the mountain with our rope to belay Conrad, who would lead the short, overhanging corner. If Mallory had indeed decided to attempt this difficult step he would almost certainly have removed his heavy and cumbersome oxygen apparatus, so Conrad did the same.

He made his way to the apex of the snow and placed a number 4 cam, wedged against a block of wood, in the wide corner crack to protect him in the unlikely event of a fall. He had been dreaming of this moment for eight years and now was his chance to make the first verified free ascent of the infamous Second Step. Whilst I faffed with the rope and tried to snap photos Conrad set off; it looked like just a few moves up the corner, perhaps two body lengths, would enable him to reach over a block to flat terrain.

Then, to my horror, the front point of his crampon skated and he pitched off backwards. I was caught completely off guard; there was loads of slack in the system and for a shocking moment I envisaged the cam wedged precariously against the wooden block ripping out, Conrad taking a 30-foot, factor-two fall directly onto me, my belay failing and both of us tumbling down the giant face below to our final resting place not far from Mallory's.

But Conrad landed feet first in the snow and managed to catch the rope himself before plummeting further and without exerting too much force onto the marginal cam. It was over in a heartbeat, Conrad was again standing at the foot of the corner but was clearly shaken. It took him a long while to recompose himself for another try. Meanwhile, I was still hanging on my uncomfortable, exposed perch. I had stopped taking photos and faffing with the rope and offered Conrad my undivided attention. So much so that I was no longer proactively wiggling my toes to keep them warm, the bloodflow to my feet being severely constricted by the leg loops of my harness in which I hung. Distracted by our near-death experience, I neglected to notice my toes slowly losing sensation.

Conrad moved a little to the right, away from the corner, finding some more secure footholds for the points of his crampons.

Then with a deep breath he committed and made a couple of moves up the face to reach good hand jams behind the block, and moments later he stood, relieved and victorious on the flat terrain.

I tried to put myself into the mindset of Mallory. Would he really have attempted this difficult boulder problem, above such epic exposure, so late in the day and accompanied by a mountaineering novice? It posed a far greater challenge than anything else on the route and they had battled desperately to make it this far. He had his beloved wife, Ruth, and three young children waiting for him at home. But he knew this would be his final Everest expedition, this was his last chance, not only to conquer the mountain but he was no doubt also conscious of the global acclaim, fame and financial security his conquest would secure. And it is such a very short barrier, the summit appearing deceptively close beyond.

Perhaps if there had been more snow in 1924 he could have simply reached directly to the good hand jams? Or my preferred theory, if the sturdy and strong Irvine had braced himself across the corner at the apex of the snow, Mallory could've climbed onto his shoulders – a common technique back then known as 'combined tactics' – and he could have easily surmounted the major difficulties. He would then almost certainly have reached the summit. Irvine would still have had to get up, but Mallory could have secured the rope and Irvine hauled himself up hand over hand, though that was no small challenge on a thin rope up an overhanging wall in extreme cold, with two sets of oxygen kit. Or perhaps Mallory continued to the top alone, though he would still have had to descend the step, quite probably in the dark.

I like to think they made it to the top. But having been faced with similar conundrums myself, the lure of the summit versus the mountaineer's instinct for survival, if I was a betting man I would put my money on Irvine's high point being the base of the scramble and Mallory continuing a little higher to the overhanging corner where he reluctantly accepted that such a major obstacle presented too great a challenge for their circumstances.

I believe they turned around and whilst retracing their steps along the ridge and across the 'slate roof', tired and in a snow squall, one of them, the inexperienced Irvine would be my guess, slipped and fell. Most likely Mallory would have been in front, Irvine may have arrested his fall but Mallory would have pulled off backwards. The rope snapped and he cartwheeled to his undisputed final resting place. Meanwhile Irvine continued alone down the ridge, but in darkness was unable to identify the point at which he must leave the ridge to descend the steep face so decided to sit out the night, eventually succumbing to exposure. Multiple expeditions have failed to find his body. It may have been removed surreptitiously by one of the early Chinese expeditions, or my hope is that his remains and possibly the camera fell down the precipice of the serac-strewn, rarely visited Kanchung Face, where they will likely never be found, so retaining the mystery for eternity.

Now it was my turn, though I would have a rope from above all but removing any risk of falling. I too removed my oxygen and pack and trudged up to the apex of the snow. The cam and wooden block came out with such ease it made me shudder; they could easily have failed to hold Conrad's fall. Opting for a different approach to Conrad, I wedged myself into the corner. Wearing thin gloves, big boots and crampons, I struggled to gain purchase on the rock but managed to grovel for a couple of moves to reach the good hand jams. Pulling up, I experienced a strange flash pump, my arms suddenly weakening due to lactic acid build-up, something that usually takes much longer to occur and never happens to me on climbs of that standard – no doubt caused by the great altitude and lack of supplemental oxygen. Breathing hard and feeling light-headed, I surmounted the block and within just a couple of minutes I too had free climbed the Second Step. Conrad was jubilant. We hugged and congratulated one another.

'What grade do you think it was?' he asked.

'No more than 5.9,' I answered.

This was the precise grade of Mallory's hardest route in the UK, virtually at sea level. Theoretically it was within his ability but climbing towards one's limit on a weekend meet in the Lakes is not the same as being so incredibly strung out at 8,720 metres. But I was no longer concerned with hypothesising. Whilst much activity began around me, the cameras being packed away and the ladders reinstated, I realised I had completely lost sensation in both my feet. All my toes felt like blocks of ice – the first stage of frostbite and the reason many have lost digits in that precise spot.

I got out of the way and quietly began the simple yet surprisingly strenuous task of wiggling my frozen toes. I removed my boots and began massaging them back to life. By now the ladders were back in place and Kevin was up with us. He unzipped his down suit and put my feet in his armpits. Gradually over the course of about ten minutes the blood and sensation began to return before I was overcome with sickening agony, by the most acute hot aches I'd ever experienced. I retched and almost cried for a few minutes until the pain subsided and the sensation in my toes was back. Ironically, less than an hour later I was overheating and stripping down to my base layer to remove the heat pads!

Our large procession proceeded swiftly up the Third Step and final snow pyramid. About 200 metres below the top Conrad and I stopped beneath a small step. Both camera teams went ahead to film us approaching the summit.

'We should do this last part without oxygen, out of respect for Mallory and Irvine,' said Conrad.

I agreed and we packed our masks inside our rucksacks whilst we waited for the cameras to get ready.

'*Action!*' Woody called over the radio.

We began the final, dramatic ridge to the summit. I realised I was walking too fast and after just a few steps felt like I'd just sprinted 100 metres and had to stop, my hands on my knees. On reaching the summit I felt extremely light-headed, almost inebriated, and I questioned the wisdom behind Conrad's suggestion. But after a few stationary minutes I felt better. It was a little chaotic as we were such a large team and everybody, including all the Sherpas, was keen to pose for their own photos and videos.

Eventually it calmed down and some of the crew descended, enabling us to film the all-important summit shots with 75 kgs of the IMAX camera gear the crew had carried up. Conrad and I spent almost two hours on the top.

For the first time in the entire expedition I called Jess on the sat phone. She was studying to be a doctor and was at that time undertaking her medical elective in a remote community on the island of Sumbawa, Indonesia – a world-class surf destination. To my great pleasure she answered. We chatted about her trip, the clinic she was helping to establish and the surf. Five minutes into the conversation she asked:

'What you up to?'

'I'm stood on top of the world!' I answered.

It is rare for people to summit Everest so late in the pre-monsoon season. It was incredibly warm on top, so much so that you could completely remove gloves for short periods. I left a photo of Jackson Corrie, my late father-in-law, on the summit and another of my wife, Jess, as Mallory had promised to do of Ruth. As predicted, the cloud thickened and it began to snow. I waited on the top until everybody else had left and was out of sight. For a couple of minutes I savoured the solitude, content in the knowledge I was the highest person on Earth. Then a sudden pang of panic coursed through my veins. *What on earth are you doing, get the hell out of here!* I thought. I quickly caught up the last of the others. I was surprised how fast we descended, the strain of altitude far less acute with gravity on our side, and we made it back to Camp IV in just two hours.

Conrad suggested I lead the way down whilst he oversaw the dismantling of the camp. The weather was seriously deteriorating, the monsoon had arrived, it was dumping snow and the wind was howling. Engulfed in thick white cloud, the visibility reduced to almost zero, I could not see anything at all save for the bright-blue rope to which I was attached that I periodically yanked out of the deep white carpet covering the ground.

Thank god for this fixed line, I thought. Navigating the descent would have been impossible in such conditions without it. Before nightfall the whole team and all our kit was back in ABC drinking celebratory cold beers!

I developed a great respect for George Mallory, both for his pioneering achievements as a climber, regardless of whether he reached the summit, but also as an eloquent and thoughtful philosopher. Amongst his voluminous writings one quote resonated with me profoundly:

'There's no dream that mustn't be dared.'

Everest was not my wildest dream. But I did have my own – many of them in fact – and I felt more driven than ever to make them a reality, no matter how far-fetched or unachievable they seemed.

Mount Asgard
Baffin Island, Arctic Canada.
66.6722°N, 65.2744°W
Inukshuk, E6/A3+, 3200ft.

Asgard North

Asgard South

6a
6a
6a

A3+

A3+

A3+

A3

A2

A3

A3

6c

Camp 2   6b

6a

5c

Camp 1   5c

Shanté Lamprey

15.

Asgard Project

The drone of the plane's engines pierced the silence of the fjord as we watched it come in to land on the gravel runway. The nervous excitement in the team was electric. All the months of planning and preparation, all the scheming and dreaming were over.

It was 2009, and the first major expedition I'd organised was about to begin in dramatic style.

'Howdy! You guys the crazy fools who chartered the air drop? I'm Rob, glad to be of service,' said our larger-than-life pilot as he climbed out of the red-and-white striped DC3 twin turboprop in his cowboy boots.

Since our arrival two days earlier in the Inuit community of Pangnirtung, an outpost of humanity in the far northeast of Canada, we had been frantically preparing and had hardly slept. Tracking down our gear shipment, meeting our outfitter, checking in with the park service, organising and packing unholy quantities of gear and supplies. Every single item and morsel of food that the seven of us would need for the next five weeks of extreme Arctic adventure was now packed into sixteen neat loads rigged with the US$50 parachutes I'd bought off eBay that were labelled 'do not use for aerial delivery'.

'I hope they work,' said Stanley.

I had managed to get permission from Parks Canada and Kenn Borek Air to parachute our gear onto the Turner Glacier right at the foot of Mount Asgard to save weeks of hiking loads. They had also agreed to let us skydive in, but the final decision lay with the pilot.

'You guys wanna jump? Hell yeah, that'll be sick! You know

what you're doing, right?' Our man had arrived and the fact that we were serious appeared to be sufficient qualification.

We removed the door from the plane, loaded the kit, donned our BASE rigs and in the mystical evening light took off on the adventure of a lifetime. We flew to the head of the fjord, up the Auyuittuq Pass and into a landscape straight from Norse mythology.

'What have you got us into this time, Springer!' Jason Pickles remarked with a smirk.

The rugged Arctic wilderness stretched uninhabited in all directions as far as the eye could see. Massive glaciers flowed between endless jagged peaks and giant walls that towered above our flight path. The speed of the plane denied the scale of the scenery. Wind ripped through the open door, the roar of the massive engines and smell of jet fuel filled the fuselage. The atmosphere was intense.

'Are you nervous?' Al asked me from behind his camera.

'I *am* nervous, man!' I replied, wide-eyed. 'We're about to fly into Mount Asgard, we're gonna throw out 700 kilos of stuff then me, Stanley and Carlos are gonna jump out and land on the glacier right at the base of the wall. Is this really happening? How cool is that! Let's hope it all goes safely.'

After just fifteen minutes, we were staring awestruck at the magnificent twin towers of Asgard. We made a couple of dry runs to assess the wind then lined the plane up along the length of the glacier at around 1,000 feet.

'Clear to drop!' came Rob's command over the tannoy. Stanley booted the first load out the door. I stuck my head out after it, relieved to see the parachute deploy correctly and the bag floating gently towards Earth. Flying super low over passes and banking hard turns close around the vertical mountain we made ten drop runs. Our cowboy pilot was loving it. Rob later commented it was the best flight of his career.

The last load we dropped had a different parachute. Much bigger than the others it required at least an 80 kg load otherwise it would float down too slowly and be at the mercy of the wind for too long, potentially landing miles away. The massive haul bag containing both of the port-a-ledges and half the climbing gear was hard to manoeuvre in the plane. Out it went and we climbed to 5,000 feet.

'Clear to jump,' announced Rob. I had a glimpse of what it must feel like to be a paratrooper about to drop into battle.

'Three, two, one, GO!' counted Carlos and we piled out the door in quick succession. The plane was flying way faster than on a normal jump run, sending us spinning and tumbling violently on exit. I gained stability as we fell past the distinct summit of Asgard at terminal velocity. Jumping BASE rigs with no reserve we pulled lower than 500 feet to minimise our exposure to any unexpected airflows, before we all landed safely on the glacier in close proximity right at the base of the wall. The plane made one final pass to check we'd all gathered up our parachutes, the signal that all was well, and then it was gone. We were totally alone.

'That was insane, that was fucking insane!' I screamed, experiencing the most intense release of adrenaline in my life. It was an utterly surreal start to what would prove to be a truly epic trip.

Mount Asgard is situated on Baffin Island, Arctic Canada, deep in the Auyuittuq National Park – the 'Land that Never Melts' in the Inuit language. The majestic twin towers lie sixty miles to the north of Pangnirtung (population 1,400), 200 miles north of the frontier capital of Nunavut, Iqaluit, and are only accessible by air or sea. Asgard is remote to say the least, a place where there are indeed more polar bears than people as Guy Lee had told my younger self on the Old Man of Hoy trip in 1991.

The 1977 Bond movie, *The Spy Who Loved Me* opens with one of the most famous stunts in Hollywood history when, pursed by the enemy, 007 skis off a cliff in a yellow jumpsuit, falls in silence towards his peril then deploys a Union Jack parachute accompanied by his signature theme tune. It was filmed on location on Mount Asgard and was at the time the most expensive stunt in movie history, with the stuntman Rick Sylvester (whom Stanley knew in California) undertaking one of the first ever BASE jumps.

I first saw that movie right around the time I started climbing and thought it was the coolest thing I had ever seen. Twenty years later, there we were, the stars of our own real-life action movie. Another boyhood dream coming true.

Following my experiences filming *The Wildest Dream*, *Take Me to the Edge* and *Top Gear*, I wanted to try to take those kinds of production values and apply them to a properly hardcore, genuine expedition without massive off-camera support, overhyped danger or false jeopardy.

The partnership Stanley and I had forged climbing El Cap and Half Dome in a day the year before was something special. I'd never found that with anybody before. We had the same skills, strength and speed, shared an adventure ethos and hearty appetite for dangerous fun. I wanted to utilise our unique relationship on a major expedition, to take our years of experience free climbing big walls, making speed ascents, BASE jumping and pushing the limits in Yosemite to a more remote, hostile and altogether more hardcore environment.

I met Alastair Lee in the Vats bar of the Brewery Arts Centre at the Kendal Mountain Festival in 2007, right after the premier of his film *Storms*, a parody of UK climbing. It was side-splittingly funny, if you were one of the few who got the jokes, but what really astonished me was the professional level of production. It looked like a proper movie with fancy special effects and slick editing but had been made on a shoe-string budget in a spare bedroom by a couple of guys who had exceptional skills and talent using recent developments in film-making hardware and software to stunning effect.

Al was of medium build with thick, dark, almost Mediterranean hair and features. He presented an air of confidence verging on arrogance that belied the insecurity of his creative genius.

'Loved your film, mate, let me buy you a beer, but what an extraordinary amount of effort for such a niche subject!' I said to him.

'You're telling me! It was a right laugh to film though,' he replied.

With a similar northern sense of humour and ambition beyond our stations we immediately hit it off.

The next year he made another film called *Onsight* that went on to win a bunch of awards. I had spent one day filming with him on the grit. I was super-impressed with the sequence he cut from what had been a fairly underwhelming shoot. Fast cuts in time to great music, modern editing tricks, engaging storytelling and good sound quality again gave the impression of a far more well-resourced and higher-end production than it really was. Al was clearly a gifted film-maker and it turned out he was a world-class photographer too.

Imagine if I gave him some really epic material to work with . . . I thought.

Ever since hearing Guy Lee's stories on the Old Man of Hoy I'd been fantasising about Mount Asgard. My old North Wales climbing partner Noel Craine had aid climbed a new route on the mighty northwest face in the mid-1990s and I'd been enthralled by his tales of the massive approach, mythical landscape, polar bears and wall of El Cap scale and quality.

Like a medieval castle of gargantuan proportions, Asgard is a striking and aesthetically beautiful mountain, the kind that I am always attracted to. The most impressive northerly aspect had never been free climbed.

I explained my idea to Al and asked if he was interested in making a film. I told him I wanted it to be like *Point Break* meets *Lord of the Rings* but real. He knew I was experienced in front of camera and understood the film-making process, that the whole crew would need to make allowances and work together with shared goals to create a film of true quality. He didn't hesitate to say yes.

I pitched the idea to Berghaus and they agreed to commit a modest budget. The marketing manager had a contact at Nokia and quickly secured the same again. Ultimately the project cost twice as much without anybody being paid a fee. Al and I both maxed out our credit cards equally to cover the shortfall. It was worth every penny.

Al had a keen eye for a shot, a knack for storytelling and no shortage of motivation. However, he had no experience of big-wall climbing when we embarked on the project. To teach him the ropes, get myself into shape and refine our systems and techniques to work efficiently together we undertook a series of training trips to more friendly and approachable big cliffs. I also knew there was a chance we might not climb anything or secure enough material for a film during the Baffin expedition. The training trips would ensure whatever happened on Asgard we would have something in the can to deliver to our financial sponsors.

Our first trip was to the spectacular conglomerate towers of Riglos in the foothills of the Spanish Pyrenees. A thousand feet tall, seriously overhanging, protected by bolts, strewn with pebbles and boulders that make for unusually dynamic climbing and just fifteen minutes from the road, it is an equally spectacular and fun place to climb. It's also a great place to BASE jump. I partnered with my friend Carlos Suarez, a typically relaxed Spaniard, ten years older than me with dark skin, hair and eyes. Well known in Spain, he shared my passion for climbing massive cliffs and a couple of years earlier I had introduced him to BASE jumping, which he had embraced with gusto.

Alastair was accompanied by Ian Burton, whom he had invited to join the Asgard expedition to assist in producing the film. A slightly awkward, aloof character a bit older than me with a quiff of blond hair, blue eyes, an intense stare and crooked smile, Ian was a product of the English public school system with confidence unmatched by competency. He was however an accomplished wildlife cameraman and possessed basic climbing skills. With a penchant for classical music and driving very slowly he didn't quite match the high-tempo vibe of the rest of the crew, but he proved to be a dependable and committed chap.

Carlos and I attempted to climb the two biggest Riglos formations, La Visera and El Pison, and BASE jump from both in two hours. A standard ascent of each would take all day but we simul-climbed without stopping using a 20-metre rope, a BASE descent taking just seconds. Whilst climbing the second tower, low cloud formed around the summit. Standing on the edge in the dense whiteness, poised to jump, was gripping. At the very moment we leapt the church bells began to ring and a huge vulture swooped past. We plummeted through the cloud and landed safely, though it had taken 2 hours and 11 minutes. Carlos was not due to join the Asgard trip but we had such a laugh and his laid-back, charismatic Spanish appeal was great on camera, so I invited him to join the team.

The next trip was to Monte Brento in Northern Italy, where Carlos and I met with my friend, the grandfather of wingsuit flying, Croatian Robbie Pecnik to learn to wingsuit BASE jump. The outrageously overhanging amphitheatre, the road that leads almost to the summit and the BASE-friendly café at the landing area 1,200m below and 2 kilometres from the exit make Brento the most popular wingsuiting cliff in the world. We hit it hard, making ten jumps in four days and both getting to grips with this more advanced style of BASE jumping. Duane was in my mind during those first wingsuit jumps. I flew cautiously and opened high.

Finally Al and I spent a week in Yosemite with Stanley. We were plagued by poor weather but managed to film a good sequence introducing our Yosemite god to the film and giving Al a taste of work on a truly big wall. Al had to attend his brother's wedding at the end of July 2009, pushing our Asgard trip a bit later than I would have liked, a delay that would prove defining but we were ready.

In Norse mythology Asgard is the land of the gods, where Odin, Thor, Freya, Loki and the other deities decide the fates of men. For the five weeks we spent in the realm of that mountain it truly felt like we were being toyed with by those gods and were at their mercy.

It began as soon as the adrenaline of our skydive entry had worn off. As we searched for the parachute loads a lone figure appeared in the distance.

'Durka Durka, Mohammed Jihad!' chanted the hooded figure as he approached.

I recognised the accent immediately and knew there was only one person who would be here and quoting from *Team America*.

'Singer, you nutter, what the hell are you doing here?' I said.

Clearly damaged by his time held hostage by Islamic fundamentalists in Kyrgyzstan, after being kidnapped during a climbing expedition with Tommy Caldwell, Beth Rodden and John Dickey in 2001, my friend from Yosemite Jason 'Singer' Smith had travelled alone, in secret, all the way from his home in Australia just to surprise us after our grand entrance.

He had been there several times before, climbed two routes on Asgard and knew the climbing in the area better than anyone. I'd corresponded with him extensively whilst planning the trip, concluding my final email saying we hoped to skydive in on 1 August.

'Bet you weren't expecting to see me here!' he said.

'No shit,' I replied.

'Dude, you should've had someone down here to meet your stuff,' said Singer. 'If I hadn't been here at least two of them would've been blown into the ice river of death and been swallowed up by the glacier. I think I spotted all of them. You know the last one cratered, right?'

Stanley and I looked at each other in horror.

The straps of the huge, well-worn haul bag containing both port-a-ledges and half of the climbing hardware had ripped off with the opening shock of the parachute pressurisation and it had exploded on impact after a 1,000-foot fall. The total devastation of the contents was impressive.

Two entire set of cams were completely concertinaed. At least eighty carabiners were twisted and broken as if they were made from plasticine, both port-a-ledges were irreparably damaged and three pairs of crampons had been destroyed. We salvaged a couple of ropes but all the hardware was a write-off.

We located all but two of the other loads that had floated down perfectly as planned. The two missing loads were the ones containing our tents and cooking gear. Loki the god of mischief was at work.

By then, around 11 p.m. in the twilight of the late Arctic summer night, it was too dark to continue the search.

We had lost half of the climbing gear and, worse, both mission-critical port-a-ledges. Although we could still climb something in alpine style there was no way we would be able to attempt one of the major lines on the northwest face, the aim of our expedition.

However, all hope was not lost. I had half-expected something to go wrong and had brought an entire back-up set of climbing gear to leave in Pangnirtung in case of such a disaster. By an incredible twist of fate we also happened to have two spare double port-a-ledges back in Pang. The gear shipment I had sent out in advance had encountered loads of problems resulting in some of it being lost. I had incorrectly deduced that amongst the missing gear were the port-a-ledges so had purchased and flown from the UK with two more. When we rounded up our gear in Pang it transpired the ledges had not been lost and we were equipped with four.

Alastair, Ian, Jas and Chris Rabone – a recent acquaintance of mine and the last member of the team – had flown back in the DC3 to Pang following the airdrop and would be catching a boat to the start of the four-day trek to Asgard the next morning on the 11 a.m. tide. We needed them to bring the back-up gear. Unfortunately we had no form of communication. Looking back, I find it hard to believe I jumped without a sat phone in my pocket. These days I wouldn't consider undertaking a remote expedition without solid communications. But this was the first big trip I'd organised and I had a lot to learn.

'There's an emergency radio in the Summit Lake shelter. The park warden in Pang announces the weather forecast at 8.45 a,m. If we can make it there by then we can ask him to pass on the message. We could be there in a few hours if we move fast,' said Singer.

By now it was midnight and we were already tired from the long journey to Baffin, stressful preparation and adrenaline-charged entry. Having studied maps of the area for months prior to the trip I knew the shelter was more like a full day's hike but it was our best option.

Singer had brought an espresso maker. We added a dram of single malt that had survived the airdrop and fuelled by the caffeine and alcohol energy bomb set off running down the glacier.

The night-time temperature drop had turned the surface of the glacier into an ice rink. With our crampons broken in the failed loads it was pure comedy as we took it in turns to slip, slide, try to regain balance then fall flat on our arses. Heavily reliant on our walking poles for balance we proceeded down in fits of laughter.

We soon encountered our first of the three appropriately named 'ice rivers of death'. They cut deep channels into the ice about 2 metres wide that flowed fast with glacial melt water along an ice chute for a mile or so before disappearing down a moulin, a terrifying hole, deep into the glacier. It had been a long sunny day and the streams were raging. If you fell in I could not see how you would stop yourself being washed away to a frozen and claustrophobic drowning.

A week later the committing leaps had become routine but on this first encounter I could hardly watch as the others launched across onto the icy surface.

'What the hell was that?' I shouted. It sounded like a bomb had exploded, followed by the rumble of thunder.

'Rockfall. This place is active right now, dude, you gotta pick your line carefully,' said Singer with authority.

The next obstacle was the death moraine that led from the glacier onto the dry land of the pass, a steep field of car-sized boulders precariously balanced on top of each other, some of which moved when stepped upon, causing the whole hillside to start sliding. There was no option but to keep moving as fast as possible across the sliding slope, trying not to think about what would happen if one of us were to be trapped underneath a boulder.

After a long, less treacherous descent, we reached Summit Lake. We paused to watch a magnificent 2 a.m. dawn before scampering 8 miles along the lake to the head of the Caribou River. Our final death obstacle was to cross the sprawling delta of ice-cold channels, one of which was waist deep and fast flowing. The sharp stones cut into our bare feet numbed by the freezing melt water.

Another few miles and finally we made it to the shelter just in time for the 8.45 a.m. weather broadcast. But our victory was short-lived – the radio was broken. Exhausted, we passed out in the warmth of the sun for few hours.

Meanwhile the others caught the boat to the head of the fjord, unaware of the failed parachute, and without the back-up gear. Most of the kit had been air-dropped but still they each carried back-breaking loads containing everything they needed for the hike in and all the fragile, heavy camera equipment.

Al's ambition was to redefine the cinematography of a modern expedition documentary. That required a small arsenal of kit, including a full set of prime lenses, a temperamental depth of field adapter that would be the bane of his trip, a medium-format film camera, a panoramic landscape camera and much more. His film *The Asgard Project* did indeed reset the bar, winning dozens of awards and quickly reaching cult-classic status.

I had moved to the Lake District in late 2008 and there I had met Chris Rabone. He was the same age as me, the same height but a far more muscular build. He ran a landscape gardening business and long hours on building sites had made him unusually fit and strong. We had only climbed together a few times and though he didn't climb that hard he was highly motivated and very positive all the time. I suspected a man of his strength and attitude would be a valuable asset in a supporting role on the expedition and though we didn't know each other well I invited him to join us. He jumped at the chance and I was right, Chris proved to be crucial.

The only member of the crew that lived locally to me, Chris had been a useful sounding board for all my hare-brained ideas. Planning and preparing my first major expedition had been a far larger task than I'd anticipated, taking months of effort raising finance, chartering planes, gaining permissions, amassing gear. Just packing the 245 man-days of food had taken a week. I pretty much single-handedly organised everything, as I would on all my future expeditions. Partly because I am a bit of a control freak, but mainly because of the geographical separation of the team and the fact everybody else had jobs.

'What do I need to bring?' asked Jas shortly before departure.

'A toothbrush and a few pairs of boxers. Everything else is sorted,' I replied.

On later trips, I'm not even sure Jas knew where he was going when he showed up at the airport!

Every year a few dozen committed hikers undertake the spectacular 62-mile trek through the Auyuittuq Pass, an ancient Inuit route from Pangnirtung to Qikiqtarjuaq. Inuksuks – Inuit cairns built from large stones that resemble human form – mark the way. A steep ascent out of the pass leads up to the Turner Glacier and the mighty twin towers of Asgard.

The trek gains altitude very gradually but is nonetheless challenging. The trail is vague, through boggy tundra and across unstable talus fields. It is polar bear country but you are prohibited from carrying a gun in the park. However, the most serious danger and cause of most accidents are the frequent river crossings. Some are wide deltas with many shallow channels over hundreds of metres. Others are narrow, fast flowing and can be over waist deep. All are freezing, serious and intimidating when carrying a heavy load. Sometimes later in the day it is necessary to camp before a crossing and wait until the morning for the flow to slow following the cooler temperatures of the night.

Jas Pickles is as tough and strong as they come but his Achilles heel is cold water. He really struggled to maintain his composure on the wider crossings, screaming like a child, much to the amusement of the rest of us.

After a few hours of sleep it was decided that Carlos and Stanley would go back up to Asgard to find the last two loads and set up base camp on the lateral moraine beneath the northwest face whilst Singer and I would continue down the pass as light and fast as we could to meet the others and share the bad news.

In one eighteen-hour push we literally ran all the way down the pass to the main crossing of the Weasel River. The bridge had washed away in serious floods the year before and a rope crossing was now in place. We had not brought harnesses or even slings. I set off soloing across the thin rope. Staring down into a torrent of certain death, after 10 feet I got the fear and retreated to the bank where we waited for the others to arrive. In the middle of the second day of their trek, wearing harnesses, they crossed the rope safely, surprised to see us waiting to meet them.

We explained what had happened.

'So are you going back to Pang to get the stuff?' asked Jas.

'No, you and Chris are,' I said. His face dropped and turned white at the prospect of repeating the traumatic river crossings.

Al, Ian, Singer and I made our way back up to Asgard shouldering what we could from Jas and Chris's loads.

Carlos and Stanley had found the two missing loads. They had also come across a very long, narrow, straight ski sticking up vertically out of the glacier that looked like it was from the 1970s and was mounted with an unusual cut-away binding. It was James Bond's ski! We took it as a good omen.

After a bit of effort creating tent platforms, building stone furniture and erecting a couple of parachutes as mess tents we had established a decent base camp. We repacked our BASE rigs on a large flat rock nearby.

Whilst we waited for Chris and Jas to return we decided to climb the much easier but massive Scott route on the East Face of Asgard. Around 4,000 feet long it is one of the finest alpine rock routes in the world, mostly easy climbing with just one, short challenging section right at the top. Al and Ian stayed in base camp and the other four of us walked around to the east side of the towers and raced up the massive route in just six hours. Traversing the summit to the north side we could see base camp. After a while exploring the edge, dropping stones into the abyss and counting how long until they struck the face, we found a perfect, safe exit point – a small, flat ledge a 20-foot rappel below the top. We also discovered a load of timber and a large wooden tripod, abandoned by the 007 film crew.

My stomach turned with the familiar anticipation that comes before leaping from a cliff as I strapped on my BASE rig. We left Singer with the gear he needed to rappel the standard descent, the rest was packed awkwardly inside our pants and jackets. I radioed down to Al on the glacier. He could just see us and had found a great profile shot of the wall from which to film.

Toes perched over the edge of the precipice I took a deep breath and tried to relax as much as possible.

The exit point and conditions were perfect. The gods were feeling kind as first Stanley, then Carlos and I dived into the void. Accelerating rapidly to terminal velocity I hurtled towards the glacier, tracking far from the cliff before deploying my canopy and drifting gently to the ground. We were down within two minutes, once again frothing with adrenaline, though it was slightly less intense than the skydive. What a day! What a way to climb! Fast, free and fly!

Stanley and I spent many hours studying the north wall with a telescope attempting to pick out a line that we thought might be free climbable. During the airdrop, to my disbelief I had spotted two port-a-ledges on the line of our primary objective, the Bavarian route on the West Face of the South Tower. I knew the super-strong Belgians Nico Favresse, Sean Villanueva and crew were in the area and suspected that they had the same idea, that route being almost continuous crack systems all the way, well suited to free climbing. Nobody has ever attempted to free climb on these mighty faces and there hadn't been any ascents for fifteen years, yet as fate would have it our Belgian friends had beaten us to it by a couple of weeks.

The Belgian crew came to visit following their descent. They had free climbed all but a few moves of the route and enthusiastically drew us a topo. But the approach gully to the base of that route was threatened by a dangerous-looking serac. We had seen a couple of serious rockfalls flush down it and didn't savour the prospect of repeatedly hiking loads through the danger zone.

They informed us that when they had climbed the gully two

weeks earlier it had been colder and much less active. On their way down they had opted to rappel the cliff beside the gully as they too felt it too dangerous in the current warm temperatures. They had been in the park for four weeks and had experienced perfect conditions, stable high pressure and sunshine the whole time, complaining it had been too hot to climb hard in the sun.

We drank whisky, shared stories and they played their ukuleles and tin whistles for an evening before they began their long hike out.

Stanley and I concluded the safest objective for a free attempt was an aid route called Inuksuk that forced an impressive line directly up the fiercest-looking area of the northwest wall. It had taken a strong Swiss team two separate expeditions to aid climb using hundreds of bolts and was unrepeated. Plagued by near-constant shade it looked extremely difficult, cold and daunting. Crucially it looked like there was a relatively safe line to the start of the proper climbing up which we could fix rope and haul our masses of gear. The sparsely featured, pink-tinged gneiss overhung constantly for almost 3,000 feet, clearly a desperate free-climbing challenge that held an ominous allure.

Chris and Jason finally arrived having had to carry two separate loads each as the quantity of back-up gear was too heavy to move in one. The very next day the weather changed dramatically. We were hammered by four days of continuous rain, wind, sleet and snow. When it cleared there was a distinctly different feel – summer had passed, autumn had arrived and it was cold even in the sun, though at least that meant less rockfall.

Dodging occasional small rockfalls, Stanley and I climbed the wandering ice and snow approach ramps that led to base of the wall, and fixed rope directly down steeper, safer terrain.

We organised and packed five haul bags the size of wheelie bins with gear and supplies for two weeks: hundreds of colourful carabiners, thousands of feet of rope, five sets of cams, a full complement of aid ironmongery, seventy freeze-dried main meals, breakfasts and desserts, a kilo of Golden Virginia and hundreds of other mission-critical items.

I felt intimidated and trepidatious, acutely aware of the weight of responsibility I held as instigator and leader. I knew that what we were about to do would be difficult and dangerous, and I could not guarantee our safety or success.

'Look, boys, this is going to be gnarly,' I said. 'I'll do my best, but you might die up there and it'll definitely be an arse-kicker. If you're not up for it, please don't feel obliged. Now is the time to bail – once we blast, you're in for the duration.'

Carlos had become increasingly withdrawn since the Scott route, spending lots of time alone in his tent and not engaging with the rest of the crew. He took the opportunity.

'I don't want to go up there. I like climbing light and fast. I don't want to deal with all this heavy stuff. It's going to be miserable and slow. Let's go climb alpine-style on the sunny side,' he said.

He was right, it would be a major suffer-fest. The other side would be sunnier, safer and far easier. But he didn't seem to understand that we had come to attempt something truly hard. Light and fast is all well and good but that style doesn't work on the greatest faces and certainly not if you want to free climb and film to a high standard.

I was disappointed but I wasn't going to try to convince him to come. If he got hurt I would feel guilty and his low morale would be detrimental to the rest of us.

However, to efficiently achieve all our goals we needed a team of five on the wall. One pair to constantly push the ropes higher up the wall using aid, whilst another pair could try to free climb and Al could film.

Without hesitation Chris piped up. 'I'll come. Don't think I can help with the leading but I'll do anything else.'

Something I've learned when the going gets tough is that attitude is far more important than experience or ability. Carlos decided to stay with Ian on the ground and Chris joined the wall team.

It took fifteen hours of ball-breaking labour to transport our 350 kgs of gear up the 350 meters of rope. Whilst we toiled, the loudest rumble of rockfall so far echoed around the glacier. Like in an earthquake, the whole mountain seemed to shake. In the darkness we couldn't tell where it fell. The next day we could see a boulder the size of a house on the glacier beneath the gully leading to the South Tower that had not been there before. Had we stuck with our original objective we would've been in that gully when that boulder came down and quite possibly all have died. I thanked the instinct that had led me to suspect and avoid such danger.

We arrived at the start of the wall in pitch darkness, exhausted and more dehydrated than I've ever been, having mistakenly buried the water supply in amongst the inaccessible haul load. We erected the port-a-ledges and lay down to sleep. Half an hour later shards of ice began to fall from the face, showering us with grape- to golf-ball-sized hail. There was nowhere to hide, but thankfully the wall was so steep most of it landed clear of our hanging camp and we were too exhausted to care.

We made good progress on the first 200 metres of the wall and discovered a flat ledge the size of a large dining table. We moved the camp up this dramatic perch. As a team of five with only two double ledges, one of us was forced to sleep outside. I was the one who had committed everybody to such hardship and thought it only fair I be the one who suffered the most so I slept outside on the ledge. To begin with it was bearable but when my sleeping mat burst and then the zip on my sleeping bag failed it began to wear me down.

I managed to onsight a hard pitch through unlikely terrain but then the wall tilted well beyond vertical and it started to get really hard. Resorting to full-scale aid, it took Stanley almost six hours to climb a single rope length, hammering in thin pitons and tiny, pointed bird beaks. Continuously hard terrain above slowed us to a snail's pace. We managed just a couple of pitches per day. Stanley and I took it in turns to lead but belaying was the worst task. There wasn't even the smallest ledge on which to stand, meaning every belay we hung uncomfortably against the wall sitting on a tiny wooden belay seat, wearing every layer of clothing we had brought up and still freezing for hour after hour, chain-smoking hand-rolled cigarettes to distract from the suffering. When we could take it no more we would rappel down to the ledge camp, leaving ropes fixed in place to ascend to our high point the next morning.

It got steadily colder, windier and more menacing each day. The cumulative effect of the punishing climbing and draining belay sessions began to take its toll.

Apart from a few sections, most of the terrain looked like it might be possible to free climb with time for rehearsal and kinder weather, but conditions were brutal and our first priority was to get to the top, which was taking drastically longer than antici-pated. We had hardly filmed any climbing so we decided to split into teams – Stanley with Jas, Chris with me – and we would alter-nate between pushing the rope higher up the route and attempting to free climb and film sections we had already aid climbed.

Stanley managed to figure out a way to free the first hard aid pitch and set about leading it with Al filming. After a valiant effort, right at the top he succumbed to frozen fingers and toes and fell. He had a violent outburst of emotion, head-butting the wall hard with his helmet.

'Bitch, fuck, crack whore, motherfucker!' he screamed at the top of his lungs. Al knew it was dynamite footage for a film.

'Sorry for all the cursing,' said Stanley after he regained self-control.

A week into the ascent another storm hit, this one much more wintery. We cursed the cold as we huddled in the port-a-ledges for four days in what would be described in the UK as full winter conditions. The ropes were covered in two inches of haw frost and an Arctic gale shook the ledge violently. It was 23 August, Stan-ley's thirty-fourth birthday. We celebrated with an Asgard cake made out of flapjack, using marine matches for candles. The Arctic summer was way shorter than I'd anticipated.

'You guys here pretty late. August twentieth, shit change round here,' Charlie, our Inuit outfitter, had warned when we first arrived in Pangnirtung. He was right.

We had persevered through harsh conditions but now the situation was getting desperate; we were not equipped for such wintery conditions with only thin gloves and mid-weight sleeping bags. Just getting to the top was starting to look unlikely.

There is a fine line between pushing hard and overstepping the mark. Getting as close to the edge as possible, without falling off the cliff. We had been treading that line the whole time but now it seemed we were in real danger of crossing it.

We had ropes fixed for 1,200 feet above our wall camp but we were still 600 feet from the top.

We only had sufficient food and fuel for three days at the most and it was now so cold that two-litre bottles of boiling water were frozen solid within a couple of hours.

The intensification of the storm the previous night had brought about the first discussion of retreat. It was getting serious. Frostbite was becoming a real threat. There was no way we were going to free it now and pushing further up the wall away from the safety of base camp and the ground was starting to feel reckless. There was a chance the weather may improve, but for certain sooner or later it would get significantly worse with the exaggerated rate of seasonal change so far north. We didn't want to be up there then.

We decided the only prudent option was to use any remaining good weather to retrieve the ropes and abort the climb before we became dangerously overstretched.

That night the wind died completely. A cloud inversion engulfed the glacier whilst a magnificent sunset filled the sky. As darkness fell we watched in awe a spectacular display of the Northern Lights dance across the stars. Early the next morning, from a clear, cold sky, the sun bathed our camp in its rejuvenating warmth for just one precious hour for the first time since we'd left the ground. On the cusp of defeat the gods gave us the slightest chance. We snatched it – throwing caution to the wind, we made a grab at the summit.

Chris and I began the long, free-hanging commute to the high point to push through the final few hard pitches to easier terrain and hopefully the top, whilst Stanley prepared to give his melt-down pitch another free attempt on camera.

On the very final section of the last hard aid pitch, with the top of the wall in sight I drew a complete blank. I had progressed slowly, sky-hooking on matchbox-sized edges between the thin bolts placed by the first ascensionists. I could see another 30 feet higher where the angle eased and more features marked the end of the major difficulties. But the face in front of me was completely devoid of even the tiniest feature and I could not envisage how to climb it. I had little hard aid experience, having always focused on free climbing, and had not seen the tiny line of 'bat-hook' holes, the size of pencil rubbers, drilled every 5 feet up to the next bolt. Instead I ventured out left, heading for a small flake, making ten consecutive hook moves on matchstick-sized edges that became progressively more sloping. Feeling sick with fear, I reached the flake and had begun to hammer in a piton when the dinner-tray-sized flake detached and plummeted to Earth. Unable to move up or down, far above the last bolt, I cursed myself for not bringing the hand drill. Visions of my Cerro Torre disaster ran through my mind. With all my resolve I tried to control the fear and made a few more hook moves on virtually non-existent placements, a clusters of crystals, an edge the size of fingernail. The next bolt was almost within reach when suddenly both hooks blew at the same time and sent me hurtling down the wall, my knuckles grinding on the coarse granite still holding the hooks.

'NOOOOOO!' I screamed in anger and terror, clearly audible to the others on the ledge far below. It was a big fall, perhaps 60 feet before the rope caught me. Blood poured from all my fingers, flaps of flesh almost revealed bone on a couple and I had no sensation in the tips. But at least this time there were no broken bones and I could still walk.

Chris helped me to tape the wounds, I took 800mg of ibuprofen and painfully and painstakingly we rappelled back to camp.

Stanley had managed to do his pitch and was in high spirits.

I was feeling sorry for myself. I removed the tape to clean and inspect my damaged fingers.

'It's nowt but a scratch, you wimp,' Jas taunted.

I couldn't help but laugh. The next day Stanley, a far more experienced aid climber than I, found the bat-hook holes and completed the pitch with ease. He could see the flake that had detached marking where I had gone and one hook still hung precariously attached to nothing at my high point.

'Aid climbers don't do that shit, man, when it gets that rad they drill holes,' he told me later. 'That's the most out-there hooking I've ever seen, you idiot.'

Stanley topped out first. He pulled up 100 feet of slack, short-fixed the rope to a belay just below the top and began scrambling up the final few metres to the summit plateau. He gently touched a boulder the size of a wardrobe that lay on the snow. It was enough to dislodge it, almost sending him with it as it plummeted off the edge directly over Jason, missing him by a matter of centimetres. We saw the huge block fall past our camp and explode on the glacier.

The gods had thrown one last death strike before relenting and allowing us to the top.

The next day all five of us ascended the ropes. In the spirit of our original objective I free climbed the very last pitch of the face with taped fingers, filmed by Al in wintery conditions.

Though we had categorically failed to free climb the wall, getting the whole crew to the top against such overwhelming odds felt like a great success. We had pushed so close to the edge and made it relatively unscathed. But the adventure was not yet over.

Stanley and I put on our wingsuits and completed our final exit checks. Just then a huge, white, snowy owl appeared from nowhere, made a close pass to inspect the colourfully clad strangers in its realm, then turned and flew directly over our heads on the exact heading of our exit, disappearing into the distance without a single flap of its wings. I am not superstitious but it was the most reassuring omen.

'Be super safe, yeah?' I said to Jas without any hint of irony as I stepped towards the exit point. I was far more concerned about Al, Chris and Jas's descent than our own. It felt wrong for the two most experienced climbers to abandon our friends facing such a long and arduous rappel with so much gear.

'Just bugger off, Captain, this was the plan all along. It's my turn to be in charge. We'll be fine. Enjoy your flight,' said Jas with a firm handshake, no doubt exuding more confidence than he felt.

'Nice and relaxed,' said Stanley, poised to dive off the edge of the massive cliff.

'Three, two, one – see ya!' I counted down and we were airborne together, diving steeply for a few hundred feet before the wingsuits pressurised and we began to fly at 120mph across the sky, carving a wide arc above the glacier to land hundreds of metres from the wall a couple of intense minutes later.

'That was the Asgard project – we came to climb that wall right there and jump off it, and that's what we just did,' I said to camera. 'That was amazing.'

'That was SICK! So ready to be off that fucking wall,' beamed Stanley to his.

That night we slept wrapped in our parachutes, our sleeping bags still up on the wall camp. My hands were pure agony the next morning, there was nothing left in the tank, we were both utterly exhausted. Face swollen, lips cracked, eyes bloodshot, I felt and looked ten years older after two weeks on that wall. Our great relief to be down was tempered by our concern for our friends.

All night they descended, removing the ropes as they went. After a few hours' rest they packed up the camp and began lowering the bags, making slow but steady progress. The choss-covered snow slopes below the wall proved to be the most taxing part of the whole descent, the heavy bags repeatedly getting stuck and dislodging loose rocks.

As if the gods were locking the door behind us it had been snowing heavily, rendering the wall unclimbable until next year just a day after we reached the top.

When they finally reached us on terra firma in the middle of the second night, the expression of exhausted relief and overwhelming joy on Alastair's face said it all.

A week of hard hiking with monstrous loads, throughout which we fantasised about fresh food, hot showers and home comforts, and we arrived at the head of the fjord where Charlie, our Inuit outfitter, would collect us by boat.

All seven of us were different men to the ones who had set out into the wilderness a month earlier. We had shared the same adventure but each of us had been on a different journey. Our roles and responsibilities, our challenges and fears, our highs and lows had not been the same, but we had all been pushed to our limits.

We had endured hardship, suffering and danger on a new scale but in overcoming those struggles had discovered reserves of strength and emotions deeper than any we had known before. The feelings of satisfaction, accomplishment and purpose were superlative. We had a look in our eyes and sensation in our souls that you cannot buy. I had never felt more alive and knew it was time for the serious expeditions I'd always dreamed of.

El Capitan, SE Buttress
Yosemite, California
37.7312°N, 119.6281°W
The Prophet, E9 7a
2000 ft.

The Nose   The Prophet

Falcon's Nest

A1 Beauty
E9 7a

Devil's
Dyno

2010
Storm

Guillotine

Dreamer
(2001 high point)

Screamer

Marginal
Belay

2004 Storm

Train Wreck

Shante Lomprey

16.

The Prophet

'If it was easy, it wouldn't be hard, would it?'

Leo Houlding

Asgard had broadened my horizons. Though I didn't realise it yet, my years as a Yosemite Stone Monkey were about to end. But I still had unfinished business there.

Back in October 2001, I was twenty-one and felt indestructible. Jas and I were in the Valley with our sights set on a new free route on El Capitan.

Free climbing on El Cap was in its infancy. The vast scale and extreme difficulty meant the few protagonists were employing new tactics borrowed from sport climbing. This involved rappelling from the top down with thousands of feet of rope to identify a line, rehearsing the pitches and moves for many weeks, chalking all the many holds, inspecting each gear placement and adding as many bolts as necessary to render it safe. The emphasis was on athletic performance, not the romance of adventure.

Still an idealist, untainted by failure or injury, I was then obsessed with climbing in the purest, most adventurous style. I felt that the way in which something was done was more important than what was achieved, and I was willing to put it all on the line to back my convictions.

I wanted to free climb a new route on El Capitan onsight, from the ground up, utilising no aid, no drill, no port-a-ledge and no fixed rope. What I considered to be the ultimate challenge. I wanted to push myself closer to the edge than ever before and add my own chapter to the sacred stone.

Jas and I spent many hazy days in the meadow below El Cap, studying the complex wall through a spotting scope and watching the play of shadows reveal and conceal the features.

An ambitious-looking line enticed us on the far-right side of the southeast face. This aspect is a mere 1,800 feet, almost half the height of the Nose. But what that sector lacks in stature is made up for by its serious nature. It contains many of the hardest and most dangerous aid routes on El Cap with ominous titles like Plastic Surgery Disaster, Surgeon General and Bad to the Bone. Tracking down the handful of climbers who knew these routes, we gleaned strategic information.

We spent one unforgettable afternoon with twelve cans of Old English, two packs of Camel no filters and the Yosemite legend Jim Bridwell. 'The Bird' was the most influential climber of his generation. In the seventies he had revolutionised El Cap climbing, making the first one-day ascent and ushering in a new era with aid climbs of visionary difficulty. He was known as much for his hard living as hard climbing and his resemblance to Keith Richards was striking.

He also had first-hand experience with our main concern, a feature called the Devil's Brow, a 25-foot horizontal roof two-thirds of the way up the wall. For a brief part of the day a shadow revealed an almost invisible ledge and a potential breach in the Devil's defences. Bridwell pointed out this subtle feature, adding, 'You kids might be able to do something with that, but be careful up there, boys. There's a fine line between badass and dumbass.'

Emboldened by this gift of knowledge from Yosemite's Gandalf – and unperturbed by its implicit warning – we began our quest.

Right off the ground it was challenging, the rock polished smooth as marble by the seasonal Horsetail Falls. The protection was minimal and the moves delicate and hard. On our first reconnaissance we only climbed three rope lengths. On our next attempt, following our chalk and knowing what to expect, we reached our high point with a fraction of the time and effort.

Above, the wall became much steeper and the rock far more friable. Serious, hard terrain. I progressed up fragile features, discontinuous cracks and grooves and after more than an hour, about 100 feet up, I reached a poor stance. I had already placed most of my gear and I wasn't keen to continue up the blank wall and hollow overhangs above. With the confidence of youth, I built a woeful belay that I wasn't sure would hold a heavy fall and warned Jason to try not to weight the rope.

Using the techniques I'd mastered on bold routes back in the UK I patiently climbed up and down familiarising myself with the moves directly off the unsafe belay until finally I had to make a move I would not be able to reverse. Absolutely committed, I made a dynamic move for a distant edge on tiptoes. To my horror it wasn't as good as it looked. My fingers slid from the edge. For a split second the unthinkable flashed though my mind – a high force fall directly onto a marginal belay and two dead Monkeys. Bridwell's warning glinted in my memory. But my survival instinct kicked in, my fingers caught a hidden hold and I stuck it, pulled a couple more hard moves and placed a tiny but solid cam for protection with huge relief. The danger of death greatly diminished, I followed less-harrowing features to a small ledge and safe belay that on subsequent attempts I would climb to directly, avoiding the death stance.

Spurred on by our success, I continued up severely fractured ground, delicately tiptoeing up a bottomless groove. Creeping upwards with patience and control, I reached a small roof and impassable terrain. I spent ages arranging sketchy protection in a crumbly crack and shaking fatigue out of my arms but couldn't see a way ahead. Then, just as I was about to accept defeat, I noticed the distinctive scratches left by aid climbers out to my left leading towards a hanging *arête*. I couldn't see around the corner but the rock quality improved in that direction. With my arms now recovered, I smeared across the hanging slab and reached a good foothold and pinch on the *arête*. Then, peering around the corner, I spotted a rusty bolt 20 feet up and left.

I took a deep breath then teetered around the shockingly exposed corner and committed to tiny crimps, a sequence I knew I could not reverse. Pulling the hardest moves of the route so far, I reached left to better holds that led to the bolt. But I was over-extended and a long way above my last gear I began to pivot and then plummeted for 50 feet, my fall held by my trusty RPs, the very tiniest of climbers' protection.

One of my ropes had been half cut on a sharp edge in the fall. I swapped ends with Jas, recomposed myself and tried again. This time I got my feet higher and stuck the better holds.

When I reached what should've been the safety of the bolt my stomach turned as I saw it was half hanging out. In a state of terror, I felt sick as I realised with gut-wrenching tension that there was more of the same to come.

I wished for the rock to be blank, impossible, to tempt me no further. But there were the slightest of holds and yet again I mastered my fear and found the boldness, or stupidity, to run the gauntlet once more. An appallingly thin sequence led to a second wobbly bolt at the limit of my reach and 20 feet above the last.

By now I was too high to lower off, and too scared to abseil, utterly committed with no safe retreat, a Braille trail of tiny holds leading to a distant belay overhead, my only way out. I cranked an outrageous mantle, then set out on another terrifying runout and made it to the sanctuary of a tiny ledge and the three solid bolts of a belay. Just three questionable runners in almost a hundred feet of desperate (E8 6c), unclimbed terrain climbed ground up, with no prior inspection, in the most exposed position I'd ever experienced. Such a feat is rare. It transpired I would never push myself so hard into the unknown ever again. I was balancing along that line between badass and dumbass like a tightrope.

Looking up, I cringed to see more of the same discontinuous, bottomed-out fissures and barely protectable hard aid terrain above. The Screamer pitch had taken it out of me. I was physically and emotionally exhausted. It was time to go down. As I descended on the safety of a rope from above I rehearsed the moves, chalked the holds and checked and memorised the gear placements in preparation for the next assault.

On the next attempt Jas fell from the crux leading the first pitch. One by one the fixed copperheads that were supposed to protect him ripped out, sending him bouncing down the slab until the single remaining wire stopped him from hitting the floor. He slammed into a big ledge on the rope stretch and cracked his pelvis. José and I half-carried him down to the road. In the absence of travel insurance, we procured some strong painkillers and he embarked on a painful journey home to Manchester.

I was angry with myself for not replacing the poor in-situ gear, resulting in Jason's accident, but I was nevertheless now enthralled by the awaiting adventure.

Perhaps unsurprisingly, I had difficulty persuading anybody else to join me on the line, now christened the Prophet (named after the epic C. J. Bolland techno record and the Lebanese philosopher Khalil Gibran's classic work). Eventually I convinced Cedar, the very first Monkey I'd met back in '98, to join me, on the condition we bring more aid gear (but no drill) and a fatter rope so he could jumar.

Well rested, now intimate with the route, the holds chalked and climbing at my best, I placed a decent piton where the fixed copperheads had been on the first pitch, and proceeded to climb quickly, efficiently and entirely free to my previous high point with much greater ease than my previous ascent.

When Cedar joined me at the tiny ledge, we had plenty of daylight but he didn't look happy. I asked him what he thought we should do.

'I think we should rap the fuck down while we still can, and take you to the fucking lunatic asylum!'

I was unable to talk him into continuing. We descended.

I was again stumped for a partner that fall of 2001, until Kevin Thaw showed up. He was up for it, but convinced me to take a port-a-ledge, though I stubbornly resisted his advice to bring a drill.

Again I reclimbed the five harrowing rope lengths. At the high point I used the ropes to lower and offset the belay, enabling me to use the bolts as the first runner, an unorthodox radical technique.

I fought my way upwards, awkwardly managing to place a knife-blade from a free position. Slightly higher, I clipped a frayed, in-situ copperhead and a comically small old piton called a RURP before reversing to the belay for a rest. From the security of the belay, I tested the gear. The head ripped immediately, though the RURP and knifeblade tentatively held. Satisfied with the gear, I committed to the hard moves above, on loose holds, to reach easier ground.

Hammering in another peg, I continued with increasing difficulty up the steep groove. A long way above the gear, a short, overhanging step of crumbly rock blocked my path. I reversed, and finally resorted to all-out aid. I struggled with the A4+ placements, angrily using birdbeaks and skyhooks for the first time.

Already pushed so far, a little over halfway up the wall I had reached my limit but didn't yet recognise it. Frustrated with the aid, I began free climbing an especially loose section. I started to get scared, then everything crumbled and I took a 30-footer onto the slab below, spraining both my ankles. Kevin and I retreated. The season was over, yet I was already planning the next offensive for the following spring with Jas.

But a few months later, employing the same push-the-limit mindset, I crossed that fine line Bridwell had warned me about, fell and crushed my talus bone on Cerro Torre. I suppose I had it coming.

I returned to Yosemite several times over the next three years, enjoying easier climbs and safer styles, but I continued to stare at the upper section of the Prophet during the hours of downtime. Reluctantly, I admitted that I was too scared to drive so hard again.

In the fall of 2004 Jas and I were both back in the Valley and on decent form. We hadn't set out to try the Prophet, but when Ivo Ninov, master of aid and dynamo of psyche, was keen we decided to compromise the original dream and try again but this time with aid, a drill and a port-a-ledge. In big-wall terms this is of course 'ground-up', though with reference to free climbing the style is 'headpoint'. The hard pitches are aided, top-roped then freed. In reality this style has more in common with top-down tactics than a ground-up free ascent.

Jason re-led the first pitch, now dubbed the Train Wreck, with typical northern black humour. This time, he slayed his demons easily with the help of the bomber peg.

Ghosts stalked me on the first of the hard pitches. Ivo offered to aid it, allowing me to refresh my memory on top rope. Hard aid is a slow process and Ivo tinkered upwards at a snail's pace. After four hours on lead, he reached the tied-off pegs where I had belayed on the first attempt. Horrified, he continued nailing up the detachable flakes above. With a scream he warned us as a flake the size of an ironing board began to peel off from the wall. One I had free climbed in 2001. It didn't quite go, and Ivo nervously tried to tie it back onto the wall. Visibly shaken, he returned to the belay and we descended to the port-a-ledge camp.

That night, the predicted bad weather grew into an epic winter storm. Our seemingly comfortable perch became a full-on waterfall. Our port-a-ledge flooded, and rocks dislodged by the flow pelted down. In a lull the next day we hastily retreated before an even more vicious front blew through, in which a Japanese couple tragically perished high on the Nose. When it finally cleared, at least eight teams had to be rescued. The Yosemite season was over. The Prophet would have to wait, again, for another year.

Jason stopped making his annual Valley pilgrimage and I spent my time in Never-Never Land climbing many other less dangerous walls, partnered with and leaning from local masters like Stanley and Dean. I had also discovered BASE jumping and a whole new way to explore and enjoy nature's finest adventure playground. The Prophet lay dormant for five years. Not a single climber ventured up there.

During the decade after my first attempt many of the great aid lines had been climbed entirely free, largely at the hands of the Huber brothers and Tommy Caldwell. These remarkable successes had all been achieved by employing top-down, sport climbing tactics and had established a new modus operandi and definition of El Cap free climbing.

To claim a true free ascent of El Cap you must make a continuous ascent, whether it takes a day or a fortnight, climbing all the pitches in sequence, without retreating to the ground or going to the top, with either one person leading it all, or both climbers swapping leads and following everything without falling. This has come to be the accepted style, particularly for first free ascents, as opposed to climbing each pitch individually over different attempts or partners freeing different sections.

In May 2010, the spring following the Asgard project, I found myself once again chilling in the sublime El Cap meadow staring up at the the Prophet for the thousandth hour. That first big expedition had completely reset my perspective and added another dimension to my ambitions. I realised I was a different person and would never again be willing to risk trying it from the ground. My desire to know what was up there finally overpowered the ideology of my youth. I walked to the top with a rack and a thousand feet of rope. With some regret, I began a wild solo rappel, laying to rest my ambitious dream of a ground-up first ascent.

Near the top I found a beautiful hairline crack, too fine to see from the meadow, equal in perfection and position to any free pitch on El Cap, but so thin it looked impossible.

The width of a pencil, it ran diagonally for 120 feet, splitting an immaculate golden slab. The sides were offset, creating a tiny edge; to my surprise, even on the thinnest sections I was able to pull on, but there were almost no footholds. The very first move looked desperate, as did the finish, with holds literally two matchsticks wide. Referencing the guidebook, I found out that this remarkable feature was the 'A1 Beauty' pitch of the aid route Eagle's Way.

Continuing down, I reached the Devil's Brow. At last I was actually up close and personal with the feature I'd eyed for so long.

Sure enough, the invisible ledge Bridwell had pointed out existed. It looked as though an exposed hand traverse offered the only free line through a spectacularly steep and blank section.

Employing complex tension traverses, scary pendulums and rope redirectional runners placed behind dangerously loose flakes I made my way down totally virgin terrain. There were holds, but the hollow diorite was gently overhanging the whole way. Dinner plates detached with a stroke, flying like frisbees and landing far away from the wall. It was terrifying to rappel; I could not imagine how horrifying it would be on lead and was glad I had not made it this far years earlier without a drill.

Towards the bottom of the pitch my feet touched a flake the size of a garage door. Attached only along its upper edge, it resonated like a gong. Reluctantly it dawned on me that this guillotine was the only free-climbable feature. I tried it, keeping as much weight on my feet as possible. It flexed several inches, but somehow it held.

Lower, a strange feeling of loss came over me as I tensioned around a corner and found myself at the ultimate high point I had reached in 2001, a little over halfway up the wall. The cams I had lowered off years earlier were still there. In exactly the same spot, I was in a completely different place. I'd become a spectator to the heroics of my youth. My top-down adventure had put to death my ground-up dream, but it gave birth to a new, more tangible goal. Except for a few short sections, I had done all of the moves on the Prophet. The game was on.

A month later Jason joined me to finish the job. In the absolute antithesis of the style in which we had begun the project back in 2001, we fixed the entire route from the top down.

Beneath the giant ceiling of the Devil's Brow, in the airiest spot imaginable that required extremely complicated work to reach, remained just one body length and half section of the whole route I hadn't figure out how to climb. It didn't look possible but I had an idea. With absolute commitment and a good deal of self-belief, a massive, extremely hard, two-handed sideways dyno overcame the blank streak. I remembered first seeing Johnny leap around the wall built for *Motormouth* and my dyno to bed every night as a kid and smiled. The Devil's Dyno provided the final piece of the jigsaw. We had found a totally free line up the southeast face of El Cap.

We replaced the rusty bolts on the Screamer pitch and added a dozen more to the rest of the climb to provide minimal protection on the least-featured sections.

I was in fighting form by now, and the A1 Beauty started to feel possible. I quickly did it in sections, but each individually felt close to my physical limit. It was going to be hard to link. We cleaned the ropes and made an attempt from the ground. In two days I led the whole route up to the A1 Beauty with no falls, with Jason following everything free except the Devil's Dyno.

In the heat of late June, I fell time and time again from the desperate crack without reaching the final peg. After many tries, and with bleeding fingertips and bruised pride, I finally admitted defeat. Even so, the ever-dependable Pickles vowed to return with me in the cooler temps of autumn. It was time to finish the quest.

'Oh well, if it was easy, it wouldn't be hard, would it?' I said to Jas, dejected, on the top. It instantly became a mantra.

Back again in October 2010, I was starting to suffer from project fatigue. Never before had I invested so much in any single climb. Some sixty days, over five seasons, four partners, two injuries and a fatal storm had passed on this nine-year odyssey. My fear of failure began to outweigh my fear of getting hurt. The route is so serious we had to familiarise ourselves once again with all thirteen pitches, but a heatwave hindered our efforts. The A1 Beauty crux catches the sun for all but the first hour of the day, requiring painfully early starts.

Rising at 4 a.m., we rapped in and with no warm-up I set off. Placing all the gear on lead, I climbed past the potential 50-footers – working the rests, calming my breathing – to the final crux. I did the long stretch out left, and massive reach to a good finger lock. A crippling flash pump took hold on the usually simple undercut crack. This area is totally devoid of footholds, and without the power to place the final cam I took a risk and pushed for the belay with trembling legs and flaring elbows. A fall from here, way above the peg, with an inevitable swing into the corner, would not be pretty. I made it by the skin of my teeth and felt physically sick from the massive physical effort and fear.

I'd led the crux pitch of the Prophet. But to claim the first free ascent I would have to do it and all the other outrageous pitches again in a continuous ascent from the ground. We were ready, but a week of bad weather forced us to extend our trip.

'Do you want the bad news or the bad news?' Jas asked as he returned with the weather forecast. 'The park service has issued a severe weather warning. A winter storm is coming. It's going to be a big one.'

The trip was already extended to its maximum. We were down to three options – we could accept defeat, and settle for having done every pitch; or we could wait for the storm to pass, then think like Tommy Caldwell and go for it in a day. In our current state of fitness – and given the extreme difficulties high on the route – success seemed unlikely with this strategy. Or tomorrow, insufficiently rested on the last day of fine weather, we could sail on straight into the heart of the storm, condemning ourselves to the tempest with no hope of rescue or retreat. We had no choice. Jason and I are neither cowards nor fools, yet once again we flirted with the line that Bridwell had warned me of all those years before.

As every other team on El Capitan either topped out or retreated, we began our ascent, setting off up the Train Wreck for the tenth time. Abandoning our shoes at the base, we carried a minute rack, climbing incredibly light save for the bottle of Southern Comfort to aid our inevitable confinement. We climbed with good pace and efficiency as big lead followed big lead. After nine stern pitches, we reached our stash beneath the Devil's Brow having both climbed it all with no falls. Already four-fifths of the way up the wall, with daylight to spare, we were tempted to continue. But with the two hardest pitches yet to come and our elbows cramped we set up the port-a-ledge.

We awoke in a cold kingdom of cloud. Magnificent, towering cumulonimbus morphed around us while an inversion obscured the valley floor. I stepped out of my sleeping bag digesting the Devil's Dyno for breakfast. Traversing Bridwell's Invisible Ledge, I felt like Jack up the beanstalk, my sense of wonder haunted by a latent menace in the sky. Despite the threat of imminent rain, I linked the next short pitch, a couple of hard moves and an easy ramp to arrive at the belay below the A1 Beauty. I was feeling good, and the temperature was perfect. Just then, the first drops of rain started to fall, and the rock was drenched in minutes. Fixing the rope, I returned to Jason on the ledge.

What began as an eerie whisper soon turned into a maelstrom as a massive Pacific front slammed full-tilt into the Sierra Nevada. Off to our left, the face of the North America Wall was engulfed by a waterfall. The ensuing forty-eight-hour tempest was the wettest anyone in Yosemite can remember. We were the only team on the wall. For the first forty hours we rode the turbulent weather with the attitude of seasoned pirates in our 4-by-6-foot canvas galleon.

'Argh! Is that all you've got!' I screamed at the more vicious gusts of wind.

But when the Southern Comfort ran out, the gusts reached hurricane force and our down sleeping bags were thoroughly soaked, it was no longer funny. Updrafts strong enough to lift the port-a-ledge smashed us around as a torrent the strength of a fire hose doused us with a deafening roar. If the thin fabric of the tent fly that was our only shelter had failed we would have been in serious trouble. No one would be coming to help in that storm.

By the third morning we were becoming hypothermic. Yet even as we contemplated the best way to surrender and considered calling to get rescued as soon as we could, the storm blew out. My beloved blue Yosemite skies returned. We were in a sorry state, like drowned rats on our flooded ledge. Our fingers and toes were utterly pruned – everything was completely soaked except my boots and chalk, which I had guarded fiercely.

Wringing out our sleeping bags, we began to dry out. Huge cascades of runoff bellowed all around us. As the great face flowed with a hundred 2,000-foot waterfalls, we recounted the night's horrors with the exhausted joy of survivors. By evening, we had succeeded in drying everything sufficiently to survive another cold night.

On day five, with far less water around, we moved the camp up to the A1 Beauty. A prominent wet streak ran down the last crux and all the chalk had been pressure-washed away. Patiently, we waited for the rock to dry.

Having barely survived ninety hours cramped and freezing in the flooded port-a-ledge, I set off to repeat the hardest pitch I'd ever done. With no chalk ticks marking the holds it felt way harder. By now intimate with this beautiful shield of gold I made it to the peg and final crux but ran out of steam. Rehearsing the moves and chalking the holds on the way down I felt confident for the next round. Less violent clouds filled the Valley, creating a tremendously atmospheric sunset.

'Go, Leo!' rang out in chorus from friends in the meadow far below.

I set off for the last try of the day. Leaving the rest at half height, I felt good – perhaps too good. Placing my foot imprecisely, I was off, and devastated. Whatever happened, we had to top out the next day.

I hardly slept; the weight of my over-ambition tore me apart. I couldn't eat and I vomited my morning coffee. But the cool conditions were perfect and I had made it all the way through the final crux to the good holds when all power abandoned me. Out of sight of Jas, I screamed, unable to move. I dropped the trophy on the podium; just a few feet from the belay, I fell. Back at the bottom, Jas consoled me with silence.

Physically and emotionally exhausted, I passed out on the port-a-ledge, waking in the heat of the midday sun. Having virtually accepted defeat, knowing we had given it our all, I ventured once more into the breach.

Fighting the poor conditions every step of the way, I made it to the peg. I worked the terrible rest for longer than on the other tries. This was it – last go, last day. Somehow I did it, once again tapping into power that seemed to come from beyond myself like I had on the early attempts, making it to the top with nothing in reserve. Relief outweighed the joy of success.

Freeing the A1 Beauty had been an immense struggle, pushing me right to my limit. I can safely say we could never have succeeded in climbing the Prophet with no aid, no bolts, no port-a-ledge and no fixed rope. Our 2001 attempts were an effort to push the limits of style of big-wall free climbing. Getting as high as we did was a bold try, but continuing in that style would have required us to cross Bridwell's thin line. Our wildly ambitious original dream had evolved and was about to become a real route on the Great Stone.

But with one last hard section to go, it was not quite over. Right off the belay I made the very hard move off an awkward undercut and heard a loud snap and felt a sharp pain in my finger. Unable to move up, I crashed down onto Jas, having sustained a ruptured tendon. I taped my injured finger to its neighbour, ignored the pain and in a fit of rage I attacked the Prophet's final defence.

The very last move of the route was the dry-laid stone wall we had previously built to terrace our summit bivi – the magnificent Falcon's Nest.

We collapsed into it elated. The Prophet was finally free. I was not expecting the short-lived but intense period of depression I suffered immediately afterwards. Like an Olympic athlete who wins gold I had attained peak performance but then lost sight of my purpose. I was deeply exhausted and it took months to regain my physical and mental strength. I think I knew I would never be able to get closer to the edge and succeed. Perhaps too that my idyllic Yosemite years were over.

17.

Yopo Wall – Cerro Autana

Alone on the lower flanks of Cerro Autana, deep in the Amazon, breaking trail through dense, near-vertical jungle in a bid to find a navigable route to the base of the wall, a palpable fear stopped me in my tracks.

The fer-de-lance is Latin America's most deadly snake. An aggressive pit viper with a hemotoxin venom that causes immediate necrosis of the flesh that can be fatal – and I was in his habitat. I didn't see the snake clearly, just a fleeting glimpse of tail in the rustling tall grass, but I could sense his presence intensely. Perhaps the yopo had put me in tune with the creatures of the jungle, or maybe it was a flashback? Or maybe I just had the fear?

José had often talked of the remarkable *tepuis* of his native Venezuela, the big walls of the jungle. His stories of the lost-world walls deep in the rainforest guarded by vertical jungle, swarms of killer bees, snakes, spiders and scorpions had me gripped. The tribal communities and shamanic ceremonies captivated my imagination.

'There are many *tepuis* but Autana is different. It is special. Sacred,' he had told me. 'Oh, and the yopo! Leo, you have to try yopo! It will change your life,' he had encouraged – or perhaps warned?

I had missed out on joining him on a trip there due to my accident on Cerro Torre. After José's premature death later the same year the logistical complications and security concerns of *tepui* climbing discouraged me from visiting Venezuela without him.

But I had not forgotten about Cerro Autana. The Asgard project had given me the big-expedition bug. In spite of all the complications, expense and suffering, the magnitude of that experience eclipsed anything that had come before. I wanted another large-scale, epic adventure. I knew Stanley and Jas were keen too. Al was psyched to make another film, this time assited by Dave Reeves, a big South African bloke, a talented cinematographer and camera grip. Dave wasn't a climber and would stay on the ground, but he knew how to look after himself in an expedition environment and had a passion for creating complex camera movements resulting in beautiful, cinematic shots that greatly elevate the production value of a film. Following Asgard in the Arctic, I thought Autana, deep in the Amazon, would be the perfect contrast.

In the decade that had elapsed since José's trip, access to Autana had become even more problematic. The jungle has not changed but Venezuela's political climate and the attitude of local tribes towards outsiders had.

Tepui climbing is prohibited in Venezuela for reasons that are not clear. Most *tepuis* are situated in the Gran Sabana in the east of Venezuela, where these restrictions are not a problem as there are few government representatives around to enforce the arbitrary law and the local communities are usually glad of the income climbers provide.

However, Autana is situated in the southwestern state of Amazonas, close to the porous Columbian border. In 2012 petrol in Venezuela was the cheapest in the world at a staggering 2p per litre – cheaper than water! In neighbouring Colombia it was more than £1. Their border is 1,275 miles of mostly uninhabited jungle, permeated by great rivers that provide perfect arteries for the smuggling of thousands of litres of petrol in one direction and hundreds of kilos of cocaine in the other. Long-standing territorial disputes and the presence of Colombian FARC guerilla fighters seeking refuge in Venezuela meant there was a heavy and visible military presence in the region. A state of semi-martial law existed in Amazonas.

The tribal people local to the Autana region are known as the Piaroa. Their culture is fascinating; they have accepted and interact with western ways but have retained a strong sense of identity with many managing to resist the Christian missionary's conversions, choosing instead to practice a form of animism. They believe in the spirits of the trees and plants, animals and birds, rivers and mountains and live in harmony with them. Numbering fewer than 20,000 across the Orinoco Basin, they are of very short stature, rarely more than 5 feet tall, with distinctive facial features. They are jolly people who treat their women as equals and have very little social hierarchy. Everything is shared equally amongst the community. Their society is renowned for its non-violence, tolerance and fairness. Farming, hunting and foraging are undertaken with great respect for their land and with minimal impact.

Autana dominates the landscape; you can see why it is sacred to the Piaroa. They believe it is the stump of the tree of life from which the fruits of all life were born, and that in a time when gods walked a bountiful Earth, a fight over a beautiful woman broke out. One of the gods swung an axe at the other, but they dodged and the sacred tree was felled, allowing evil and hardship to enter the world.

The Piaroa treated us outsiders with respectful suspicion, hardly surprising after centuries of persecution and exploitation by conquistadors, missionaries, miners, oil prospectors, loggers and drug cartels.

In order to climb Autana we first had to gain the trust, permission and support of the Piaroa. A month before our expedition our Venezuelan partners Alejandro 'Alejo' Lamus and Alfredo 'Yupi' Rangel travelled to Ceguera, the closest village to Autana, to begin the negotiations.

They met with the community representatives led by a man called Juan Pablo. Along with gifts of food, fuel and tools, they set up a laptop as a cinema and showed them a Spanish translation of our movie *The Asgard Project* to introduce we gringo climbers and convince them that we were there solely in pursuit of adventure and not to search for gold, diamonds or oil.

The community were suitably impressed by the film but remained unconvinced of our intentions. They simply could not understand why anybody would put so much time, energy and money into something so pointless as climbing their sacred *tepui*. They had a point.

They agreed to let us come, though they demanded a handsome ransom for their permission and support. Alejo, Yupi and Juan Pablo devised a strategy to smuggle five gringos along with half a ton of gear into the jungle without detection by government officials or other communities who, if they caught wind of our mission, would either shut us down or also demand hefty financial compensation.

Smuggling is a local speciality – a network of trusted contacts, corruptible officials and secret river ports usually used to move contraband would serve just as effectively to smuggle haul sacks full of racks and ropes in secret.

They decided that the gear must travel separately from the gringos. Juan Pablo stressed the importance of keeping a low profile. Not a single carabiner could be carried on our persons, no big cameras could be in our possession and there should be no loose talk about our plans in public.

Alejo relayed all this information to me by phone. We had never met. I had tracked him down through a very loose connection as I knew we needed help on the ground in Venezuela. He had a rumbling basso voice and Latino accent to his fluent American English that made him sound like a gangster. He seemed to know his stuff regarding expedition logistics and it was he who suggested a seasoned Tepuyero – *tepui* climber and beat-boxer Yupi – join the team.

Alejo explained the situation with exchanging money into the local currency of bolivars. Officially pegged to the dollar at 4 to 1, on the black market the going rate was double that. However, it would be difficult and dangerous to exchange large sums in a short period on the street when we arrived in Caracas, so we agreed I would wire all the funds to his US bank account in advance. I must admit I thought twice before wiring a five-figure sum to my Facebook friend with the gangster voice!

As we collected our bags and made our way to the arrivals

lounge in Caracas Airport it was only half in jest that we joked our Venezuelan partners would be nowhere to be seen – phone numbers dead, emails bounced back, Facebook profiles deleted! To my relief they were of course there, ready and waiting.

After a massive gear sort Alejo and Yupi set off on the fourteen-hour drive to the frontier town of Puerto Ayacucho, the last town before Autana. They needed a five-day head start with the gear so Team Gringo made our way to a deep-water soloing (DWS) area on the Caribbean coast that also happened to be the Ibiza of Venezuela. Perfect limestone tufas rose for 45 feet above a lukewarm, emerald sea. Latin beats cranked out of a distorted stereo, a dozen bronzed gyrating beauties sipped rum and Coke and cheered the wide-eyed white boys as we climbed and dived from the desert island rocks.

By night Puerto Cruz really came alive. Venezuelans are a fun-loving bunch who know how to party. With the highest ratio of women to men on the planet, a sun-drenched tropical climate, penchant for rumba dancing and last orders at 10 a.m., more than once we discussed substituting our intended jungle sufferfest with a DWS/DJ club exploration of Venezuela's Caribbean coast.

Nursing hangovers in local DWS explorer Francisco's kitchen, we were brutally reminded of Venezuela's other superlative claim at the time – murder capital of the world. On his way home from the bank in broad daylight, Francisco was mugged at gunpoint on his own doorstep a few metres from where we sat. It was time to flee the girls and guns and take our chances with the bugs and Piaroa in Amazonas.

Alberto's baggy jeans and shiny smartphone did little to disguise his indigenous Piaroan features. His beaming smile that never wilted would accompany us for the next three weeks. He and Juan Pablo had helped Alejo and Yupi source all the necessary supplies and successfully smuggled all our gear upriver and into the jungle towards our goal.

Before we followed we had one more important obligation.

Yopo has been an integral part of Piaroan culture for thousands of years. It is an extremely powerful hallucinogen extracted from the seeds of the *Anadenanthera peregrina* or yopo tree. A sophisticated mix of several other entheogenic plants are combined to denature gut enzymes and significantly increase the duration and intensity of the psychoactive ingredients DMT and bufotenin. The Piaroa believe it gives the skilled user powers of clairvoyance, longevity and wisdom, amongst other blessings. However, for the uninitiated the first dose has a reputation for inducing a fiercely bad trip.

Juan Pablo presented us to the incredibly wrinkled, impossibly old-looking man. Dressed in full ceremonial attire, complete with bone jewellery and feather headdress, he played the role of Amazonian shaman convincingly. Inside his large conical hut made of thatched palm leaves half a dozen Piaroans sat on low stools around a small altar covered in a collection of exotic feathers, skulls, rattles and other shamanic paraphernalia. Delighted with the coffee, fresh fish and small sack of marijuana we offered him, he invited us to join them.

For an hour or so joints were rolled and passed around before we were all given a small piece of root to chew that made our mouths go numb. A little later each of us was offered a small gourd of a bitter, ayahuasca tea that soon gave a gentle buzz. The shaman prepared the yopo concoction, grinding seeds in a ritualistic manner accompanied by chanting song. Aromatic smoke filled the space. I was excited. Previous experiences with magic mushrooms and peyote had been positive and enlightening. One by one the shaman invited us forward. Through eyes like minute galaxies he looked into our souls as he held out a small shell containing a tablespoonful of an emerald-coloured crystalline substance and an ornate double-nostril snuff bone. The mound of caustic green powder went up my nose.

'Oh fuck!' I said two seconds later.

My eyes glazed over, I began salivating as profusely as a rabid dog and collapsed onto the floor.

Overwhelming visual hallucinations started immediately, so intense I couldn't tell if my eyes were open or closed. For the next ten hours I went on an ineffable journey more terrifying, powerful and revelatory than I can ever hope to describe.

I was in and out of consciousness, hyperventilating and vomiting. But the acute emotion of despair, of being confined to hell for eternity, was far worse. I completely lost control of myself in every way. Trapped in a nightmare, it was like a Hollywood depiction of an exorcism, or a violent epileptic fit accompanied by my blood-curdling screams.

'This is awful, this is fucking awful. No, no, no, NO!!!' I bellowed at the top of my lungs in panic.

I honestly felt I was dying. It was the worst trip ever.

Finally, after what literally seemed like eternity, I reached a state of serene euphoria. Amidst the delusions of grandeur and divine communication there were moments of supreme clarity. Like the facades of perceived reality had been stripped back, I could see the atomic structure of the universe, feel my connection to its vibrations and knew my place within it.

Certain thoughts rang clear as crystal in my mind like a revelation and remained there beyond the ceremony. One was to write a book. Another – to have children.

No doubt these were things that had been deep in the back of my mind.

I knew Jess had always wanted a family. I however did not. Unwilling to concede the lifestyle compromise that dependants would inevitably bring, I was happy with my high-risk life of extreme adventure the way it was, without the unending responsibility of fatherhood. Or so I thought.

Jess was entering her mid-thirties. We had been together for a decade and happily married for six years. I knew she wanted to try to start a family soon. Up until that point I was adamant I didn't want kids.

But the thought resonated with such intense clarity and lingered in the forefront of my mind for months. The same voice in my head that had told me to marry Jess was back with a new message.

'*Have children.*'

When I came round with the dawn I felt weak, humiliated and like I'd taken a severe beating.

'Whatever happens, DON'T MOVE. It's all in your mind,' Yupi had prophetically warned before the ceremony.

I had broken this sacrosanct rule. Battered and bruised, my bare feet were covered with deep friction burns from thrashing around on the hard earth floor like a man possessed. The wounds were quite severe. Not the ideal start to a month-long journey into the mud and infection-rife environment of the jungle.

Al and Dave, who had opted out of taking yopo, looked exhausted and traumatised. They had physically restrained me for half the night to stop me causing myself more serious injury.

The shaman asked to see me. I thought I'd blown it and that we would not be allowed to climb Autana. On the contrary, he was far warmer and more welcoming than previously. He poked and prodded me, examined my eyes and foot wounds, then laughed and slapped me on the back, smiling knowingly. Juan Pablo and the other Piaroans didn't seem at all fazed by my reaction; apparently it is not unusual. After the ceremony the Piaroa interacted with us in a totally different manner. Their suspicion was gone, they were friendly and tactile. It seemed we had passed our intense initiation into their system of beliefs and they gave us their full support for the duration of our time with them.

Of the five of us who partook in the ceremony, only I had reacted so violently. The others had abided by the golden rule not to move and undertaken their trips statically and silently. As we tried to find words to describe our journeys it became apparent that we had all experienced some similar visions and equally intense, terrifying emotions.

Though yopo was terrible, there was also a very positive element of self-purification, higher understanding, subliminal acceptance and profound euphoria. It remains one of the most profound and powerful experiences of my life and, traumatic as it was, I did not regret it.

Somewhat dishevelled after the night's revelations, we began the physical journey in a large dug-out canoe, known as a bongo and powered by a burly outboard motor, up the Rio Orinoco, Rio Siapo and Rio Autana towards the sacred peak. As darkness fell our Piaroan friends navigated the rivers' hairpins with skilful flashes of a torch and a photographic memory of the river.

Arriving in Cegurea, we hung our hammocks and mozzie nets in an open-walled thatched hut and passed out. We awoke to an idyllic scene. Joyful children played in the rapids of the river. Friendly faces tended allotments and fished. Curious teenagers giggled at the strangers in their home.

On the far bank of the river a thousand shades of green formed the dense jungle behind which a magnificent view of Cerro Autana's west face, framed by a celestial double rainbow, completed the delightful picture.

We savoured the tranquil calm, correctly suspecting that as soon as we entered the jungle our surroundings would become considerably more hostile.

To begin with the jungle was benign. A good path led through allotments, across log bridges and sandy clearings with relative ease. But soon enough the burden of our excessive packs combined with the ever-intensifying heat of the sun, suffocating humidity and onslaught of flies, mosquitos, ants and cockroaches began their insidious offensive.

Within a couple of hours the gringos were suffering badly. As the day wore on the clouds consolidated and the downpour began, quickly creating a quagmire.

The jungle grew ever more dense, the trail less obvious. Machete marks in trees and the cut stumps of saplings marked the way but also created lethal punji sticks lining the slippery path. Jason fell, spearing his skin-tight T-shirt, missing his arm by millimetres.

This was my first jungle expedition. I have been on many since and found the cliché horrors of the jungle to be overstated. Rainforests can actually be very pleasant environments.

But not that one. It was everything we had feared and worse, living up to and beyond every cliché. For the second time in days

I felt I was in hell! Imagine a high-intensity workout in a steam room. Throw in a plague of Scottish summer midges, the mud from a wet Glastonbury and the dehydration of a bad hangover and you begin to get the picture.

Our one saving grace was that the plethora of menaces tended to take turns in their assault. The unbearable sweating would subside after a pause but within minutes the clouds of sweat bees would spur us forward. The rain would replace the stifling heat of the sun with a soaking and slippery trail.

After a day of brutal hiking we reached our equipment, exhausted. A million termites had colonised our stash and already turned some unimportant gear to dust. Thankfully they had not yet devoured the ropes or harnesses. Most of the villagers immediately set off back to Ceguera whilst we set up our hammocks with built-in mozzie nets amidst a growing storm of biting flies. Retreating into our cocoons, spirits dropped as profuse sweating continued. The only way to cool down was to calm down, slow one's breathing and try not move.

Dawn offered a brief respite before the sun and bugs returned. Beneath the thick canopy of the rainforest the great monolith of Autana was completely hidden.

We planned to recce the approach to the wall. However, no sooner had we decided this than it seemed the whole village turned up to help carry loads. They told us we were only an hour from the wall and they were keen to hustle as they must return home that night and would not be coming tomorrow.

Keen to utilise their support, we soon discovered the Piaroa are not good porters.

Usually when they venture into the jungle they are either hunting or gathering on day trips. They travel light carrying little more than a machete in one hand and a plastic bag of their food staple *manioco* in the other. When they find what they want they skilfully construct an ultra-light back-basket out of leaves called a *warashi* and transport loads of less than 10 kgs. They simply chuckled out our giant haul bags and grabbed a load as they saw fit.

A boy not older than eight carried a handful of carabiners, a pregnant teenager a rope, the young men day-pack-sized loads at most. Only a toothless grandma carried a decent load of two long fixing ropes. Our huge pile of kit was split into countless disorganised loads.

A ripped guy with a big grin called Alfonso took the lead, relishing the challenge of opening a trail with his Samurai machete skills. Behind him followed an unlikely procession of sweaty gringos carrying oversized bags and chattering Piaroans with tiny baskets of gear. Whenever the terrain got steep or technical they would remove their shoes, opting instead for the support and grip of woollen socks or bare feet.

Eventually the terrain started to become significantly steeper. Through a gap in the trees we caught our first glimpse of the wall to double disappointment. First we were at the wrong end of the long mountain, miles from where we wanted to make base camp. Second, the east face we had come to climb looked small, loose and unbelievably overgrown. Had we come so far and suffered so much for that? Suddenly the Piaroa decided it was home time. They chirpily downed bags wherever they were and departed. Disheartened we retreated to camp to regroup. Throughout the toil of the day we had made significant negative progress. Our gear was now strewn all over the jungle, we were probably only halfway to a suitable base camp, had lost the bulk of our porter power and our objective looked unappealing.

Yupi, the seasoned Tepuyero, lightened the mood.

'Only the second day and we have already seen the wall! In the jungle this is good!'

Over the next four days, with the help of a select group of Piaroa, we continued the trail to the far end of the peak. Alfonso and his friend took turns to sharpen their machetes and cut a path through what at times looked completely impenetrable jungle, constantly going up and down through small valleys. Every tree and plant seemed to be covered with vicious spikes. Progress was measured in days per mile as opposed to miles per day.

We retrieved and transported all our gear and established base camp in the correct spot. From directly below, the wall looked far more impressive. It was heavily vegetated at the top and bottom but the middle thousand feet was clean, featured and outrageously overhanging. A clear line stood out that would take us directly though the steepest part of the cliff via the face of the Shaman created by the multiple entrances to the spectacular Autana Cave at half height.

Base camp was situated by a trickle of running water in a slight clearing in the dense trees on a steep, muddy slope. With nowhere to pitch a tent, it was a sprawling collection of hammocks strung underneath tarps, with a communal area under a large sheet of plastic, a gear room and a studio for all the film kit.

Our unlikely habitation benefited from exquisite views but soon turned into a ghetto with the daily afternoon downpours. A tarantula the size of a hand paid us a visit, Yupi discovered a scorpion in his hammock and Alejo had to have a live earwig removed from his ear. Dave had more mosquito bites than I've ever seen and Stanley squeezed a live botfly larva from a boil on his cheek.

Conditions could hardly be described as comfortable but with DEET and determination we all relished the harsh delight of life in the jungle. Proper Indiana Jones-style adventure!

Transpiration from the forest pumped clouds into the air and flooded the atmosphere. Rainbows and waterfalls would appear and vanish at random. At night fluorescent frogs illuminated the dark with their song and iridescent hummingbirds would hover by our hammocks in the morning.

Finding a way from camp to the start of the wall was the scene of my fer-de-lance encounter and a route-finding triumph. A snakes-and-ladders course up vines and roots, across terraces, through trees and death-defying boulder problems wound a way up near-vertical jungle for a thousand feet, requiring only a couple of short sections of rope. Ferrying all the loads, particularly in the wet, was hazardous but exciting.

The first pitch of the wall was overgrown beyond belief. Yupi took the lead, demonstrating expertly the arduous, dirty work of *tepui* climbing. A waterfall growing next to us was the only indication it was raining as the wall above was so overhung. I led another filthy pitch literally digging my way upwards. Then the wall became remarkably clean. The extremely compact quartzite sandstone proved excellent for climbing. Cracks and crimps, corners and chimneys led with unexpected ease up the leaning wall.

The greatest challenge was the plethora of creepy crawlies who made their homes in the cracks and crevices of the wall, the same features we climbed.

'Argh! I just uncovered a scorpions' nest! There's hundreds of them. Tiny see-through things. Are these the ones that make you puke blood?' Stanley yelled down in alarm after dislodging a microwave-sized block.

'I think so!' I replied, feeling guilty at the hint of amusement in my tone.

It was intimidating to lead, reaching blindly above our heads, unsure if there might be a venomous snake or scorpion in the hold. We encountered birds, bees' nests, more scorpions, centipedes, and dozens of spiders of all shapes and sizes. I almost took a big fall when a bat I had disturbed flew into my face and became briefly entangled in the gear I carried.

After six pitches we reached the astounding Autana Cave. A marvellous cavern of deep-red stone, cathedral in scale, the walls covered in a thin veneer of quartz crystal that sparkled when the sun hit at the right angle. One passage penetrated all the way through the *tepui*. Inside it was completely sheltered from the daily torrential downpours, it was pleasantly cool, there was a gentle breeze and there were no bugs. There was even a freshwater spring!

The view across hundreds of miles of uninhabited jungle to the east, little changed from the pre-Cambrian age, was breathtaking. It was hard to believe that wonderful campsite was halfway up a giant cliff. It was the perfect antithesis to our woeful base camp in the jungle directly below. We based ourselves in the cave for the remainder of the climb.

Alberto, our smiling guide, was desperately keen to join us in the cave. Yupi undertook a crash course in jumaring and patiently helped Alberto become the first Piaroa in history to climb inside their sacred cave. His smile grew to epic proportions for the days he spent in the magical labyrinth.

Above the cave the wall became so impending it was almost horizontal. A subtle line of hanging walls, grooves and chimneys led diagonally through hundreds of feet of the most overhanging terrain with surprisingly vertical climbing. I led a scary, wandering pitch through steep blocky terrain we dubbed 'the Blocky Horror Show'. Stanley took the flying bottomless chimney, displaying fine technique of high-end back and footing.

Another hard pitch brought us to within 50 feet of the end of the wall. Unfortunately, a 20-foot horizontal roof put an end to our free-climbing aspirations. The compact blank ceiling looked like it would require a bolt to be drilled and force us to break our self-imposed ethical code to not tamper with the sacred stone.

Stanley was about to start hammering the hand drill when he noticed a pair of tiny holes in the roof right where a bolt would be required. He took a piece of 4 mm cord and pushed it into the wormhole. To his great joy it popped out the other hole, creating a perfect thread and enabling him to reach a cam placement and overcome the final obstacle without having to place a bolt. A welcome consolation prize after the disappointment of having to use three points of aid on the last few feet of our route.

Stepping onto the tiny ledge on the lip of the giant roof Stanley dislodged a huge block that plummeted into our forest base camp directly below. Thankfully nobody was harmed, though one of our hammocks was damaged by the fallout.

The fixed line down to the cave now hung hundreds of feet out in space. Like spiders on a thread of silk we dangled high above the forest in a most abstract position. It was the most overhang cliff I've ever seen.

From the lip of the wall, 500 feet of extremely steep vegetation stood between us and the rarely visited summit. No longer sheltered,

I bore the full brunt of the afternoon thunderstorm as I forced a path up the vertical forest. I simply threw myself into the comically dense thicket to break trail. Intimidating vertical steps were negotiated by standing on Stanley's shoulders, arborist gymnastics and brute force. After several hours we emerged from the undergrowth onto the somewhat anticlimactic summit before we retreated hastily down our ropes through space for one final night in the amazing cave.

We descended back into the perilous toils of the forest heavily laden with reams of gear, a growing collection of infected cuts and bruises and another bank of unforgettable experiences from our journey into the lost world.

The Autana expedition almost seemed to mirror the yopo ceremony. We went through hell and suffered extreme physical and psychological duress in the darkness of the jungle at the beginning, but perseverance led to a place of heavenly serenity, sublime beauty and a higher perspective as we climbed. Both ordeals brought their own form of enlightenment. The wounds would heal, the bites and scars fade, but the doors of perception would remain a little more ajar. The lessons learned, friendships forged and magical memories would last a lifetime.

I thought of José, of my accident, of Jess, of future expeditions – but most of all I contemplated fatherhood with no small amount of anxiety.

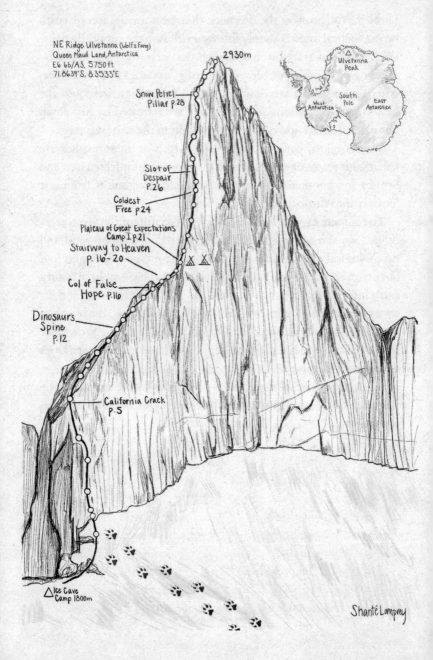

NE Ridge Ulvetanna (Wolf's Fang)
Queen Maud Land, Antarctica
E6 6b/A3, 5750 ft.
71.8639°S, 8.3533°E

2930m

Snow Petrel
Pillar p.28

Slot of
Despair
P.26

Coldest
Free p.24

Plateau of Great Expectations
Camp I p.21
Stairway to Heaven
P. 16-20

Col of False
Hope P.16

Dinosaur's
Spine
P.12

California Crack
P.5

△ Ice Cave
Camp 1800m

Ulvetanna
Peak

West
Antarctica

South
Pole

East
Antarctica

Shanté Lamprey

18

The Last Great Climb

'I may say that this is the greatest factor – the way in which the expedition is equipped – the way in which every difficulty is fore-seen, and precautions taken for meeting or avoiding it. Victory awaits him who has everything in order – luck, people call it. Defeat is certain for him who has neglected to take the necessary precautions in time; this is called bad luck.'

Roald Amundsen

The third and final expedition in the trilogy was something I had been quietly working towards my entire adult life. It had begun when Rolf gave me Ivar Erik Tollefsen's book *Queen Maud Land Antarctica* in Norway when I was eighteen. Throughout my Yosemite years I had acquired the skills and formed the vital partnerships. Lucrative TV and movie work had shown me a model that might fund a trip that cost double what I paid for my first house. Asgard and Autana had cemented the relationships and given me the project management and leadership experience necessary to tackle the epic scale of the challenge. We started in the Arctic, went through the Amazon and later that very same year we embarked on another trip of a lifetime: to Antarctica to climb the unequalled Ulvetanna. We saved the best for what would tragically prove to be our last. The Autana crew, plus sturdy Chris from Asgard, who would again prove his worth, departed for the far south in December 2012. Two weeks before, Jess had found out she was pregnant.

It weighed on my mind so heavily that it wasn't until we reached the conclusion of the expedition that I could bring myself to even tell my closest friends.

Ulvetanna is the jewel in the crown of the Fenriskjeften range that lies in Queen Maud Land, eastern Antarctica. Ulvetanna translates from Norwegian as 'the fang' in the Fenriskjeften – 'the jaw of Fenris', a wolf from Norse mythology so fierce the gods feared it could destroy the world.

The prodigious granite spires emerge from an endless white desert, just like the jaw of a gargantuan beast, to create a landscape from the realms of fantasy. It does not look like Earth.

Such is the remoteness and obscurity of these peaks, whose perfect form and ferocity rival those of Patagonia, the Himalayas or anywhere, that they were not even discovered by the wider world until Ivar Erik Tollefsen's remarkable 1994 expedition and his book that put Queen Maud Land on the climbers' map.

With Robert Caspersen and Sjur Nesheim, Tollefsen made the first ascent of Ulvetanna, widely regarded as the hardest summit to reach on the harshest continent. They returned in 2008 to climb the difficult north face. Only two other teams had ever set foot on the top, including my uber-strong friends the Huber brothers.

The reason so few had climbed Ulvetanna was not only the extreme difficulty of the peak but that just reaching the foot of the mountains in Queen Maud Land was prohibitively expensive. The only way to get there was to share logistics with the limited government and scientific establishments that operate in eastern Antarctica at grotesque cost. The flight alone, in a charismatic Soviet-era cargo plane from Cape Town, South Africa, to the Russian logistics hub and science base of Novolazarevskaya, cost £15,000 per person and the total expedition budget was ten times that.

After fifteen years of building goodwill and trust, following the remarkable success of Al's film *The Asgard Project* and the marketing value the brand had leveraged from our expeditions, I had finally managed to convince Berghaus to foot the lion's share of the bill.

I researched the area extensively and realised that the longest and most spectacular line on Ulvetanna remained unclimbed – the mile-long dinosaur's spine and massive vertical headwall of the northeast ridge. You do not need to be a climber to appreciate the line, as aesthetically perfect and compelling to climb as the Nose of El Capitan or any other route on any wall or mountain. Certainly, one of Earth's last great climbs.

Once again I single-handedly organised every detail of the expedition. The arduous government permits, amassing and packing the ton of highly select gear and supplies into a huge wooden crate and arranging for it to be sea- and air-freighted to Novo. Dealing with six-figure payments to sketchy Russian companies; the design details and colour combinations of the Berghaus kit we would each be wearing. What tents, sleeping set-up, boots, skis and climbing gear we would need, right down to the Christmas crackers and crate of champagne we would bring to celebrate the festivities in base camp.

The art of expedition leadership is to ensure that precisely what is needed – be it an obscure piece of climbing gear, a spare battery for a camera or a pole for a tent – is in the hands of who needs it at the exact time and place it is required. It is far more complex and challenging to successfully achieve than it may sound. Amundsen was a master.

Unbelievably it was the same cowboy pilot who had dropped us into Mount Asgard in the same iconic DC3 that flew us the 100 miles from Novo to the Fenriskjeften! The Canadian airline he worked for specialised in polar aviation, in the Arctic north for one summer, followed immediately by an austral one in the Antarctic south.

'You guys again! This is gonna be fun.' Rob grinned, slapping me on the back when we saw each other for the first time since I'd bailed out of his plane in Baffin.

The two massive engines of his beautiful plane roared, blasting six lonely souls and our small mountain of kit with the wash from its propellers and we were left alone on the ice, staring at the most impressive and intimidating peak I'd ever seen. To my pleasant surprise, under a clear blue sky without a breath of wind it was calm and warm enough for Jas to roll and smoke without gloves. 'I've just had an amazing thought: I've never been this far away from a policeman!' he said with glee.

It came as a shock when the very next day during our routine daily comms check, status report and weather update I was told, 'There is coming typhoon. Will be eighty-two knots of the wind. Be ready,' by the stoic, monotone Russian chap on the other end of the satellite phone.

That is almost 100 mph, a category 2 hurricane combined with cold temperatures that can create a windchill feel of -60°C and we were not ready! We were camped in the open, 3,000 miles from the closest hospital in Cape Town on a different continent and none of us had any polar survival experience. We set to work creating storm defences of which a Roman legion would've been proud, Chris Rabone putting his skills as a landscape gardener to good use building formidable snow walls. We double-poled all the tents, tied ropes between them in preparation for the blizzard and braced for impact. Thankfully the swirling tempest powering across the South Indian Ocean changed course slightly before making landfall so we were spared its full brunt. Though we only experienced wind of 40 knots, three days of white-out in temperatures of -27°C served as a very effective shot across the bow.

Even in the relative safety of base camp we had been genuinely scared of the storm. Just existing and taking care of ourselves in that extreme environment was a battle. Frostbite was an ever-present threat, as was acute sunburn from the ferociously intense solar radiation, less filtered by the thin ozone layer above the Antarctic. Simple tasks like making a cup of tea or going to the toilet were serious challenges that carried considerable risk. And that was on the ground! Looking at the mile-long northeast ridge, the longest rock climb I'd ever seen, and the impending headwall, I shuddered to think how hard life would be up there and how gnarly it could get if another storm came. Big-wall climbing is a struggle in the dreamy conditions of California. But an unclimbed route of that scale? Out there in the last great wilderness, with the massive added burden of being committed to producing a high-quality film, the promise of which had financed the trip? I simply couldn't see how we were going to succeed. The task ahead was so herculean and hazardous. I felt a burgeoning weight of responsibility towards my friends but refrained from sharing my doubt and concerns with them too openly. Jess's pregnancy lingered almost as daunting as Ulvetanna in the back of my mind.

Though just 2,000 metres above sea level, the thinner atmosphere at such an extreme latitude made it feel more like 4,000 metres. We all suffered more than anticipated. Headaches, lack of appetite, gasping for breath in the night – classic acclimatisation afflictions plagued our first week.

We had to move half a ton of kit 3 miles by ski and sledge then up the 1,000-foot snow slope to the start of the wall. In bad conditions that journey would be perilous, so we established a sturdy advance base camp complete with a hurricane-proof snow cave carved deep into ice beside a double-decker-bus-sized boulder right at the foot of the wall.

The conflicting goals of climbing the mountain and documenting the ascent were pronounced. If we spent too much time and energy on the film we would not reach the top, but if we focused only on climbing we would not have a film. Al is as fast as anybody I've worked with but it takes time to achieve a high standard of cinematography. Our heavyweight, cautious approach and ambitious filming aspirations meant we didn't start climbing until day twelve.

'I feel heavy, weak and tired. Let's do this!' I said to Jas, starting up the very first pitch. I was feeling the strain of leadership. Our cause felt almost hopeless.

But the conditions were incredible and the rock quality on the northeast ridge much better than we had expected, having heard tales of horribly rotten granite on other lines. After the typhoon we enjoyed twenty consecutive days of stable high pressure and no wind.

Stanley led a dreamy and difficult 200-foot-long overhanging pitch we called 'California Crack'. To our amazement we were able to free climb in rock boots without gloves though had to constantly battle frozen fingers. Slowly we progressed up the initial steep, 1,000-foot buttress to reach the lower-angled terrain of the ridge, fixing rope as we went and descending to the snow cave camp when we were too tired to continue. The twenty-four-hour daylight wreaked havoc with our body clocks but enabled long sessions on the wall between sleeps.

From the Col of False Hope we faced a serious logistical challenge. It would be nigh on impossible to move the vast quantity of gear and supplies we needed for the headwall up the long, low-angle, diagonal route we had climbed and fixed. Stanley, Jas and I decided to pull up all the rope and refix directly down the 1,800-foot north face from the col. No small task, completed in a tiring twenty-six-hour camp-to-camp mission.

Above the col, I felt truly privileged to be the first human in history to set foot on the utterly remarkable Stairway to Heaven.

I led four rope lengths up the wildly exposed knife-edge ridge, no more than an arm's span wide, like the spine of a dinosaur with vertiginous drops of nearly 2,000 feet on both sides. It was the most unique and unusual piece of rock architecture I have ever seen. If Ulvetanna were in the Alps or US, it would be as famous as the Matterhorn or El Capitan, I thought.

The climbing wasn't too hard but there was absolutely no protection. I ran out the full length of the rope between hand-placed bolt belays. It got gradually steeper and trickier towards the end.

'Don't fall now or you'll die!' I said to myself whilst reclimbing the whole feature with Al above to film a few days later.

The Stairway to Heaven terminated on a flat terrace the size of a golf green – the Plateau of Great Expectations. Above, the nature of the face changed to true big-wall territory. The vertical headwall soared skyward for another 1,000 feet before a massive horizontal roof, which would have to be negotiated, obscured the view of what lay beyond.

Regrouped in base camp we welcomed in 2013 with a well-stocked party. Just like on Asgard, I decided ground-support Chris with his strength and positive motivation should be requisitioned to the wall team, meaning just like on Autana poor Dave would be left alone on the ground in the wilderness for up to two weeks.

Now we felt ready. Acclimatised to the alien environment, feeling fit and rested, we were practically, physically and psychologically prepared.

In two herculean, thirty-hour efforts we hauled our 300 kgs of bags with supplies for five men for two weeks up the north face to the col, then repeatedly jumared the many loads along up the Stairway to Heaven to the Plateau of Great Expectations. We pulled up all the rope on our way, severing our retreat route to the ground, casting off from terra firma and committing to the wall. We hung our two port-a-ledges and this time Chris gallantly offered to bivi in a coffin-like feature in the rock.

The headwall delivered the goods for which we'd travelled so far. Steep corners and splitter cracks of world class enticed us upwards with a lot of effort but without the need for hammer on piton, save for two bolts on the initial blank slab just above wall camp.

I climbed a hard pitch (E6 6b), the twentieth of the route, at the very lower limit of free-climbable temperatures using handwarmers in my chalk bag to stave off numb fingers.

We had unexpectedly managed to free climb the whole route thus far, but just as the idea of a completely free ascent began to smoulder it was promptly extinguished when the stable weather suddenly collapsed and we were hit by another storm. Temperatures plummeted to -30°C and a gale ripped up and across the face. We occupied ourselves playing cards and drinking whisky, confined to our port-a-ledges for three days through the worst of the weather. We emerged to a very different scene. It didn't look like it would possible to descend the Stairway to Heaven, which was plastered with fresh snow. The atmosphere had become much more malign.

The wolf snarled and showed her teeth.

But with no sign of good weather in the Russian forecasts we reluctantly resorted to full-on aid climbing in alpine boots, big gloves and full winter gear, up terrain that would certainly have been free climbable were it warmer.

In brutal conditions, using a combination of aid and free shenanigans, with much loud cursing, Stanley led the Slot of Despair, a desperate flared offwidth chimney that led through the giant roof. For the first time we caught a shadowed glimpse of success, but the weather was against us.

Armoured in Gore-Tex and down, armed with rack and rope, I continued the upward crusade. Progress was slow, yet consistent. A battled-hardened team, we knew our only chance of success was to push the rope two pitches higher every day, come what may.

It started snowing as Jas and I reached Chris and Stanley's high point. The crumbly, parallel offwidths continued for another full rope length up the endless wall. It was scary and awkward to climb in full winter gear but was worse for Jas, who hung motionless and exposed for hours.

We reached a big ledge perched directly on the ridge where the pretty white snow petrels nested, the only other living things we saw for the duration of the expedition. The blizzard intensified; in the shade, in the wind, the anemometer read -27°C and dropping. Jas was really suffering. I massaged his feet back to sensation, ignoring the trace of fear in his brow and my own urge to run away.

'We really need to bag another pitch, but let's not exhaust ourselves, mate,' I encouraged him.

'Just let me know when you've had enough,' replied Jas with a wink. His manly tone wavered as he realised dropping the gauntlet in such a position might lead to frostbite.

'It's like that, is it? Right then, pass me the sharp ends, dickhead,' I said as I set off up another worrying pitch.

This dry humour, tolerance for suffering and banter even in the most harrowing situations is why Jas and I had become so close and done so much. He is dependable and will do anything he is asked. But if you don't ask, he won't do anything!

Waking each morning warm and comfortable in our down-filled nests, as fatigue cumulated and we were plagued by agonisingly painful hands, it became increasingly difficult to motivate ourselves to face the battle of the day.

I'm not sure we would've been able to continue were it not for Chris, who every morning would diligently prepare a large mug of rocket-fuel-strength espresso in his coffin then deliver it along with a double dose of ibuprofen to each of us in bed. Fifteen minutes later, pain would subside and sudden bowel movements would force us to hurriedly dress, gear up and get out of the hanging tent to take a dump.

Jess was constantly on my mind and slowly, amidst the battle of the wall, I was beginning to get my head around becoming a dad. Perhaps it would be fun to one day share some of the wonderful places and extraordinary adventures I had discovered with my own child, I thought. Maybe family expeditions would offer an alternative path to satisfaction to that of these increasingly extreme ones, and would certainly carry far less chance of death.

It felt like we were close to the top, but time was running out. On another brutally cold and windy day all five of us jumared half a mile up to our high point. As Stanley and I took turns to lead we teetered on the brink of throwing in the towel and retreating to camp. It was -35°C and gusting to 30 knots. Warm pee instantly turned to yellow crystals of ice on hitting the rock. Beards and eyelashes were caked with frost. A blister of frost nip developed on the end of my nose.

Upper lips frozen stiff, chins held high but buried deep in layers of hood and scarf, the climb had become the sternest test of determination. Just as we were about to accept defeat, I pulled over a vertical step and stumbled across a magical flat spot protected on all sides from the onslaught of wind. The others joined me and we paused for hot drinks and food, savouring the salvation of shelter.

Jas even managed to roll and smoke! The unmistakable summit was just a rope length higher.

The decades of dreaming, years of scheming, months of planning and weeks of prolonged, desperate struggle had paid off. Balanced on the tiny summit pinnacle no larger than a coffee table, all five us howled with joy like the Fenris wolf itself. Our triumphant outburst was greeted by a momentary break in the cloud and we bathed in golden light.

'We made it!' I said triumphantly. 'Didn't seem like a summit day, but we're here. It's pretty brutal, we're a long way from home, man, but we're on the top! We did it, guys, this is what we came for. Well done, everybody! That was hardcore."

Al was fighting with desperately frozen fingers to capture that ephemeral moment on camera. Dave could actually see us from his position so far below on the ground with his big lens.

Just before we began the massive and complex descent from that most remote summit I decided it was time to share my other news.

'What an adventure, got to be the biggest yet, eh?' I said to Jas on camera. 'And guess what – I'm going to be a dad! Oh my god, Jess is pregnant! Oh my god! Summer baby! Arghhhh, the next adventure!'

'Holy shit, Springer, now you've really gone and done it!'

We made the long, complex and gruelling descent from Ulvetanna without incident, packed up every trace of our presence in Antarctica, save for our rappel anchors and a few patches of yellow snow, and left for home.

Six months after I'd reached the elusive summit of Ulvetanna, Jess gave birth to Freya. Our daughter spent the first night of her life sleeping on my bare chest and my reservations about becoming a dad melted along with my heart. Overnight I discovered a new, deeper emotional level to existence. Jess, and my yopo revelation, were right.

★

A little over a year after we stood together atop the last great climb, Stanley was dead. He crashed his wingsuit whilst proximity flying in Zion National Park in Utah. His wife, Meika, was seven months pregnant. I have not BASE jumped since. Dean Potter also died wingsuit proximity flying in Yosemite a year after Stanley.

Stanley and I had shared so much together over many years. From the carefree days of youth, dirtbagging in the valley, through these wild expeditions, and along with Jas, whose wife was also pregnant, were on the cusp of entering the next phase of maturity: fatherhood, a prospect that had filled us with more fear than excitement but that we expected to share.

I had envisaged sitting outside Stanley's trailer in Yosemite for decades to come, drinking strong coffee in the morning and cold beer at night. Watching our kids play together and introducing them to our incredible games in that awesome playground. Perhaps they too would become solid partners? I imagined we would sit there still when we were all too old and worn out to run any more laps up the Nose or flights from Half Dome, content to reminisce about the epic times we had shared. But it was not to be. Part of my life died with Stanley, my connection to California and those Yosemite years was severed.

He died pushing it. He was flying a difficult and dangerous line very close to the ground. He was alone, nobody even knew where he was, and his body was not recovered for a week. He was charging hard on one last rampage before planning to tone it down and embrace fatherhood.

The last time I spoke to Stan, a few weeks before he died, it had been to reassure him that the deep emotional reality of becoming a dad offsets the countless compromises a thousand times over. I recognised the same sense of panic in Stanley's voice in that last conversation that I had felt on Ulvetanna, but I was confident that his heart would change as mine had as soon as he met his child. But he never did. Just a month after Stanley's death, his son, Finn, was born.

Stanley's untimely death affected me deeply. Everything I had thus far believed and lived by was now thrown into question.

Living life to the full, not being afraid to die in order to fully live and all the other extreme sport clichés had been the backbone of my life philosophy. 'Dangerous fun,' Stanley had called it. Of course, if you play with fire you will get burnt. Stanley wasn't the first friend I'd lost in the mountains, but when José, Duane and the others died I wasn't holding my adorable six-month-old baby in my arms and their wives weren't heavily pregnant.

I was already in turmoil trying to reconcile my passion and profession that entailed long absences and high levels of risk with the responsibility of parenthood. Losing Stanley almost pushed me over the edge. For a few months following his accident I struggled to come to terms with my predicament. Was there no way to balance risk and responsibility, ambitious adventure and domestic stability? To be a good dad and continue the life I loved?

I began to question whether I could ever justify going on another serious trip. Perhaps it was time to hang up my harness, settle down and get a real job?

Then a freak coincidence reminded me that we are less in control of our destiny than I had come to think. That though we can limit and manage our exposure to risk, it is inherent in life and we cannot eliminate it. By accepting this and playing a little more cautiously, perhaps there was a way of continuing to lead a full and fearless life as well as being a devoted family man?

Soon after Stanley's death I landed a great TV job for Discovery Channel. One of the shoots was to take place in the jungles of Borneo. Production sent through the schedule and flight options. I would be travelling on 17 July 2014 from Manchester to Mulu via Amsterdam and Kuala Lumpur. In the schedule I had four days to climb and film a new route up an unclimbed 300-metre limestone cliff in a remote rainforest gorge. I knew this wouldn't be enough time so suggested I travel out early to prepare off-camera and unpaid. Production agreed. Whilst I was safely high on the wall in the Malaysian jungle, Russian separatists shot down my original Amsterdam to Kuala Lumpur flight over eastern Ukraine. A seat on the doomed Malaysian Airways flight MH-17 quite literally had my name on it. My last-minute change of plan was the only reason I had not perished with 298 other innocent souls.

For all my questioning of high-risk escapades in pursuit of fun I had overlooked the proverbial 'might get run over by a bus tomorrow' that had once been my mantra. The simple act of changing a flight had saved my life and given me the chance to watch my daughter grow up.

I had been on the verge of turning my back on the life of adventure I adored, something that may well have kindled bitterness and resentment, but this close call totally reset my perspective. I found this random near-disaster strangely comforting and it reignited my drive, which had been all but quelled when Stanley died.

I would like to instil my own values and beliefs in my children, to inspire them to reach their furthest potential. To be brave and believe they can do anything they set their hearts and minds to. Surely a good parent must lead by example? Is it not hypocritical to preach about aiming high and working hard to achieve goals, only to abandon our own ambitions for the sake of theirs?

I wanted to be there for Freya and Jackson but I also wanted to show them what dreaming big and going all in to make those dreams come true really means. Or perhaps I am just too selfish to stop doing what I love.

I organised another major expedition to climb a new route on an Arctic face even bigger, steeper and more obscure than Mount Asgard called the Mirror Wall in northeast Greenland. This time I led a new crew of young guns who, although talented and strong, lacked any experience of such a serious expedition. We spent fifteen days living on that huge, hard wall and though we shared a great sense of solidarity, I was acutely aware, more than before and I dare say more than the others, that the consequences of our actions could affect many lives and most of the critical, potentially life-threatening decisions fell to me alone.

Although on an expedition life is day-to-day and most concerns are immediate, again and again I found my thoughts reaching beyond the crevasse field or blank wall, back to the rolling hills of my home in the Lake District, to Jess and Freya, who turned two whilst I was absent, and for decades into the future. I had spent months in the domestic comfort of home planning the trip, lusting for the excitement and risk of expeditionary adventure, only to find myself out there, up an on epic wall surrounded by danger, pining for my family and the simple, safe life I'd left behind.

I thought too about the mothers, fathers and loved ones of my companions, people whom I had never met and perhaps did not realise that their lives too may be altered for ever by the small but significant decisions I had to make at every turn that carried mortal consequence. Perhaps these deeper reflections were simply a sign of growing older, and wiser, I hope? The innocent naivety of youth replaced with a more empathetic, parental view of risk and responsibility? We had a couple of the usual close calls that are what make expeditions so memorable but thankfully completed our mission safely and successfully and made another first-class film. Within weeks at home, again my mind began to wander to ever greater adventure.

Inspired by Mallory, captivated by Antarctica and reinvigorated by surviving MH-17, it was time to dare my own wildest dream.

19

My Wildest Dream – Spectre Exped

Spectre (noun) – something widely feared as a possible unpleasant or dangerous occurrence.

My skis grated across the blue ice. Flying a kite the size of a paraglider, in 20-mph winds, I hardly noticed the load of my 200-kg sledge.

Jean, Mark and I raced across the white stripes of hundreds of snow-filled crevasses down a 100-mile glacier, so massive it could only be in Antarctica.

Then I saw it. Over a col, between two snow-covered peaks – my first glimpse of the Spectre. A summit so remote and hard to reach it had almost become fantasy. Standing proud over all the other mountains, it looked just as impressive as Patagonia's Fitz Roy, the South Spur as prominent as the Nose of El Capitan. A giant, granite canine, its surface smooth, almost featureless, as shiny and unbroken as the enamel of a tooth.

Prodigiously vertical, far too steep to hold snow, one face of the buttress glowed a pale gold in the polar sun, full of allure. In contrast, the other face hid in the blackness of menacing shade, exposed to the battery of the tireless katabatic airflow from the deep-freeze of the Antarctic plateau.

We were 270 miles from the South Pole, where the cold of shadow makes it hard to breath, where the mountains are magnificent but murderous, and a climber without shelter could not survive deteriorating conditions on a bottomless scale.

I slowed down to marvel at this mythical mountain, so

inaccessible and impossible to see. Thinking of the steep chapters ahead, I took my concentration off the demanding tasks of controlling my kite, navigating and maintaining speed.

Whump. I catapulted violently backwards, my ski blades screeching and dragging uselessly across the ice like the skidding of tyres before the terrible smash of a car crash. My reduction in speed had caused a snow bridge to collapse under the load of my pulk and it had fallen down a crevasse into the belly of the glacier.

In the time warp of near-death milliseconds, no sooner had I realised my fate than the violence abruptly ended, and all was calm, still and silent save for the whistle of the wind. I was saved only by the overhand knot in my trace, the 25-foot rope attaching me to my pulk, wedging into the tight groove at the mouth of the crevasse.

'Well, slightly alarming but all's well that end's well. Pulk looks OK, I didn't lose any of my stuff and I'm not dead. Result!' I said to Jean, resorting to dark humour to cope with near-disaster and the constant threat of danger after he rescued me and my pulk.

Ulvetanna had been a wild adventure, but it had given birth to another idea that would make it seem tame. Almost immediately after that success my mind had wandered to an even more remote, committing and extreme expedition. Another turn of the dial.

Kite skiing has revolutionised modern polar travel. It enables long-distance travel at high speed with heavy loads. In optimum conditions the record for distance travelled in twenty-four hours is an astonishing 370 miles. My friend Ronny Finsås kited the classic route from the South Pole to the coast in just five days. It usually takes fifty in the other direction without kites.

Wouldn't it be cool to combine a long polar journey with a technical climbing objective? Something that had never been attempted. I thought so, and I knew just the place.

Ulvetanna happens to be just 100 miles, or an hour by plane, from the main logistics hub for the whole of eastern Antarctica, Novolazarevskaya. A well-managed base, where medical and rescue services are located and from where help or resupply could be requested.

The Spectre is on the other side of the continent, 1,500 miles away from Ulvetanna and 1,000 miles farther south, making it even more inhospitable. The closest human habitation is the US base at the South Pole, 300 miles away, and the closest logistics hub and source of support or rescue is the ALE (Antarctic Logistics & Expeditions) Union Glacier camp (UG) nearer to 1,000 miles away, beyond the range of any capable aircraft without refuel.

The Spectre Trans-Antarctic Expedition was the most ambitious, complex, difficult and expensive trip I had ever imagined, let alone undertaken, the culmination of everything I had learned in a life full of adventure. It would combine an unsupported, wind-assisted journey of over 1,000 miles across the interior of Antarctica, with climbing arguably the most remote technical summit on Earth, the Spectre in the Gothic Peaks, at the southern end of the Transantarctic Mountains.

Even some of my closest confidantes told me it was crazy and would be impossible, if not the journey, then just raising the finance – twice that of Ulvetanna.

But if it was easy, it wouldn't be hard, would it! No great feat ever was and I relish a challenge.

It took me five years to raise the funds, acquire the skills and find the partners. A lot of effort and a bit of luck just to make it to the start line. Generous contributions from Berghaus, the Mount Everest Foundation and the Wally Herbert Award were hard-won and supplemented by remortgaging my family home to cover the absurd cost. But this time I had another element to contend with. It broke my heart to leave Jess alone to care for Freya, now four, and Jackson, one, who had just taken his first few steps, to embark on a three-month expedition, my most ambitious and hardcore to date. But I could not let go of my desire for adventure.

It was no small task to find partners with the ability, skills and desire to attempt such a trip. Very few people are highly skilled in kite skiing, polar travel, big-wall climbing, alpinism, photography and film, and also have a career and family life that can support or withstand a three-month unpaid expedition. I had scoured the world to find the two best of men by my side.

Jean Burgun, thirty-seven, is the epitome of humble strength. He lives in the peaceful foothills of the southern French Alps with his wife and two young boys. A kind-spirited soul, he is quick to offer help in any situation, and his gentle, humorous demeanor conceals his hard core.

A member of the French youth alpine climbing team, where leading alpinists partner with promising youth climbers, he served his apprenticeship with winter ascents on the big north faces of the Alps as well as trips to Yosemite and Patagonia. He had been close to completing the notoriously difficult French Alpine-guide exam before a skiing accident left him with a broken back and a change of path. He worked as the custodian of a mountain hut half of the year, while the other half he works in rope access, specialising in complex, high-risk jobs such as replacing the lightning rod at the top of the rotten spire òf a thousand-year-old cathedral.

He discovered kite skiing in the relatively early days of the sport, logging over 1,200 days under wing, becoming part of a French crew at the vanguard of alpine snow-kiting, using kites to ascend classic alpine routes when the conditions are just right. It is utterly astounding to see him looping his kite up a 50-degree *couloir,* dodging rocks and in minutes reaching the top of a peak that would normally require an early start and a whole day.

Mark Sedon, forty-eight, is a mountain guide who lives with his wife in Wanaka, on New Zealand's South Island. An understated, low-key Kiwi with a very dry, dark sense of humour, Mark started out as a ski bum, then got into rock climbing and mountaineering, and is an accomplished sailor and surfer who spends a couple of weeks every year exclusively kite-surfing a secret spot in Peru. He is also a chief guide for New Zealand's biggest heli-ski operation and has spent a decade organising and leading expeditions all over the world, including twenty to the Himalayas, ten to Antarctica and the seven summits. It was in this role that he almost met his end in a terrible helicopter crash in 2014. There was nothing left of the machine, and the other passenger was killed, but somehow Mark survived and after several months in hospital returned to his former life, albeit with a damaged spine.

Mark and I met in Camp 4, Yosemite, on my first trip to the Valley in 1998. He was there ticking off El Cap classics as I was just discovering the wonderful world of big-wall free climbing.

Mark was actually a very late substitute on the Spectre trip. The original team member was dealt the terrible news that his father had been diagnosed with terminal cancer and given three to six months to live. That was in July, and we were due to depart in November. As it happened, when I got the call saying we were a member short I was in New Zealand, drinking a beer with Mark, who is also the director of the Wanaka adventure film festival I was attending.

He said casually, 'I can do all that. I'd love to come.'

Although I have spent many weeks over multiple winters kiting in Norway and completed a 1,000-mile, unsupported kite expedition across Greenland, I was by far the least experienced kiter on the Spectre crew.

On 20 November 2017, our ski-equipped Twin Otter aircraft had dropped us off precisely where we requested: 140 miles from the South Pole – the point of no return, the maximum range it could fly and get back to base without refuelling.

We brought 650 kgs of gear: sixty-five days' worth of food and fuel supplies; two sets of skis per man, three kites of different sizes for varying wind strengths, kite harnesses, ski helmets, down suits, crampons and more gloves than an outdoor store; three tents, three sleeping bags, three stoves, repair kit and medical supplies; three ropes and rack for alpine-style big-wall climbing; and as much weight in camera and tech equipment as climbing gear.

The flight took six hours across an endless ocean of wind-sculpted ice and snow. We disembarked the aircraft at an altitude of almost 10,000 feet, struck by the extreme cold: -37°C compounded by 15 mph of wind.

Struggling to release the frozen latch on the plane door, our veteran polar pilot said, 'Nothing's easy out here!'

We were to repeat this mantra almost hourly for the next two months.

Within minutes the plane was gone, and the magnitude of our isolation and scale of our undertaking dawned upon us. Had we immediately begun the journey back, the physical challenge would have been enormous, but the psychological strain of knowing we were going to continue hundreds of miles in the opposite direction, to climb a 2,500-foot big wall, before commencing our return required serious mental strength and massive faith in every ounce of the collective experience we had all spent our lives accumulating.

'Now we've gone and done it!' I joked through frozen lungs to my comrades.

Mark, the seasoned Kiwi mountain guide, said only, 'That looks like a storm on the horizon.'

Sure enough, a full-scale blizzard hit on the very first day of our two-month expedition, with four days of winds up to 50 mph and wind-chill temps close to -90°C.

'We're all laughing, but if the tent rips or the stoves break, we're gonna die!' said Mark with a wide-eyed chuckle.

'Warm in the tent, you said, light winds from the south? This is not what was in the brochure!' joked Jean. It was -22°C inside.

We anticipated our kite approach to the Spectre would take a week or less. In fact, delayed by the welcome storm, then strong wind, extreme cold and poor visibility, it took seventeen gruelling days to reach the mountain.

'In all my life, I never 'ad such a week. The kiting 'ere is so 'ard,' Jean said in his French accent after a particularly epic session. I could only shake my head and be thankful I was with such seasoned kiters as Jean and Mark, as I felt so far out of my depth.

'I wanted the most hardcore trip ever, and I got it!' I said to my GoPro.

We were less than a mile from the Spectre when my pulk disappeared into the crevasse, almost ending the expedition and perhaps my life. It was another near miss. Jess and the kids were constantly in the back of my mind but I tried to banish them from the front and focus all my attention on the dangerous tasks at hand. We retrieved the load from the slot, cached our kiting gear and supplies, and turned our attention to the mountain.

The only previous climbing in the Gothic Mountains was in 1980, the year I was born, during a science expedition led by the American geologist and professor Edmund Stump, travelling by snowmobile with the massive logistical support of the US government. Stump's field guide during the expedition was his brother, the renowned alpinist Mugs Stump (who by circle of fate was mentor to Conrad Anker). In the name of science the two brothers completed several very impressive climbs, including the first ascent of the Spectre, which they named, via its north face.

During my planning, I had tracked down Edmund, who had recently retired from work at Arizona State University in Phoenix. I visited and spent a memorable day talking with him and poring over his meticulous archive of slides, which included a whole box of route shots taken by Mugs and not opened since 1981.

'You know, it was one of the best times of my life out there with Mugs,' Ed reminisced. Mugs died in 1992 at age forty-two in a crevasse fall on Denali.

He recounted a line Mugs had said to him as they entered the cirque of the Spectre: 'Ed, welcome to the most beautiful place on Earth.'

Two days after my crevasse incident we set out to make the second ascent of the Spectre via an unintentional variation to the Stump Route. On entering the cirque I could see what Mugs meant – a natural cathedral encircled by Gothic spires, surrounded by the vastness of Antarctica. A place only a handful of people have ever witnessed. We felt privileged and alone.

Ed had described their ascent as fairly straightforward save for one memorable crack on which he had required help from the rope; he couldn't even understand how Mugs had done it.

Anticipating a fairly casual day, Jean, Mark and I decided to go super light, no stove or bivi gear, nor even our huge down jackets, as we expected to move quickly with few stops. We began in very cold weather: it was -20° but clear, sunny and windless. Front-pointing unroped up the 60- or 70-degree snow *couloir* to the col in thin gloves and light jackets, we entered shade for 200 feet.

'Oh my god! This is panic cold,' yelled Mark.

Such cold takes your breath away; almost as if you're being strangled. Your body begins to seize up, as if an evil witch is turning you to stone. Too cold to stop to change gloves and add layers, we pushed through the patch of shadow, emerging into the sun gasping for air.

Above the col we found an extremely complex face, much steeper than it looked from afar. Astoundingly blank granite slabs were crisscrossed by a maze of snowy ramps and interspersed with vertical steps up to 50 feet. The steps were occasionally split by snow-choked chimneys and offwidths but offered few gear-sized cracks, presenting many possible paths but no clear line.

Slowly we exhausted the options, crawling upwards, overcoming dry-tooling cruxes up to M7, all far in excess of the difficulties described by Ed. At one point we came across a piton and sling left by the Stumps. Clearly Mugs had been a master route-finder as well as one of the best alpinists of his generation and had chosen a better line through the maze than we had.

'The problem is we're just not seventies men!' I joked.

'They were 'ard as fuck!' Jean said.

I led one pitch protected by a single fist-sized cam that culminated in an awkward chimney, powder snow dissolving out of it as I tried to gain purchase for my feet in a position where a fall would be unthinkable.

Mark looked towards a bank of cloud coming from the north. 'That doesn't look good,' he said with uncharacteristic severity. 'It's the start of a weather front. If we were in New Zealand, I would say we should bail right now.'

'Let's keep going until the wind picks up, and that'll be our sign to run away,' I replied, knowing this could be our only shot at the summit.

It took fifteen hours to reach the summit ridge, climbing more than twice the actual distance due to constant traversing and occasional down climbing. The way ahead was less difficult but not simple, and the summit at least two hours further, guarded by steep gendarmes and requiring more devious route-finding.

The sky had become dark and ominous, and our mood deteriorated with the weather. The usual banter and joking were long gone. Mark's usually relaxed expression was full of concern, deep furrows in his brow, and Jean had become mechanical in his words and actions.

We would certainly have turned and fled had anybody suggested it, but, aware that we might not get another chance, we pushed on almost in silence.

By the time we reached the top the storm seemed ready to break at any moment. Exposed beyond belief, we could see the tiny red dots of our tents far away at the base, knowing they contained everything we needed to survive and that it would take many hours to reach them.

'We are the most remote people in the world right now,' I said, concerned about the descent.

'We are a long way from 'ome,' Jean agreed.

'Let's get the fuck out of here!' declared Mark.

We hastened off, the pedigree of the team ensuring the long, complex rappels were thankfully uneventful. It was a joy to be reunited with the safety and shelter of our tents. Being away from them and the kit needed to survive out there had been harrowing. It is a constant survival situation, always one step away from disaster. Within an hour of reaching camp from the twenty-four-hour round trip, the death wind began to blow over 35 mph outside. A disaster, had it caught us up on the wall.

★

From the inception of the expedition idea, I'd had my sights fixed squarely on the magnificent 2,500-foot line of the South Spur of the Spectre. Another last great climb, as regal and more remote than any climb on Earth.

Due to the extreme length of our journey we had opted not to bring a port-a-ledge or gear for a full wall-style ascent, while as an ethical statement we had omitted to bring a drill, bolts or fixing rope. We were committed to the most pure and hardcore, alpine-style ascent. To rise to the challenge with minimal aid, to see how far we could go, to push the adventure envelope right to the edge.

The South Spur was far steeper and much more big wall in nature, as well as even more beautiful than anticipated. To attempt it in the light and fast alpine style for which we were equipped, in a place already so remote and exposed, we needed a spell of stable high pressure and good weather. Yet during the two weeks we spent in the Gothic Mountains the wind seemed to change every six hours: sometimes without warning a 30-mph wind would appear and blow for the rest of the day, bringing a cold I would be happy never to experience again and that could kill quickly. Our weather forecasts were unreliable. At best the weather was very cold but calm, and when the Spectre basked in sun it was seductive, but just a few hours later a full-scale blizzard could arrive, and even in the safety of camp we feared the tents could rip apart.

It was a bitter realization. I had worked so desperately hard to reach that point on Earth and knew I'd likely never set foot there again. My fingers were touching the prize, but my heart knew it was not mine.

There was a clear line that would be right at the limit of what we could achieve with what we had if we got lucky. I cursed myself for not bringing my 6-kg carbon-fibre port-a-ledge. With that shelter we could survive a storm and it would've provided an acceptable margin of safety for an attempt. But I wasn't willing to rely on luck. I didn't want my kids to end up without a dad or with one who was crippled. There were so many wonderful places I wanted to show them, so many exciting things do. Out there on the ice I thought of many ideas for family adventures and expeditions.

'I don't have good feeling about this. I can't see it ending well,' I finally said to Jean.

He agreed. 'This is a real big wall, port-a-ledge territory, not alpine terrain. We would not climb in the Alps in these conditions. Why would we consider it 'ere?' Jean said matter of factly, without seeming to display the profound disappointment that I felt.

But I knew it was the right decision. We were too close to the edge for such a demanding climb.

I had learned the hard way what happens when you push too hard in the wrong place at the wrong time. We had to be conservative, we still faced a month-long trans-Antarctic crossing to get home to our families.

Hard-earned experience, skill and wisdom can enable you to undertake and accomplish great things with an acceptable margin of safety, but you must be in tune and pay heed to your intuition.

Jean and I decided to attempt to traverse the Organ Pipe Peaks. Mark stayed behind knowing two would be faster than three. Starting on the north face of what we dubbed Alpha Tower, we again encountered far steeper and more difficult terrain than expected, including a desperate 15-metre 5.11/A3 offwidth, and dangerous, unconsolidated snow gullies with sustained difficulties up to Scottish VII, 7. We summited in sublime conditions before a committing descent rappelling over the most compact, crack-free granite I have ever encountered. It had taken fourteen hours. With clouds building, we cancelled the traverse, escaping on snow slopes down the north side of the col. Winds of 30 mph struck two hours after we reached camp.

'Good call bailing, boys,' Mark chirped on our return. 'It was getting lonely here.'

All too soon it was time to leave the Gothic Mountains and begin the most arduous leg of the expedition. For 60 miles, dragging our giant pulks, we battled by ski or crampon into the biting wind, roped together, retracing our route up the heavily crevassed Scott Glacier.

Traditional man-hauling couldn't be more different than kite skiing. We settled into the routine: fifty minutes of movement, then ten minutes to eat and hydrate, in segments repeated for eight to ten hours before erecting camp, cooking, sleeping and repeating. Void of excitement or fun, this was the phase of the expedition I had dreaded.

'We must have come at least ten miles?' enquired Jean after a gruelling ten-hour day negotiating wide crevasses.

Keeper of the GPS and knowing the answer, I shook my head.

'Eight then? Surely six?' he continued with increasing dismay. He tried again.

'Five?' He sounded disgusted. I nodded.

Jean did the majority of the endless, arduous task of melting snow and preparing food throughout the expedition, whilst Mark managed the camera equipment, backing up data and charging batteries, and I wrote daily dispatches for sponsors and faffed.

Thankfully after four days we entered the much safer terrain of the plateau, with temperatures almost 20 degrees milder and wind half the strength than we had experienced a month earlier.

Accepted wisdom is that travelling upwind by kite with expedition loads over long distances is not viable. Still we were hopeful that by utilising the latest wing technology and new-school tactics we could make better progress tacking upwind by kite than walking. Our kiting set-ups consisted of World Cup giant slalom-race skis mounted with ski mountaineering bindings, high-performance race kites, and sophisticated carbon-kevlar-hybrid pulks.

During our very first upwind session, zigzagging diagonally into the wind as if in sailboats, we were thrilled to be gaining about one mile on the desired heading for every three miles of ground covered: eventually totalling 75 miles of kiting and gaining 25 miles in the right direction, or five times the previous day's walking and a hundred times more fun!

After a few days becalmed and a couple more tacking we encountered the McMurdo South Pole Traverse, a graded road used to supply the US South Pole station with fuel. Apparently the convoy of giant bulldozers towing a million gallons of fuel had just passed through and created a freshly groomed ski piste. We kited 75 miles in seven hours, on a leg of the journey we had expected to man-haul over seven days.

We celebrated Christmas in style, exchanging presents of fudge and clean undies, and enjoyed a frozen feast of real food after the dehydrated meals of the last six weeks, accompanied by hangover-inducing quantities of single malt whisky. Mark surprised me with a card Freya had drawn, saying she loved and missed me. I cried.

Then blizzards, white-outs, lack of wind or wind from the wrong direction conspired against us, and in twelve days we travelled just 185 miles.

Pushing hard, underpowered but trying to tack upwind, we got dangerously separated on one session before the wind dropped off completely. It took almost three hours dragging our still hugely heavy pulks through ankle-deep snow to regroup. We got annoyed with each other, exchanging the few terse words of the trip.

Frustration grew, and we began to question whether we had the time and supplies to finish the mission. The last flight out of Antarctica was on 27 January. On 26 January, the ski plane would come for us wherever we were, using the US$100K evacuation bond we had paid upfront and I had personally financed by remortgaging my family home.

As hope was dwindling, Antarctica's Almighty intervened. I got out of the tent to take a pee and was dumbstruck.

'Get out here, guys!' I yelled.

'Oh my god,' Jean said. It's the sun dog of my dreams!'

Two perfect circular rainbows showed around the sun, while a pillar of light was mirrored on the horizon. Bright sun dogs burned on each side of the sun, with multicoloured arcs above them. Most entrancing of all, an iridescent white circle of light, or parhelion, traversed all the way around the sky.

Though lightplay of refraction and reflection is not uncommon in Antarctica, such a combination is rare. As we gazed in reverence, the tent began flapping. The wind was picking up – from the right direction.

We took down camp and in the last remnants of the vision launched our kites. Wind, surface and visibility conditions improved, and on this day, number forty-four of the expedition, we travelled over 125 miles in a single eight-hour session. In four almost perfect days we covered close to 500 miles, floating across a sublime river of sparkling diamonds, with a top speed of 32 mph and smiles ear to ear.

A couple of days of poor conditions were followed by another glorious and extremely technical day of kiting through a final group of mountains and we arrived at the finish line, the Union Glacier logistics hub where we had begun. After 1,100 miles and fifty-two days of extreme adventure, autonomous in the deep field of the frozen continent, the three of us were still laughing and joking like schoolboys. Should we have been required to, we all felt in good enough physical and psychological shape to have begun the whole ordeal again the very next day. That is the sign of a successful expedition.

Within just a few days the constant challenge, hardship and joy became a distant memory. Our cravings for cleanliness and comfort, were so soon fulfilled. The fantasy of fresh food and cold beer which we had been grasping for weeks faded with shocking speed when those things were again available in abundance.

I couldn't wait to see Jess and the kids after such a long, hard absence. I had missed them so dearly. But within days of arriving home my mind began wander back to the great white wilderness and that virgin South Spur.

With the knowledge we gained on the trip, particularly with regard to upwind kiting, I think it might be possible kite all the way from Union Glacier to Spectre and return via our route, adding 600 miles to the journey and turning the dial yet another notch. We had shown the way to a new kind of polar exploration and opened the door to climbing in one of the least-explored ranges on Earth. I had already begun planning my return to the

Transantarctic Mountains for the South Spur, though it is yet to take place. It seemed the two great loves of my life, my family and extreme adventure, being at home and being away, were destined to be in perpetual conflict. But the summer after the Spectre expedition, I found a way to reconcile them.

20

Family Outings

'Daddy! I'm scared,' whimpered Freya, age seven, wide-eyed with a furrowed brow framed by her golden hair. As she stepped around the corner above the abyss, wispy clouds swirled far beneath, a cold updraft blowing whilst the summits of white-topped Alps, now level with us, glittered in the summer rays.

'Don't worry, sweetheart, I'm right here. Remember we just have to find the hidden staircase the fairies made for us. Ah ha! Here's another step!' I reassured her with a gentle smile.

A few metres below, Jackson, three, continued to beam and giggle from his happy place, strapped to Jess's back inside his harness and carrier, seemingly oblivious to the great drop below. His infectious positivity along with Daddy's relaxed composure helped to calm Freya. With bravery beyond her years she took a breath, composed herself, found the fairy steps and struggled upwards.

She had every right to be sacred. Not many children can have found themselves on that exposed step, high on the North Ridge of the Piz Badile. This was not your average family outing. As I often tell her, 'Only stupid people never get scared.'

Fear and danger are not the same thing. People who never experience fear are a liability, destined to get hurt. But equally those who surrender or flee at the slightest whiff of danger will never achieve their potential. Fear is a valuable tool that lets us know there is potential for harm. Learning to manage fear and avoid panic and irrational decision-making and how to harness the powerful internal forces that danger can unleash and turn it to our advantage is an invaluable life skill. One I've spent years learning to master and I certainly hope to impart to my own kids.

Resilience can't be taught theoretically nor self-belief built without risk. Under careful guidance, Jess and I have grown our kids' zones of comfort by taking them on some pretty wild adventures and putting them in harm's way to show them what they are capable of and how to manage risk. To nurture the perfect balance of confidence and competence. But most of all because we enjoy sharing the journey and elevated perspective from up there.

Our first serious family outing was an ascent of the highest mountain in Slovenia, Triglav (2,600 metres), in the beautifully preserved nature of the Julian Alps. We took the long seven-lakes route to enjoy more time up high in the mountains. Freya had just turned five and Jackson was only eighteen months old. He spent most of the journey strapped to his mum's back in his Happy Baby Carrier. I would be carrying the daddy-load, a rucksack as tall and heavier than Freya with everything required for a family of four to camp and climb in the mountains for five days. That meant Freya and her skinny little legs would have to complete the journey without being carried. Above the clear turquoise water of Lake Bohinj we gained height through pine forests and meadows of wild flowers, past ancient farmsteads to a mountain hut above the treeline. We had not booked a bunk in the rudimentary hotel and it was full. I was surprised to learn that camping was prohibited in the Triglav National Park but knew with our minimalist bivi tent we would be able to find a discreet spot. The kids love camping whether in the garden or on a mountain. Tents are dens, there are fun tasks they can help with, and we all get to snuggle in one giant sleeping bag.

We decided to take an alternative route via what is known in Slovenia as a difficult path. It transpired to be a jaw-droppingly exposed death path, a climbers' trail along a narrow ledge system that traversed for a mile above a 1,000-foot precipice with towering cliffs above. Storm clouds brewed and though we were roped together there was no way to anchor to the mountain. Jess was scared. I reassured her. Freya was completely unfazed but seemed to recognise the seriousness of the situation. She stopped messing around and became unusually obedient as she held my hand and talked about fairies. The family dynamic added a completely new dimension to the alpine experience that had become so familiar to me. It was like starting afresh, rediscovering the wonder of big walls and awe of exposure that had captivated me as a child. Intense, rewarding and meaningful without having to push the edge at the end of the world. I remembered the terrifying gorge descending Akdağ in Turkey with my dad and uncle when I was seven. How Dad had encouraged me to face my fear and how formative it was.

The storm broke into a torrential downpour just as we regained the main trail. Lightning and thunder exploded across the sky. Properly equipped, led by Mum and Dad's explicit display of calm positivity and reassurance, far from being intimidated the kids laughed and shouted excitedly into the eye of the storm, feeling the raw power of nature, learning to connect and channel its energy.

Thankfully we soon arrived at the welcome warmth and shelter of another hut. This one made space for us and we enjoyed a hearty broth followed by hot chocolate with cream whilst watching the storm rage in the night outside.

The summit pyramid of Triglav is a technical ascent from all aspects. Several via ferratas, with metal steps and occasional ladders protected by steel cable, ease the way. The storm blew through and after breakfast, Jackson, helmeted on his mum's back, and Freya, roped to me, seemed to thrive as the terrain got steeper. I've often noticed that most kids prefer the engagement of climbing to the monotony of walking uphill.

Though a challenging climb, it is a popular summit. The hardy Slovenians, who as a cultural norm are all expected to one day climb Triglav, were full of praise and admiration for little Freya. The descent with another night in a hut along the way was long. I was tired when we made it back to the van but Freya still skipped and played, her skinny legs still strong after twelve hours on the trail. I was impressed and understood the meaning of fatherly pride. Spending time together in the mountains, combining my two great loves of family and adventure, was special and a powerful bonding experience. I thought about Stanley, his widow, Meika, and son, Finn. Of what he had missed out on, pushing too close to the edge that one last time.

In the summer of 2020 we turned up the family adventure dial and undertook a more serious Alpine ascent.

Sitting on the border between Switzerland and Italy, the North Face of the 3,300-metre Piz Badile is considered one of the six classic north faces of the Alps. The North Ridge forms the sharp edge to the right of this face. A thousand metres of uninterrupted, clean granite towers into the sky, it is one of the most classic easier rock climbs in Europe. Nevertheless it is a big undertaking in the high mountains and not to be underestimated

The biggest threat on any mountain is the weather, the next most serious hazard is falling rock and ice. The knife-edge nature of the North Ridge minimises this danger, whilst 4G phone connection throughout the Alps to accurate forecasts and helicopter rescue has drastically reduced the commitment and potential for disaster of climbing there. The unique mountain infrastructure of the Alps has turned formidable peaks into amenable, even family challenges.

Though the approach to the climb alone, from the chocolate-box Swiss valley of Bregaglia, would be beyond all but the most hardy children.

We began the gruelling but delightful hike past picturesque wooden chalets and tinkling cow bells. Deciduous trees of birch, chestnut and poplar soon gave way to scented forests of spruce and pine above.

Freya, then seven, again displayed remarkable stamina for walking uphill as long as you hold her hand and keep her constantly entertained with stories about adventurous animals or games like I Spy and Twenty Questions. Even little Jackson, three, made it most of the way before Mum scooped him onto her back.

We had recently learned that Jackson's eyesight was very poor and he sported adorable, thick-lensed new glasses and seemed even happier than usual to actually be able to see the Alpine glory. We had also realised that Freya is neuroatypical. She struggled more than most with social interaction and suffered from irrational anxieties. Her astute intellect and exceptional stamina were also unusual. Jess, who is a GP, had noticed these and other telling traits and we had sought professional advice. As I looked deeper into neurodiversity I began to recognise that I too displayed characteristics that I had long been told were not normal but had only just realised could probably be described as neurologically atypical. That was also true of most of my close friends and partners.

'Fuck normal life' was a Stone Monkey mantra. It had never occurred to me that reacting to situations and stimuli in a way that is not usual is, by definition, atypical. Perhaps the lust for adventure and dangerous fun ran deeper than I had realised? Many of the greatest thinkers and artists are neuroatypical. And the more I thought about it, so were many of the greatest climbers that I had known.

We arrived at the immaculate hut beneath the Piz Badile.

'I've only known very few children to walk up here and all much older than you,' the custodian, Heidi, praised. Freya glowed with pride.

We told Heidi our plan to make a family ascent on the North Ridge and to my surprise she wasn't at all condemning.

'I can see you know what you are doing. What a joy for them! I only wish I had children of my own to share such adventure,' said Heidi. I felt for her.

Conscious that little legs would be tired after the long approach, we spent a whole day frolicking our way through the blooming Alpine meadows, where bees buzzed and butterflies fluttered amongst a bouquet of colourful, perfumed flowers. We picnicked and played amongst the boulders and snow patches before roping up to cross the snow field at the foot of the mountain and climb a short section that leads to a col beneath the start of the true ridge and a wonderful promontory just large enough for our bivi tent.

I'd carried up some firewood and we toasted marshmallows over an open fire on our magnificent pedestal in the sky, surrounded by precipitous drops on all sides. I'd often told them stories of Daddy's dramatic cliffside camps and they were thrilled to experience their own for the first time, tied to a rope all night.

Before dawn, I left Jess and the kids sleeping and climbed up the first few hundred metres of the ridge without a rope to check out the terrain. Although certainly not scrambling, and by no one's definition walking, it was really quite easy rock climbing as long as you found the right way.

We fried sausages for breakfast, packed up camp and set off just after another party ahead.

We used an unorthodox climbing technique, developed for extreme ascents but a game changer for family climbs, known as 'fix and follow'. I would lead with an extra-long rope then fix it in place, leave the heavy bag at the top and rappel back down to the others. We would then all climb together attached to the fixed rope using a progress-capture device called a micro-traxion. Being right beside the kids to help and calm them is revolutionary on big routes.

In this fashion we made rapid progress up the seemingly endless ridge. At a spacious ledge we stopped for a lunch break and allowed Jackson out of the carrier. Close up, the scene was a typical family picnic in the outdoors, but seen from afar it was anything but, the four of us perched eating biscuits in terrain usually reserved for hardened mountaineers.

I was operating comfortably within my abilities and knew that if necessary I could carry Freya with the same system as Jackson, either to the top or the ground.

Jess trusted my judgement and ability as a climber; I was completely confident in hers as a mother who is highly in tune with the needs of our children. You have to push your kids to do anything, but knowing precisely how hard to push is a subtle art at which Jess excels.

After the picnic we continued to make good progress, albeit a bit slower on the steeper terrain. Freya was still going well but understandably beginning to tire. Time to deploy the Haribo sweet treats, a trick we usually avoid as in a child's mind it quickly becomes more about the sweets than the experience, but on this occasion the sugary energy kicks were worth the risk.

Freya methodically uncovered the fairy staircase for hour upon hour without complaint; she struggled on the hardest sections but gave it her all, proving the true grit a seven-year-old girl can possess. Jackson singing and laughing in his carrier on his mum's back looked increasingly out of place the higher we climbed.

Eventually we reached lower-angle terrain of the summit ridge. Jackson escaped his carrier to climb the last few easier pitches. I took a photo of him standing on the sharp edge above the almighty precipice and swirling cloud just as the golden sun splashed onto his face. He looked incredibly cute with his shock of platinum hair, adorable smile and thick glasses that made his eyes look huge like a Disney character, topped off with his bright-orange, slightly too-large helmet.

I knew it was a keeper.

The sky began to explode deep crimson as the sun edged towards the horizon. Just as I began to feel the unpleasant knot of anxiety in the pit of my stomach that always accompanies the onset of darkness in the mountains, we rounded a pinnacle and found ourselves literally on the doorstep of the summit bivouac hut.

Safely inside, Jess made a cosy nest out of the hut's mattresses and blankets and the thick down sleeping bag I'd carried up. We all snuggled together to drink hot chocolate and listen to a few chapters of Harry Potter on Audible. All four of us couldn't have been happier.

The next morning we opened the door to a magnificent dawn above a cloud inversion. Promptly tied in again, the kids gazed in awe at the spectacular colours illuminating the dramatic peaks floating like islands in a sea of cloud.

'What's that big thing in the sky, Mummy?' piped Jackson as a pair of golden eagles, seemingly the size of sunloungers, majestically soared from the horizon without twitching a feather then circled close by before an impressive display of courtship aeronautics and they were gone. It was my fortieth birthday. I can think of no way I would rather have spent it.

We made half a dozen retrievable rope rappels. I went down first with Freya hanging from my harness between my legs, then Jess came down with Jackson on her back. It felt abstract to be in the gnarly Alpine arena I knew so well with the kids, who enjoyed rappelling as much as a fairground.

Once on the ground, Freya holding Jess's hand and Jackson mine, we literally skipped the whole way down the luscious Val Masino, where fourteen years earlier Jess and I had spent our honeymoon. We arrived in the village just in time for pizza and ice cream, having descended as quickly as a standard team.

Our first big climb as a family added another dimension to the realm I already held so dear. Though the children had little grasp of what they had achieved, I felt a sense of accomplishment and joy equal to that of any of my great expeditions.

'Do you think it's wise to post these on Instagram?' I asked Jess, reviewing the remarkable photos I'd taken. 'We're bound to receive plenty of flak for being irresponsible parents.'

'We care more for our own kids than anybody, who cares what they say? I think there'll be more people out there who find it inspiring and will aspire to do more adventurous stuff with their own kids if they see it,' was her considered response.

I posted a selection of the best. The stand-out image was the one of Jackson high on the ridge, but I made sure Freya was given the credit she deserved, as well as Jess for her uber-mama performance.

Within the hour I received a message from a journalist I knew from a news distribution agency. He asked if we'd be willing to do a short interview and allow them to put the photos and story out on the wire. Realising this would certainly open us to much wider scrutiny, I thought of my dad's favourite advice – 'Tell 'em, fuck 'em!'

Within a week Jackson's photo had gone viral, generating millions of views and creating a small media frenzy. It was published in titles across the globe including *the Sun*, the *FT*, the *New York*

Post, New Zealand Herald, and many of the European and Asian majors.

Next came a barrage of TV interviews. We conducted a live interview on BBC Breakfast from a hut in the high mountains of Slovenia during another alpine adventure.

Finally we spoke to CNN Global, with a staggering reach of over 500 million viewers, from a remote beach in Croatia before we decided the kids had had enough of the awkward Zoom interviews.

One question that we were constantly asked was 'I find it difficult to get my kids out for a walk around the park, how did you do it?' to which we repeatedly responded: 'Yes, so do we, but once you've gone through the tedious motions of getting them dressed, teeth brushed, breakfasted, etc., when you finally do get going, don't stop! Kids are capable of far more than people think and it's *always* worth the effort of getting them out on any kind of adventure.'

Unsurprisingly a quick comments search did indeed reveal the expected tirade of 'They should be reported to Social Services', 'Who would do that to their own kids?' and such. More remarkable and reassuring to me was that for each criticism there many more positive reactions along the lines of 'What an incredible upbringing!', 'I never imagined we could continue our lives of adventure with kids' and my favourite: 'I wish you were my dad' from a grown man in Lancashire.

Our family outing up the Piz Badile had been incredible and the media storm entertaining. But my deepest passion lay in climbing steep mountains in truly remote places far from human infrastructure.

I wanted to share with my children the wonder of real wilderness, away from mountain huts, internet connections, resupplies and quick rescues. To unplug for a while and experience the rawness of nature, the empowerment of self-reliance and connection to a wilder world, to undertake our first family expedition. And I had an idea.

★

As we drove up the increasingly steep hairpins, twenty miles down a dirt road heading deep into the back country, the black sky erupted into a violent storm. Apparently it hadn't rained for months.

I was driving a minibus towing a beaten-up old horsebox. We'd removed the back two rows of seats and added a Walmart mattress topper to create a budget RV for our 2021 summer holiday. My wife's dual citizenship had gained the kids and me entry through the US border that was all but closed due to Covid.

Just a few miles short of the trailhead the rear-wheel-drive van suddenly lost traction on a particularly aggressive switchback and slid into knee-deep mud on the inside of the bend, jackknifing the trailer. The kids, now eight and four, cuddled, distressed, into Jess, who was understandably flustered.

A peculiar groaning noise came from the trailer – apparently Tiberius and Titan, our recently rented llamas, weren't too happy either.

Not exactly the start to our first family expedition I had planned.

'Don't worry, we're totally stuck so at least we won't slide off the mountain! And besides, uncertainty is what adventure's all about!'

Jess and the kids didn't look at all convinced.

The Wind River Range is in western Wyoming, USA, a subrange of the Rocky Mountains that form the US continental divide. The Winds are a collection of wilderness areas that together create 2,800 square miles of truly wild west, a vast area of forest, meadows, rocky peaks, lakes and glaciers. Part of the Greater Yellowstone ecosystem, it is home to moose, elk and bighorn sheep as well as black and grizzly bears, mountain lions and wolves.

No motorised transport is allowed, there are no roads, no permanent human settlements, no shops or lodges. Other than a well-maintained trail network there is no infrastructure at all. It's much more akin to the remote regions I love than the Alps.

American wilderness areas are protected by law but not subject to the same stringent restrictions of the national parks, allowing far greater freedom for personal recreation and exploration, with far fewer visitors.

The kind summer conditions are fleeting short, further compounded by a horrific mosquito hatch in the early season. We visited at optimum time in early August.

With all the camping kit, climbing gear and most critically food required for a family of four to spend fourteen days of autonomous adventure, we had around 100 kgs of stuff.

Enter Tiberius and Titan. Unlike horses, llamas are extremely easy to handle and are hardy creatures, requiring very little food or water and able to travel over surprisingly rough terrain carrying up to 35 kgs. Highly social, always kept in at least pairs, well-trained llamas like Tiberius and Titan are curious, friendly and pleasant to be around. And of course the kids loved them.

Our mis-adventurous start was overcome that very evening with the selfless help of a passing Native American chap called Darwin and his massive 4x4 truck who towed us out.

'Do you think they like sweeties?' said Jackson, kindly offering a Werther's Original to Tiberius. We were at the Big Sandy trailhead, loading up the llamas, two days after the incident with the van on the opposite side of the range.

Freya adores all animals and our heavily laden new friends seemed to appreciate the doting attention as we set off into our adventure.

Within an hour we came face to face with a huge moose. The potentially dangerous beast was obviously more terrified than us as it took off from the trail at a gallop through the thick forest – quite a spectacle.

As the sun began to set, its alpenglow setting alight the spectacular Cirque of the Towers, Jess cast her line into the calm waters of Billy's Lake by our camp.

Using a spinner, frowned upon by local purist fly-fisherfolk, she landed a rainbow trout that very first try. A clutch more followed in the most successful hour's fishing of a lifetime. Jackson was beside himself with excitement and we cooked them on a fire.

We left the llamas tied in a meadow by a stream and accompanied by Stephen Fry's melodic voice recounting tales of the boy wizard (Audible stories played by phone being our secret weapon when the kids start to flag) we hiked over a steep pass and down into the jaw-dropping Cirque of the Towers.

Another terrific storm struck, the excitement of thunder and lightning this time souring as Jess and I had to physically shield the kids from hailstones the size of marbles that left bruises.

The storm blew through and we camped by a glistening emerald lake at the foot of the giant granite towers that give the cirque its name. Rejuvenated, we played hide-and-seek amongst the boulders.

Our first summit was Pingora Peak, a formidable granite dome, near vertical on all sides and once dubbed 'impossible' by the first Europeans to lay eyes on it. The East Ledges route is in fact a relatively easy climb though grand in scale with 1,000 feet of technical terrain, a major outing for a four-year-old. This time Jackson climbed the whole route 'by his own', as he says. I rappelled with him and Freya hanging from my harness, bouncing and giggling the whole way down.

The next day Freya and I tackled the fantastically exposed East Ridge of the Wolf's Head, considered to be one of the most classic climbs in North America. A much longer, more committing and complex alpine outing that I felt was too much for Jackson.

One especially dramatic section known as the Sidewalk is a spine of rock set at a 50-degree angle, just 3 feet wide with vertiginous drops in excess of 500 feet on both sides – enough to make the most seasoned alpinist gasp. Like a smaller version of the Stairway to Heaven on Ulvetanna, shared with my little girl. It is outrageously exposed and Freya was frightened, but with gentle encouragement she faced her fear and padded her way up the knife-edge ridge on all fours into less exposed terrain.

'Dad, being in nature is like opening a window into your heart to let in the happiness that was always there, only you just did not know it before,' said Freya. My heart almost burst. Beaming from ear to ear, she romped along the remainder of the thousand-foot, world-class alpine climb and literally skipped past a party who had started hours ahead of us on the long and treacherous descent.

Tiberius and Titan were thrilled to see us and looked as relaxed and healthy as ever, though there was a noticeable pair of very short-munched circles of grass in the meadow.

We continued deeper into the wilderness to the more austere, seldom-visited Mount Hooker, where we were met by my friend and climbing partner Wilson Cutbirth.

Mount Hooker's West Face is a 2,000-foot-tall vertical wall of the most beautiful jade granite, comparable in scale and severity to Yosemite's El Capitan. We camped in a small meadow surrounded by large boulders and whitebark pines, close to a shallow lake littered with playful stepping stones.

Wilson and I set off early to climb a long, sustained and difficult route called Gambling in the Winds. We committed to an audacious alpine-style ascent, climbing the fourteen continuously hard rope lengths, carrying very little, in a single continuous push from camp to camp.

High on the cliff, long into the night on the very last hard section, we both 'hit the wall'. Wilson doubled over with abdominal muscle spasms and I suffered the most debilitating finger cramps caused by dehydration, exhaustion and exacerbated by the 12,000-foot altitude. We were forced to pull on a few pieces of gear, forsaking a 'free' ascent but safely reaching the top.

Down at camp, Jess woke to distinctive snuffling and grunting sounds outside the tent. Instinctively she grabbed the bear spray and a hiking pole, her only means of defence. With two kids and nobody else for miles around – save for us, 1,800 feet above, locked in our battle and powerless to help – she was too scared to unzip the tent to find out whether it was a relatively harmless black bear or a far less common but much more aggressive grizzly.

She frantically banged pans together to try to scare it. The kids woke up but the bear lurked on for hours. Jess had to reassure them whilst controlling her own fear and repeatedly trying to scare it off, until it eventually lost interest and left. Jess is a brave woman and inspiring mum.

Uncertainty is indeed what adventure is all about. Clearly we had not planned a bear encounter, but what is certain is that the 50 miles and 10,000 feet we trekked and climbed with our llamas during our fortnight in the Wind River wilderness, both the highs and perhaps even more so the lows were deeply bonding and hugely formative to share as a family. To combine such a major and majestic climb with Wilson and the fantastic family ascents on the same trip into such pristine wilderness was a dream. It felt like a culmination of life experience, bringing together all the things that I love.

I don't know if Freya and Jackson will choose a life of adventure but I've no doubt our time in the wilderness will have made them more self-confident, resilient, brave and better able to face the challenges of whatever path they choose.

That first taste of real adventure and high exposure in the Akdağ Mountains in Turkey with my dad when I was seven profoundly influenced the way I saw the world. Discovering rock climbing and the Old Man of Hoy trip gave me a higher perspective and revealed a heartfelt passion for exploring places that are hard to reach, where few people can go. I feel so lucky to have found such passion and clear purpose so early in life and to have been encouraged to pursue it by my mum and dad. To have met such interesting and influential people like Malcolm 'Pike' Cundy, Johnny Dawes, Doug Scott and Chris Bonington when I was a child, who inspired wild and daring dreams when the world was still in my imagination.

I feel grateful to have had the opportunity for those first times, even more so to have survived the wild times, and truly blessed to enjoy the big times that I hope are not yet over.

As my dad likes to say, 'Try hard, take risks.'

Author's Note

It has been a challenge to know what to include and more difficult still to decide what to leave out of this story. Some chapters could easily have filled books. To condense fifteen Yosemite seasons into three was almost beyond me. I'm not sure I've done the human and geographical characters the justice they deserve, but I have tried to tell an honest tale and paint an interesting picture of the wild things in wild places with wild people I feel so privileged to have done, seen and met.

There are a dozen other expeditions that will have to wait to be told another time; kite skiing the length of Greenland and discovering Norway's winter wonderland, the Hardangervidda Plateau, during the training; the first ascent of the 4,000-foot-tall Mirror Wall in the Arctic with a new, strong but inexperienced crew; an exploratory free tree-climbing trip to the giant strangle figs of the Lamu Auro crater on the flanks of an active volcano in New Britain, Papua New Guinea; the first ascent of the steep face of Huan Shan, a sacred Taoist mountain and the birthplace of kung fu in China.

Most recently there was the largest scale and most complex project I've organised and led so far, to the Great Northern Prow of Mount Roraima, deep in the Amazon rainforest of Guyana. That story is too big to tell here. On these trips I have begun to take a mentoring role, giving others opportunities to go to places and do things that they could not have done otherwise and sharing some of the knowledge I've gained along the way. It's been fulfilling and I've formed deep friendships and strong partnerships with a handful of characters who do not feature in this book. Those people and our stories warrant more than just a passing mention.

In 2020, with a couple of old Stone Monkeys, we discovered an area of world-class, unclimbed desert towers in the recently opened Kingdom of Saudi Arabia. That we climbed them with local royalty seems like fiction even to me.

I am currently planning return expeditions to Asgard, Queen Maud Land and the Spectre as well as others to new savage and exotic lands. I hope to visit all the places in this book and more with my family and to continue to share with them quality time in wild places.

As I write we are about to depart on this summer's family holiday to Northern Norway. Amongst other adventures we plan to spend a week sea kayaking to and then climbing a huge granite mountain called Stetind and to make a film. Family expeditions have definitely proved to be a hit on many levels. But they have complemented not replaced my grown-up trips. I haven't lost the desire for ever more extreme adventure, I just have the risk addiction better in check and I have come to value simple pleasures more than before – our comfortable home and the idyllic life Jess and I have built here in the Lakes, gentle strolls through bluebell woods, stand-up paddle boarding on the lake, bike rides on the miles of bridleway from our door.

I never imagined when I left home at sixteen that I would end up putting down fresh roots just a few valleys away from where I was born and raised. But the incredible round trip that brought me back to where I began has been full of learning.

There are so many people who have helped on that journey and this book. None more than Jessica, who has endured and encouraged much that is written here, sharing my risk but not the rewards and taking care of the kids for long periods alone. Freya and Jackson have been an inspiration, breathing new life and joy into adventure for me. My mum and dad, whose support, encouragement, liberal parenting and progressive embracement of risk has enabled everything here.

Then there were inspirations, mentors, many partners and expedition members mentioned in this book who I would like to mention again and thank here:

Malcolm Cundy, Guy Lee, Doug Scott, Chris Bonington, Haydn Martin, Johnny Dawes, Paul Pritchard, Noel Craine, Andy Cave, Tim Emmett, Patch Hammond, Jason Pickles, Thomas and Alex Huber, Ivo Ninov, Cedar Wright, Dean Potter, José Pereyra, Kevin Thaw, Conrad Anker, Jimmy Chin, Sean 'Stanley' Leary, Shaun Ellison, Robbie Pecnik, James Boole, Alastair Lee, Chris Rabone, Dave Reeves, Ian Burton, Carlos Suarez, Jean Burgun and Mark Sedon.

The photographers Eric Whitehead, Adam Long, Adam Wainwright, Ray Wood, Chris 'Douggs' McDougall, John Dickey, Alastair Lee, Matt Pycroft and Mark Sedon.

And for the ongoing support of Berghaus, the owners the Rubin family.

For the contributions and help with the book, Steve Backshall, Shante Eide, Ed Douglas, Iain MacGregor, Jill Cole and Holly Purdham.

And there are a few characters who have played important roles in the most recent chapters of my life, who do not feature in this, my first book, but I felt were deserving of a name check here: Waldo Etherington, Wilson Cutbirth, Joe Möhle, Matt Pickles, Anna Taylor, Dan Howard, Edward William and Troy Henry.

I hope the experience, skill and wisdom of maturity will enable me to keep pushing closer to the edge, but with a higher margin of safety. I am not naive to the risk and still question the morality of indulging in such dangerous pursuits as a father. But it is the danger that makes it so exciting. It is who I am and what I love and I try to be cautious.

Perhaps I am not normal – but then, who would want to be?

Glossary

Climbing Disciplines

The word 'climbing' covers a very broad spectrum of activities that are in fact completely different sports. Consider it like 'running': at one end of the spectrum there is a 100 metre sprint, at the other a 100 mile ultra-marathon. Here is a very basic outline of the different rock- and mountain-climbing disciplines. It is not an absolute system: they can be combined, there is much crossover and most climbers practise multiple disciplines, though few practise all.

Aid Climbing Ropes and equipment are used directly to aid ascent. The climber hangs in a harness from gear placements and stands in short rope ladders called aiders to reach and place the next piece of gear. Historically it was common practice, but these days it is generally only employed on very tall cliffs.

Alpine Climbing An advanced form of mountaineering practised on steep faces that usually involves climbing with ice axes. Many big walls are in an alpine environment and may involve elements of alpine climbing.

Big-wall Climbing Simply climbing very tall cliffs. These can be up to 1,500 metres high and can require multiple days, weeks or even months to climb, although elite climbers can climb routes in hours that would take most teams a week. Requires specialist techniques and equipment and is an advanced form of rock climbing.

Bouldering Climbing close to the ground without ropes or harnesses. Crash pads are used to protect the landing. The focus is entirely on physical performance. The very hardest climbing movements are made in bouldering.

Free Climbing   This is what most people think of as climbing, where appendages are used to climb a rock face or mountain. Ropes and equipment are used only for safety and, if weighted or used to directly to assist the climber, negate a free ascent.

Free Solo   Climbing alone without a rope or gear. A fall from height almost certainly results in death.

Ice Climbing   Climbing frozen water using ice axes and crampons.

Indoor Climbing   By far the most common form of climbing. Practised on man-made structures indoors. Developed in the 1990s, climbing walls or gyms brought the sport to the urban masses and led to great advances in rock climbing standards and popularity.

Mixed Climbing   Climbing steep faces that are a combination of ice, snow, rock and sometimes frozen turf.

Mountaineering   Climbing mountains. Usually involves snow and/or ice and sometimes the use of ropes, an ice axe and crampons. Generally, it refers to less steep ways of reaching a summit. Steeper, harder faces are considered alpine climbs. There are many styles of mountaineering, from commercial, guided 'high-altitude tourism' with miles of fixed ropes and massive logistical support – as practised on Everest – to exploratory ascents of unclimbed, unnamed peaks by small teams in obscure, remote ranges.

Rope Solo   Climbing alone using ropes and gear for safety. Can be practised free or aid.

Speed Climbing   There are two styles of speed: the Olympic, indoor version where athletes race up a fixed route on a 15 metre artificial wall in a matter of seconds; and the outdoor version where ascents of cliffs or mountains are timed against the clock. It is common to use whatever tactic is fastest, be that aid or free.

Sport Climbing   A type of free climbing that originated in the 1980s, where safety bolts are permanently installed into a rock face. This greatly reduces the element of risk; the focus being entirely on the gymnastic aspect. Routes are often rehearsed with the aid of the bolts before a free ascent can be claimed.

Traditional/Trad Climbing   Free climbing when there are few or no bolts, as was traditionally the case. A variety of gear is carried and placed by the lead climber as they ascend and is removed by the second climber. It is a much more adventurous style than sport climbing and adheres to the 'leave no trace' wilderness ethos. Sometimes climbs are rehearsed with the aid of gear or a rope from above before a free ascent.

Climbing Grades

There are multiple scales used to assess the difficulty of a climb. In this book the UK grading scale is used mainly, with occasional references to the US system and Aid grades.

The UK system is explained on p. 47. In the lower standards it is antiquated and confusing, but from intermediate to expert it is simpler and runs from E1 to E11.

The US Yosemite Decimal System begins at 5.1 and runs to 5.15c. From 5.10 it is subdivided into 5.10a, 5.10b, 5.10c, 5.10d, etc.

Aid grades run from A0 to A5+. They consider both the technical difficulty of the gear placements and potential consequences of a fall.

Climbing terms

Alpine style   Attempting a climb or peak in the most minimalist, lightweight fashion. Usually as a team of two or three carrying everything required with no support and without fixing rope. Regarded as a superior style.

Arête   A small ridge-like feature or a sharp outward-facing corner on a steep rock face.

Back cleaning   Down climbing or lowering on rope to retrieve previously placed protection equipment to be used again higher on the pitch.

Back and footing   A technique for climbing chimneys where both feet are on one wall and the back and hands on the other.

Belay   1) To protect a roped climber from falling by controlling the movement of the rope with a friction device known as a belay device. 2) An anchor point on a cliff that forms the beginning or end of a pitch.

Bergschrund   A crevasse that forms between a glacier and steep face that often signifies the start of a climb.

Bird beaks   Very small, pointed pitons hammered into rock. Only a few millimetres of metal make contact. Regarded as marginal protection.

Bold   Lack of protection or dangerous climbing.

Bomber   In reference to protection it means very secure, i.e. bombproof.

Bivi   Bivouac, to sleep outside; usually without a tent. Can be intentional or unintentional.

Cams   A spring-loaded camming device placed into cracks and clipped to the rope to protect a climber. Come in various sizes from 00 to 6 covering a range from 1 cm to 30 cm.

Carabiners   A metal link with a spring-loaded 'gate'. Used to secure climber to rope and protection.

Chimney   A crack wide enough to fit your whole body into.

Choss   Loose rock encountered on a climb.

Cirque   A geographical term to describe a group of peaks arranged in a semi-circle formed by glaciation.

Cloud inversion   Or temperature inversion. When a layer of cold air is trapped at ground level by warmer air, often creating a layer of low cloud.

Col   A small pass or 'saddle' between two peaks.

Copperheads   Aid-climbing protection. Small pieces of copper or aluminium wedged to wire that are hammered with a chisel into poor placements. Usually regarded as marginal protection.

Corner   Open-book corner or dihedral. An inside corner of rock, the opposite of an *arête*.

Couloir   Mountain feature. A steep gully filled usually with snow.

Cracks   Fissures in rock faces that can be climbed using various techniques and provide placements for protection.

Crank   To pull hard on a hand hold.

Crimp   Small finger holds that are grasped by placing thumb on top of fingers to increase strength. Also used as a description of this technique.

Crux   Or cruxes, the hardest move or section of a pitch or route.

Dry-tooling   Using ice axes to climb on rock.

Dyno   A jump or leap in which both feet and hands leave the rock face.

Exit   BASE-jumping term for exit point, a place from where one can jump.

Front-pointing   Using the front points of crampons to ascend steep ice or hard snow.

Gneiss   A igneous rock type similar to granite.

Grovel   To struggle.

Ground-up   Attempting a climb from the ground to the top without prior inspection (which you might do by descending on a rope in advance).

Headpoint   The practice of top-roping a hard traditional climbing route before leading it cleanly.

Headwall   A region at the top of a cliff or rock face that steepens dramatically.

Heel Hook   Using the back of the heel to 'hook' hold for balance or leverage.

Jamming   Wedging a body part into a crack. Can be done with hands or feet: hand jamming, foot jamming.

Jumar/Jumaring   1) A type of mechanical rope ascender. 2) To ascend a rope using a mechanical ascender.

Kernmantle   Type of rope with separate sheath (kern) and core (mantle).

Leading in blocks   One climber leading multiple blocks of pitches, as opposed to both climbers alternating between leading and seconding.

Line   The line a climb takes up a cliff or mountain. On first ascent, the intended line of features the climber(s) will attempt.

Mantle/Mantle shelf   A move used to surmount a ledge or feature in the rock in the absence of any useful holds directly above. It involves pushing down on a ledge or feature instead of pulling one-self up, like getting out of a swimming pool.

Offwidth   A wide crack not quite sufficient to fit your whole body inside. Notoriously awkward to climb.

Onsight   A clean ascent made on the first attempt without prior practice.

Opening   The deployment and pressurization of a parachute. Modern skydiving and BASE parachutes are more correctly known as RAM air canopies or wings.

Pitch   Portion of a climb between two belay points. Can be as short as 10 metres up to the full length of a rope (usually 60 metres).

Piton   A flat or angled metal blade of varying sizes that is hammered into the rock for protection. Can be left in place (*in situ*) or removed.

Port-a-ledge   A portable, foldable ledge. Usually an aluminium or carbon-fibre frame with fabric platform like a stretcher. Can be fitted with a fly sheet to create a deployable hanging tent.

Post–holing   Breaking trail or leading the way in snow.

Protection   Equipment including cams, nuts or pitons placed by a climber into a rock face and clipped to the rope to catch a fall.

Proximity flying   BASE-jumping term used to describe gliding in very close proximity to terrain, either a cliff face or mountain side. Usually practised in a wingsuit. Considered to be very dangerous.

Prusik   A knot used for ascending a rope.

Pumped   Build-up of lactic acid in the forearm muscles, caused by hanging from arms, which ultimately results in fingers uncurling and no longer being able to hold on.

Flash pump   Sudden onset of pumped forearms, often due to lack of warm-up or sometimes high altitude.

Puntering   Easy climbing or incompetence such as practised by beginners or 'punters'.

Quickdraws   Two carabiners attached to a 10–25 cm sling. Used for attaching the rope to climbing equipment.

Redirectional   A piece of gear used to change the position of a rope from an anchor point either to the side or down overhanging terrain.

RP   Tinniest protection. Brass wedges the width of a pound coin.

Runout   1) A long portion of a route with minimal protection. 2) A lengthy distance between two points of protection which, in some but not all cases, might be perceived as frightening or dangerous. May also be used as an adjective to describe a route or a section of a route.

Runners   Running belays. Pieces of protection clipped to rope whilst climbing to catch a fall. A fall that will be twice the distance of the climber above the last runner.

RURP   A miniature, postage-stamp-sized piton. An acronym for *realized ultimate reality piton*.

Simul-climbing   An advanced technique where both climbers move simultaneously, forsaking the need to stop and belay. Greatly increases speed but also risk.

Skyhooks   Aid gear. Finger-sized metal hooks used to hang from rock features.

Slider-up/Slider-down   A BASE-jumping term linked to the height of a jump. Taller jumps result in faster fall rate. Above 500 feet a fabric 'slider' is attached up the canopy lines that slows down the opening and reduces the forces involved in rapid deceleration as it slides down. Below 500 feet rapid pressurization is desirable and opening shock is lower due to reduced air speed at deployment.

Serac   A large tower of ice on the surface of a glacier or a glacier that flows off a cliff that may collapse at any time, making travel beneath them extremely hazardous.

Stuck   To successfully catch a hold.

Splitter   Term used to describe perfect cracks to climb. Usually suggests very straight, vertical and hand-sized.

Scree/Talus   Areas of rocks on a hill or mountainside. Scree refers to smaller rocks, talus to larger.

Technical   In the context of mountains or terrain, it means difficult or steep and usually requiring specialist techniques and equipment such as ropes or ice axes.

Tension traverse   Using tension from the rope to progress sideways.

Topo   A map of a climb.

Traverse   Moving sideways on a climb.

Via ferrata   'Way of iron'. A route on a mountain where the safety is provided by steel ropes or chains that are permanently fixed to the rock. The progression is often aided by artificial steps or ladders.

Whipper   A fall.

Wingsuit   A suit with fabric under the arms and between the legs, used for skydiving or BASE jumping, enabling the wearer to reduce his or her rate of fall.

Wire   Aka Nut, Rock, Stopper – A metal wedge attached to a wire placed in cracks as protection.

Image Credits

First Image Plate Section

Page 1. Shepherd's Crag © Eric Whitehead

Page 2. Angel of the North © Adam Wainwright

Dinas Mot © Ray Wood

Old Man of Hoy © Guy Lee/Leo Houlding Collection

Stanage © Adam Long

Page 3. Screamer © John Dickey

Devil's Dyno © Alastair Lee

Patch Hammond, Leo, Thomas and Alex Huber © Thomas Huber

Page 4. Cerro Torre © Leo Houlding

Leo post-injury © Kevin Thaw/Leo Houlding Collection

Page 5. Kjerag © Chris 'Douggs' McDougall

Conrad Anker and Leo as Mallory and Irvine 1 © Atlantic Productions Limited from *The Wildest Dream*

Conrad Anker and Leo as Mallory and Irvine 2 © Atlantic Productions Limited from *The Wildest Dream*

Page 6. Mount Asgard N. W. face © Alastair Lee

Free climbing, Arctic wall © Alastair Lee

Winter conditions © Alastair Lee

Inuksuk © Alastair Lee

Page 7. Aid climbing © Leo Houlding

Shredded fingers © Leo Houlding

Wingsuit BASE jumping © Alastair Lee

Leo, Jason Pickles, Chris Rabone, Ian Burton, Sean 'Stanley' Leary, Alastair Lee and Carlos Suarez © Alastair Lee

Page 8. The Prophet © Alastair Lee

Second Image Plate Section

Page 1. N. E. Ridge of Ulvetanna © Alastair Lee

Page 2. Cerro Autana © Alastair Lee

Yopo Wall © Alastair Lee

Page 3. Sean 'Stanley' Leary and Jason Pickles © Alastair Lee

Shaman Boliver and wife © Alastair Lee

Cuevo de Autana © Alastair Lee

Page 4. Ulvetanna Peak © Alastair Lee

Sean 'Stanley' Leary © Alastair Lee

Page 5. Arrival at Ulvetanna © Alastair Lee

Ice cave © Alastair Lee

Jumaring © Alastair Lee

Serious weather © Alastair Lee

Jason Pickles, Chris Rabone, Leo, Alastair Lee and Sean 'Stanley' Leary © Alastair Lee

Page 6. Jean Burgun snow-kiting © Mark Sedon

Jean Burgun, Leo and Mark Sedon © Leo Houlding

Antarctic plateau © Mark Sedon

Parhelion © Mark Sedon

Exhausted © Mark Sedon

Page 7. All images © Leo Houlding

Page 8. All images © Leo Houlding

Index

Page numbers in **bold** refer to illustrations.